# LITTLE HORSE OF IRON

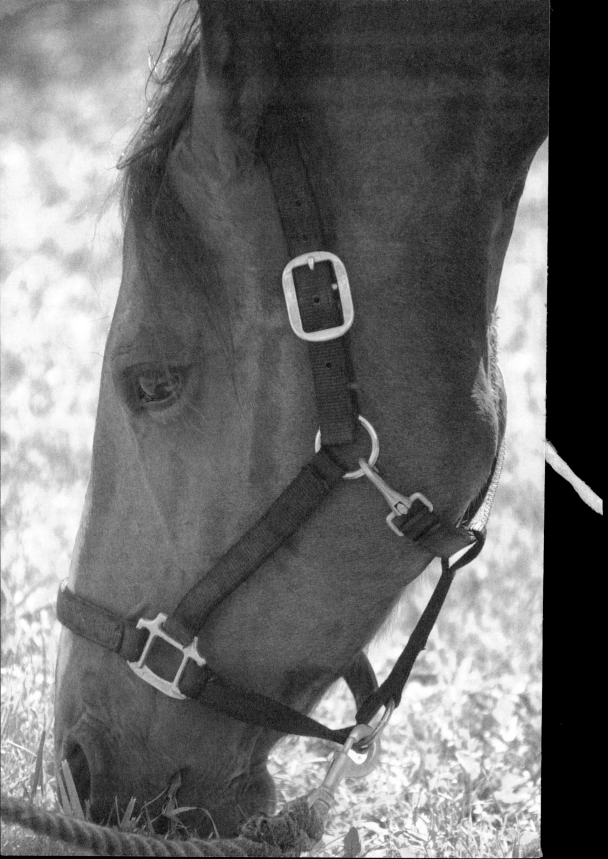

# LAWRENCE SCANLAN

# LITTLE HORSE of IRON

*A Quest for the Canadian Horse*

RANDOM HOUSE CANADA

*For Kathi and Patricia, and, of course, for Dal*

NATIONAL LIBRARY OF CANADA CATALOGUING IN PUBLICATION DATA

Scanlan, Lawrence

Little horse of iron : a quest for the Canadian horse

ISBN 0-679-31047-9

1. Canadian Horse. 2. Dali (Horse). 3. Scanlan, Lawrence. 4. Human-animal relationships. I. Title.

SF293.C29S32  2001          636.1          C2001-900851-1

www.randomhouse.ca

Text design: CS Richardson

Printed and bound in the United States of America

2 4 6 8 9 7 5 3 1

# CONTENTS

Chapter 1    The Gift of the Sun King    *1*

Chapter 2    Wanted: One Little Horse of Iron    *17*

Chapter 3    The Great Sell-Off    *36*

Chapter 4    Riding High on a Little Horse    *47*

Chapter 5    The Canadian Horse as Warhorse    *58*

Chapter 6    Coming to Blue Haven    *71*

Chapter 7    On the Brink of Disaster    *96*

Chapter 8    *"He* Won't Blow Over in a Stiff Breeze..."    *105*

Chapter 9    Horse Rescue    *125*

Chapter 10    The Education of Saroma Dark Fox Dali    *139*

Chapter 11    Show Time    *159*

Chapter 12    "He's *So* Quiet..."    *183*

Chapter 13    The Canadian Horse as Sport Horse    *208*

Chapter 14    Seven Falls Makes a Rider    *226*

Chapter 15    The Loneliness of the Long-Distance Rider    *249*

Chapter 16    Dark Fox Dali in the Year 2000    *263*

Chapter 17    The Canadian Horse Hall of Fame    *289*

Chapter 18    The Sweet Second Summer    *306*

*Epilogue*    *336*

*Bibliography*    *346*

*Image Credits*    *351*

*Acknowledgements*    *352*

*Index*    *354*

# CHAPTER I

# THE GIFT OF THE SUN KING

---

### 1665

*The Sun King sent to New France 2 stallions and 20 mares from the royal stables . . .*
*The ship was much weighed down by its cargo of horses, their ample fodder, 80 maids of*
*honour and 70 workers. "The whole," wrote one historian, "formed a sort of Noah's ark."*

MY FOLKS' HOUSE IN EAST TORONTO harbours an eccentric collection of old toys to keep grandchildren amused during visits. Some items date back to when I was a boy growing up there in the 1950s: an astonishingly resilient Etch-A-Sketch, a plastic set of ball and bowling pins, a tiny wooden hammer and its companion pegboard. One of the sturdiest toys, and most called upon, is a palomino rocking horse made of rigid plastic with red stirrups set over a metal stand on heavy

Above: *Louis at Maastricht* by Pierre Mignard, 1673.

---

coiled springs. Acquired for nothing years ago at a yard sale down the street, my mother recalls. The lineup to ride that horse is always long and queue jumpers risk being set upon.

The attraction speaks to the ancient and primal bond between humans and horses. And all children—whether rural or urban, whether they've ever seen a real horse or not—seem to know about it. *Little Horse of Iron* harkens back to my own boyhood desire to ride.

The local riding establishment, called Hilltop Stables, was half an hour away. I rode there occasionally in the early 1960s with my brother Tommy and over the protests of my mother. Her upbringing on rocky farmland north of Kingston in southeastern Ontario cured her of any romantic notions about horses. Besides, she would point out, trail rides cut deeply into our paper-route money. My favourite mount was a big horse aptly called Chocolate, and I well remember his gentle nature and the thrill of gallops back to the barn.

I remember, too, vividly, riding a smaller horse across busy St. Clair Avenue as part of a trail ride one bright summer day when the blue sky seemed to have beckoned us to the stable. My horse paused in the middle of the road as a bus crested the hill and bore down upon us. It's funny how moments such as this, which endure only thin seconds, occupy fat folders in one's memory banks. The other riders had all gone ahead and were safely out of the way, their horses settled in the low hills beyond the road, and I can't recall whether my horse paused and I tried to move him on, or whether he simply froze and I did likewise. What I do remember is cold panic. Perhaps the trail guide was shouting as the bus kept coming, kept coming.

By then my focus had shifted from the horse to the bus. I could see the driver's face. Then the guide, a boy likely not much older than I, dashed out from the roadside, circled my horse and lashed out at the poor creature with the length of chain he held in his hand. Only later did I wonder why he carried such a thing, but it did have the desired effect. My horse charged forward and I managed to stay on, though my heart was beating furiously and was not where it should have been, but in my mouth.

I was not one of those who grew up on a ranch or a farm and who took to riding as a tadpole takes to swimming. I liked horses but the art of riding was not something I studied or pondered. The Hilltop barn was eventually swallowed by malls and bungalows and I didn't ride again for a long time.

In my late thirties, I took up riding more formally when I was asked to help the prominent equestrian Ian Millar write his memoirs. It seemed I could have no real entry into this man's heart and mind until I had mastered at least the rudiments of correct riding. I was living in the country then, took riding lessons once weekly and continued doing so for years. I later went on a cattle drive in Alberta and twice rode the Wyoming outback on rugged week-long treks.

By my late forties, I had written several books and magazine articles about eminent horses and riders and trainers. I had developed a special interest in all this; some mistakenly called it expertise. I knew, or thought I did, a great deal about the history of horses and horsemanship, but my knowledge was long on theory, short on practice. If I was a rider, I was only a fair one. And I could not, by any stretch, call myself a horseman, for I had yet to realize a long-held dream—to ride my own horse.

At the age of 50 I finally bought my first. That I came to buy a Canadian horse owes everything to a librarian named Patricia Cooper, who lives north of Toronto near Palgrave. She owns two Canadians, a young chestnut mare named China and an older black gelding called Tom, and she wrote me several years ago, wondering if she and I might collaborate on a children's book about the Canadian horse. I knew the heritage breed only vaguely but I did agree to go to Patricia's house, meet her horses, and look at her research.

Patricia is a modest, soft-spoken woman, but there is a sense of mission about her. Over tea in her airy kitchen, we talked about the breed, my interest now warming in the face of Patricia's own zeal.

She had compiled eight binders of magazine and newspaper articles and other historical documents, all logged and cross-referenced on filing cards in a plastic box the colour of dark amber. She was, after all, a librarian and she was urging me to take over her project.

I carried away this great load in a cardboard box and we agreed to confer again. What I read took my breath away. The Canadian horse is a storied but unheralded breed and I knew immediately that I would buy such a horse and tell the history of his kin. Over time, what took shape in my mind was not a kids' book at all, but one that would weave two tales—the history of Canada's national horse (or is it Quebec's?), and my own tale of taking on as my first horse a young, unschooled, peppery one.

Hardy, quick, and pound for pound perhaps the strongest horse on the planet, the Canadian has been called "the little horse of iron" yet few know about the breed, whose roots go back 350 years to the very early days of colonial Canada.

Twenty years ago, the Canadian horse almost disappeared, but the numbers are surging now, with some estimates putting the count of registered Canadian horses at more than 4,000. Still, the breed is rare and two decades ago was endangered. Despite the low numbers and their reputation as multi-purpose horses, Canadians have won North American and world championships in the sport of combined driving.

The Canadian makes a fine trail horse, some are capable eventers, others are notable jumpers or endurance horses. Their bloodlines played a pivotal role in forming the Standardbred, the Morgan and several other well-known breeds. And, of course, their proud history as farm horse and warhorse goes right back to the very beginnings of New France. The more I read of this horse, the more I came to appreciate him.

Being a Canadian, though, the horse has historically been admired elsewhere and undervalued at home. Cecily Ross once wrote a piece in *Harrowsmith* magazine about this heritage breed. It was entitled "The Little Horse That Could." "I wonder," she wrote, "how a country so hungry for symbols and unifying myths has managed to overlook such a great Canadian." We know the Pony Express saga but not an equally proud bit of horse history closer to home. Even American author Bonnie Hendricks, who wrote the definitive book on international horse breeds a few years ago, called the Canadian horse "one of the best kept secrets of the twentieth century."

It's possible, and intriguing, to view Canadian history through the eyes of this horse. If the horse-proud Louis XIV has a place in the story (for he sent the first horses to New France), so do all these elements: a small cavalry unit fighting for the French on the Plains of Abraham, *les habitants* racing each other in cutters on frozen lakes, Cornelius Krieghoff painting horse-rich pastoral scenes, and the many thousands of *chevaux canadiens* who perished in the American Civil War or who turned heads on Kentucky racetracks. The Queen's Plate, that famous horse race that feels so English, so rooted in Toronto, was first run in 1836 at Trois-Rivières as the King's Plate and its prize of 50 royal guineas was restricted to horses bred in Lower Canada, many of them horses whose ancestors were a gift of the king to a distant colony more than a century and a half earlier.

The king of France was a small man with an eye for the dramatic gesture and a keen sense of his own wigged, powdered and perfumed place at the very centre of the universe. His extraordinarily long reign, 72 years, only partly explains why the memory of Louis XIV, the Sun King, remains so vivid.

In the 17th century, all Europe feared him and his unpredictable appetites—for conquest, for self-glory, for the pure exercise of power. The man who once said "I am the state" (*"L'état c'est moi"*) meddled with impunity even in the courts, issuing some 9,000 *lettres de cachet* to pluck the favoured from the grasp of the law. The citizens of France, wrote one biographer, "regarded him with Asiatic humility."

Louis's thoughts wandered only occasionally to the colony of New France across the Atlantic. But when, in the 1660s, the colony's transplanted bluebloods began discreetly asking for horses to ease their travel over muddy and snowy roads, the king complied. He would have bestowed his gift to the colony in the same way he did everything: in a grand way. This was the man, after all, who constructed the Palace of Versailles and the Louvre, devoting fantastic energy, immense wealth and several decades to these tasks. Like a Roman emperor, he issued medals and coins (the *louis*) to help imprint his image on his subjects; the vast territory of Louisiana (the entire watershed of the Mississippi River) was claimed in his name. At the palace it was considered a great honour to join the select audience gathered to catch a glimpse of the king eating—which became as much a ritualized performance as his retiring to bed at night and rising from it in the morning. To be spoken to by the king as he supped, or, better, to join him at table, were seen as exquisite honours.

The homage was like that paid to a god; indeed, several images remain of the king as Apollo in a celestial chariot pulled by four spirited horses. It became an offence to turn your back on the many portraits of the Sun King. In the same way, courtiers wore hats when he did not, and doffed them when he donned his.

The Sun King's attendants would deploy high-heeled shoes and wigs to hide his low frame (five foot, three inches tall, or 1.6 metres) and his baldness (the result of an illness). Painters, in their works, for the same reason, carefully placed him on a dais or an elevated throne. And the dozens of equestrian statues of the king—one so enormous that 20 men could sit comfortably inside—might lead one to conclude that his horsemanship was similarly inflated by image-makers. But there is evidence to suggest that Louis XIV was a born architect, a wonderful dancer—and a consummate horseman.

In 1662, one of the major spectacles of his reign was held in a square near the Louvre. Called a *carrousel*, this competition among horsemen harkened back to similar events in the Middle Ages when knights displayed their equestrian skills. By Louis XIV's time, it had become more balletic, but still tested the horse and his rider, who would rush at baubles with the tip of his sword, or lance ring-shaped targets on the fly.

The scale of the event almost defies imagining. Five teams, involving in total some 12,000 individuals dressed in fabulous costumes to represent Roman, Persian, Turkish, Indian and American themes, vied with each other. The king, all in red, appeared as emperor of the Romans, carrying a shield inscribed with his personal device, the sun, and the words *Ut Vidi Vici* ("As I saw I conquered"). An entire volume of engravings, with text, has survived to help us remember the event. That the king fared quite well in the competition should have come as no surprise: He loved to hunt deer from his horse, and one of his mistresses, Louise de la Vallière was, reputedly, an excellent horsewoman.

A portrait, *Louis at Maastricht*, painted in 1673, shows the king, again in Roman garb and sandals, and he appears quite handsome: aquiline nose, delicate moustache, the hair of his black wig as curly and shaggy as a rock star's. He's on a black horse with a long tail, a mane as curly as the king's, a powerful, thick neck and distinctively high cheekbones. The horse looks very like the horse we know now, more than three centuries later, as *le cheval canadien*, or the Canadian horse.

Time and circumstance would shape the French horse into a distinctive breed in the New World, and the first step—to cross the Atlantic Ocean—may have been the most trying. The passage took anywhere from 19 days to 4 months and could be hideous, with both humans and animals packed like sardines in the holds of ships that soon reeked of vomit. Many horses died in transit. Sailors of the day ranked the voyage to New France as one best avoided. Captain Vaudron wrote in 1716 that "the very best of these voyages gave me more white hairs than any others I have ever undertaken elsewhere. It was a perpetual torment of mind and body."

The first horses actually came to Acadia in 1610—to Port-Royal (now Annapolis Royal, Nova Scotia) as part of an attempt by the

Sieur de Poutrincourt to revive the colony. But (and this is a recurring theme in the history of the Canadian horse) raiders from across the border came north in 1616 and carried off most of them. Samuel Argall—he would later win fame for abducting the Indian princess Pocahontas—and his men from Virginia must have admired the horseflesh they saw.

In 1647, Louis XIV sent another horse as a gift to the governor of New France, the Sieur de Montmagny. The colonists had been astonished, and even a little embarrassed, that this knight, a representative of the king, had no horse: He was a *chevalier sans cheval*. That horse, though, did not seem to last long and may well have died of loneliness; other accounts suggest he was killed by First Nations people who had never seen a horse before and may have mistaken the creature for a moose. Later, the sight of an animal being ridden by men and obeying their commands would bewilder indigenous people, for they had never seen a trained animal.

Finally, in 1665, the Sun King sent 2 stallions and 20 mares from the royal stables, of whom 8 mares perished on the voyage. All horses from the royal stables bore on their left haunches the capital letter *L* surmounted by a crown. The ship was much weighed down by its cargo of horses, their ample fodder for the long crossing, 80 maids of honour (so-called *filles du roi*, many of them orphans without dowries or prostitutes, and all meant to be married and boost the colony's numbers) plus 70 workers. "The whole," wrote one historian, "formed a sort of Noah's ark."

These horses arrived close to what is now the old town of Quebec City, on the beach of a little bay at Anse au Foulon, on July 16 of that year. Today, Anse au Foulon is an industrial zone, with a dock for freighters, and the view south across the river is of white pillbox refineries. But in 1665 the landscape would have looked bleak and rugged, for permanent settlement had only begun with Samuel de Champlain's trading post in 1608. These were the very early days of New France. Like all animals then transported across the ocean, the king's horses would have had to swim ashore, since docks had yet to be built.

And while they may have looked bedraggled and pitiful from the rigours of their voyage as they climbed wet and exhausted onto the rocky shore, in truth they were exceedingly fine horses. The king had instructed his lieutenant and closest adviser, Jean Baptiste Colbert, to send to the colony only the best animals of France. (In letters to the king, Jean Talon, Intendant of New France and the king's representative in the colony, did complain that some of the first horses sent by French agents were of second quality, but Talon was a shrewd empire builder likely putting pressure on the agents to do as the king had requested.)

They were warhorses, descendants of the Norman horses that took knights-at-arms into battle. Look at the 11th century Bayeux Tapestry and you will see knights riding *le cheval canadien*'s ancestor, with its black and distinctively wavy mane, long tail, feathered legs and sturdy build. Refined somewhat in Louis XIV's time by the addition of Barb blood from Spain, these horses were nevertheless imposing and immensely strong.

Royal horses came from Normandy and Brittany, at the time the two most renowned horse-breeding provinces of France. The then small Breton horse was noted for his soundness and vigour. The Norman horse reflected other imported strains—the Andalusian and the Percheron.

By Andalusian, I mean the Arab horse, introduced into Spain in the 8th century by the invading Moors of North Africa. The Arabs were lighter, faster and more agile than any horse the Europeans were used to. Forerunner to the racehorse, the Arab infused the French horse with its special qualities. As Canadian historian Robert Leslie Jones put it, "There can be little doubt that the hardiness, the bottom, and the prepotency of the old French-Canadian horse were traceable to this Andalusian inheritance." Other authorities point to the influence of Dutch Friesian horses, which had come to France prior to the 16th century from Spain or the Spanish Netherlands. The great trotting ability of the Canadian, the feathered legs, the general appearance and the abundance of mane and tail are all cited as evidence of Friesian blood.

The young Louis XIV had lost in wars to Germany, and he apparently blamed the equipment—the horses. What he wanted were horses of quality equal to those of the German enemy, and so his lieutenant, Colbert, decreed that in every region of France the best stallion and mare were to be matched in order to improve the standard.

Whatever their ancestry, the quality of the horses sent to New France reflected the majesty of their owner. All the king's horses, ironically, may have cowered a great deal less before their monarch than did the courtiers of Versailles. Cruelty in the breaking and training of horses was then the norm in Europe, but perhaps less so in France, where an enlightened trainer named Antoine de Pluvinel wrote a book on gentling horses called *L'Instruction du Roi*. The book, published in 1666, was written in the form of a dialogue between the author and Louis XIII, the Sun King's father. De Pluvinel urged kindness in schooling horses. The whip, he admonished, was a poor way to inspire confidence in a horse.

I would like to think that the comparatively sweet temperament of the breed can be traced by some long thin filament all the way back to the time when the Canadian horse's ancestors were trained and handled with discretion in the royal stables. Alas, every horse, no matter his temperament or bloodline, reflects his handlers, cruel or kind as the case may be.

In 1667 and 1670, the Sun King sent more horses to New France—another 27 in total. The newly arrived horses were meant as rewards from the king to certain noblemen and to farmers who had shown the greatest zeal in clearing and cultivating land. Many horses, though, failed to adjust to their dramatically changed circumstances. The benign climate of France had left them ill-prepared for the shock of bone-chilling winds that howled along the St. Lawrence River in February. Working horses sought what shelter they could in rough shanties; foals were given no shelter at all. The *habitants* cured little or no hay for their horses, who lived on straw and whatever else they could find in the forest. Maybe a little grain.

Some were fed frozen fish! And some, of course, perished from the cold and deprivation.

The next generation of horses lost a little in size but gained in toughness; the strongest survived and passed on that vigour to their offspring. These horses would develop the marvellously thick winter coats for which the Canadian is today well known. The change was remarkable and quick. A Swedish naturalist, Pehr Kalm, who travelled in Canada in the mid-1700s, remarked on how well the horses managed in the cold. "The horses," he wrote, "are left out of doors during the winter, and find their food in the woods, living upon nothing but dry plants, which are very abundant; however, they do not fall off by this food, but look very fine and plump in spring." The phrase "easy keeper" describes the horse who thrives on little—the horses of New France would epitomize that notion.

The gift of the Sun King, though, came with strings attached. The horses remained royal property but were rented to gentry and farmers who paid either one foal or 100 *livres* (pounds) per horse per year over the course of three years. At that point, any colts not turned over to the Intendant as rent became the breeder's property. Since only the privileged could afford the fee, the *habitants* opted to produce foals instead. And any colts taken in by the Intendant were raised at government expense until they were three, then offered under the same terms just described.

Most of the early Canadian horses were bays, but black soon became the favoured colour as the number of horses grew. After 1670, the king of France was no longer sending horses. The incentive program to produce them in the colony had proved wildly successful. By 1700, the colony had more than 700 horses. They were small (about 14 hands) but sturdy—some 1,200 pounds. Sure-footed, the horses pulled *calèches* (carriages) and *carrioles* (cutters), as well as *berlines* (heavy sleds for transporting people, wood, blocks of ice and farm supplies) and *berlots* (a more open variation of the carriole, with poles on the sides and designed to carry three standing passengers).

While the calèche offered a rough ride, especially on crude roads, the carriole ran smoothly over the snow. The gentry would have the seats upholstered, and heated bricks were placed on the floor and covered with a linen cloth. The seat was covered with a bearskin or moosehide, known as the carriole skin.

The big, powerful draught horses of the day, such as Percherons and Clydesdales, did not pass muster with the French colonial farmer. He wanted a versatile horse to pull the plough or wagon, to clear land, to take the family to church in carriage or cutter, or to be ridden, often bareback, in search of errant cattle. The farm horse, because so often and widely used on the farm, became a personality. Owners of these sturdy horses praised their strength, their ability to get by on little food, their tirelessness as trotters through spring mud or winter snow. The horses continued to work long after other breeds were ready for retirement. The mares were unusually fertile and would reproduce until 20 years or older.

Farmers typically owned three horses, but practically every child in New France had his or her own horse; 10 children sometimes meant 10 horses. The horses never seemed to suffer from the cold. Like Mongolian mothers of the 11th century who used to bathe their infants in cold water to toughen them, the farmers of New France did not coddle their horses. On the one hand, the horses' workload did not seem onerous: harrowing, and hauling grain, wood and goods to and from the nearest town. Sometimes they were asked to plough fields alongside oxen. On the other hand, the horse might be asked to drive at great speed on winter roads, then stand wet and uncovered in the cold for hours. The extraordinary stamina of Canadian horses and the lightness of the cutters meant that covering 150 kilometres a day was not unusual. Often the *habitant* would spend the day hunting deer in the woods, and the horse's task was to haul the venison home.

In summer, the horses were released into the woods where the flies tormented them, all the more when the horses' tails were docked. This was commonly done out of fashion or because drivers feared that horses driven in a tandem hitch—that is, one horse before the other—were vulnerable to eye damage from the constant swishing of the lead horse's tail.

Racing these horses with calèches or carrioles became so common and the drivers so hell-bent that in 1708 a law was passed forbidding horses from trotting or galloping within 10 *arpents* (or acres) of churches or towns. By 1709, Montreal had so many horses that laws were passed (and ignored) restricting townspeople from owning more than two horses and a colt. The Intendant grew alarmed when it became clear early on that settlers were devoting themselves entirely too much to horse breeding; cattle and sheep, needed by the colony and clearly a better source of profit, held less interest.

Administrators worried aloud that the horse-proud *habitants* had stopped using snowshoes and would thus be ill-equipped if called upon for military service. Or was the concern more about wounded pride? Peasants in France did not own horses, but it seemed that peasants in New France did. "It is hard to escape the conclusion," remarked one historian, "that [administrators] were simply scandalized at seeing common people on horseback. It was the horse as a symbol of upward mobility and liberty that caught the eye of the administrator and caused such consternation. Thus the horse was a doubly important acquisition for the habitant."

The breeding of horses in New France took on new importance because importing them was so costly and, owing to the wars ravaging Europe, unreliable; Britannia, not France, ruled the waves. By 1719 there were some 5,000 horses in the colony and horse-drawn vehicles were becoming standard equipment.

What mattered a great deal to the *habitant* was "the promenade," a Sunday stroll in his carriage. At first, only the better off could afford a calèche. Such carriages would be used at weddings to lend colour and a greater sense of fun: The calèche would be ribboned and adorned and the newlyweds would tour the village with their wedding party in tow.

The calèches and carrioles, always pulled by Canadians, were also employed in a remarkable transportation system that ran in the 18th century between Montreal and Quebec. The network, government-run and regulated, was better than anything then available in North America. Every nine miles there existed "post houses" where calèches and carrioles (usually four of each along with others that could be called upon) were kept in readiness. Travellers could expect that during the day one of these vehicles would be made ready within 15 minutes, or at night within 30 minutes. Otherwise, the postmaster paid a fine. There was no schedule per se; when you came to the post house, a carriage was arranged, even if you were the only passenger. The speed was also regulated—seven miles an hour.

By 1760, New France was home to 12,000 horses—"the French moose without antlers," as the Hurons called them. And so it was that a small cavalry unit of 200 Canadian horses—the creation of a certain Chevalier la Pause—fought on the side of the Marquis Louis-Joseph de Montcalm on September 13, 1759, on the Plains of Abraham. The men wore a distinctive blue uniform with a red flash at the neck and a cross at the stomach. This was the final chapter in the British siege of Quebec that had begun in May of that year.

Some 400 mounted men, including volunteers, earlier fought against General James Wolfe's men on August 9. But they came under withering English fire, and 300 were either killed or wounded. A smaller French troop had better luck on August 17 when soldiers and cavalry under Monsieur Louis-Antoine de Bougainville turned back English forces that had landed at the village of Deschambault upriver from the main battleground. Ironically, more than 200 years later, Deschambault would again figure in the story of the Canadian horse, and in that of my own Canadian horse, whose roots trace back to a government-run breeding farm at Deschambault.

Montcalm himself was mounted on a horse, an ancestor to the Canadian (only in the 1800s was the breed formally recognized). The general rode up and down the line of his troops, shouting out the question, "Are you tired?" to his exhausted men, who insisted they were not. "Vive le Roy!" they declared and went into battle. This would be Montcalm's last ride. A painting in one history text shows the mortally wounded commander on a black horse returning from the battlefield to Quebec City. The battle had begun at Anse au Foulon, the precise spot where the horses had come ashore in 1665. General Wolfe had landed some 500 British troops there at midnight and ordered them to scale the 50-metre cliffs. At the summit, the British overcame French sentries as a precursor to their victory.

During the long siege of Quebec, when the British naval blockade cut off supplies from France, starving farmers had been urged by Montcalm to slaughter their horses for meat, but the people declined. It would be, they said, like killing a member of their own family and God would surely punish them for such a crime.

The sure-footed horses fell into legend, and there exist innumerable documented stories of their speed, endurance and spirit. Pehr Kalm, the Swede, tells the story of a British officer leaving Berthier for Trois-Rivières one January morning and encountering a terrible snowstorm. He was obliged to leave his pureblood horses at Maskinongé and to replace them by *marche donc* ("Giddyup"). "This," he wrote, "was the nickname of Canadian horses which were the only horses which could keep to the road in such terrible weather and such bad roads."

The isolation of New France also meant that for almost 200 years no other breeds intermingled with these horses and they developed unique and distinctive characteristics. The Canadian horse was typically small, with powerful legs and shoulders, round frame, voluminous and crimped mane and tail, and broad hooves that seemed tailor-made for heavy snow.

In time, the horse came to be called *le petit cheval de fer*, the little horse of iron. Perhaps the tag arose from the horses' ironlike feet, for which they became famous, or their sturdy constitution, or their immense strength, which was all out of proportion to their size. In any case, as the 18th century ended and a new one dawned, the future of these wonderful horses seemed unassailable, as bright as a *louis* in the noonday sun.

The history of the Canadian horse, like the history of Canada, has a defined chronology, one I could plot. But when I started writing the personal part of this book about buying and training my own young horse, I had no idea how it would unfold. My notions were warm and fuzzy. I imagined that the horse of my choosing would greet me at the paddock gate like a close friend, that we would ride the trail on sunny perfect days. A real horse, especially a raw and spirited horse like the one I eventually bought, is more complicated than that. I had ridden school horses for years and had never fallen off. That would change.

Much about owning a young horse took me by surprise. The highs were higher, the lows lower than 10 years of walking the perimeter of the horse world had ever prepared me for. My horse, a burly, handsome bay called Saroma Dark Fox Dali, made incursions into my heart and brain and taught me much about fear and trust. My diary plots a journey (though some days it felt like an odyssey). I was embarrassed to record some darkly comic moments along the way, delighted to chronicle others.

The diary begins in the spring of 1999 when it seemed my task was pure and simple: Find the horse meant for me. A part of me dreaded making that decision, for however the choice unfolded, I was bound to chronicle it. My horse, I knew, would reveal aspects of my character and what passed for my horsemanship, and I was wary about operating in such a bright and unrelenting light.

And yet there was also delight in this pursuit, and I leapt to it with the same glee that my tiny nephews and nieces display as they ride that palomino rocking horse in the old family rec room. By the way they test those springs and never seem to tire of the ride, and by a certain faraway look in their eyes, I know that the little horse takes them to places they've never been before.

# CHAPTER 2

# WANTED: ONE LITTLE HORSE OF IRON

SPRING 1999

*My horse-buying file is home to all manner of horses not bought, directions not taken to far-flung farms and stables. To browse it is to remember the kind of excitement a fisherman feels in spring the first time he drops his lure in the water. I had plenty of bites but for a long time I caught nothing.*

IN APRIL OF 1999, AS I SET OUT TO BUY my first horse, a registered Canadian horse, it dawned on me how much I had to learn. I had never gone through a saddle fitting. I had never clipped or lunged a horse. Never walked a colicky horse. Never had to make hard decisions about a horse's life, walked a horse into a trailer, watched a horse enter the world, or leave it. Most of the horses I had ridden—

Above: A Canadian horse trotting in a paddock.

and I've been riding intermittently for 11 years now—had been waiting for me all tacked up and ready to go. A lifelong renter had suddenly decided to buy. But houses are static things; a horse is very much alive.

When you buy a horse, you buy that horse's history: the pastures (rich or weedy) where he grazed, the manner (rough or kind) of his handling, the skill (even or not) of the one who had schooled him, even the water (sulphurous or sweet) he drank every day of his life. Horses bear the sins of their handlers with astonishing good grace, but somewhere in that sculpted form every bout of lost temper, every shortcut, every attempt at economy, each little loss of faith in that horse leaves a legacy. We chip and chip away, or we build and buttress, and leave a little of our character on that horse's heart.

You hope that the seller who perhaps bought the horse as a colt had a good eye. You hope the breeder had good instincts and high standards. You hope all those stories about horse dealers, like the ones about used car salesmen, are just old coinage. Surely car dealers no longer put sawdust in crippled transmissions? Surely horse dealers no longer drug crazy or lame horses to dupe buyers?

I had a specific job in mind for my horse: competitive trail rides and, some day, our bodies willing, endurance rides of 50 kilometres and more. I didn't want a sleepyhead, nor did I want a firebrand. I just wanted a good horse.

April 1, 1999
Fool's Day. Been looking for a horse only two days and already the divergence of opinion is comical. In the same day, an hour apart, I spoke on the telephone with two old guys in the Ottawa Valley, both with a strong Celtic shading in their voices, both lifelong horsemen with hardened views.

Old Guy #1. Never ever push a three-year-old horse. The leg bones are attached to the rest of the body only by muscle. You can do terrible things to a young horse if you ride him hard before he's fully mature, and in the case of the Canadian horse, that's five years old. A light hack is fine, but competitive riding and cantering? Forget it if you have the horse's best interests in mind.

Old Guy #2. [When told the above.] I can tell *you* don't know a lot about horses. In 1942, I sowed an entire field with a two-year-old Canadian pulling the plough. Are you telling me that a 1,200-pound horse can't carry a man? Call my daughter and see if she's got horses for sale, but don't tell her a three-year-old can't be ridden. She'll laugh you off the phone. . . .

As I make my calls, casting an ever wider net in search of a horse, I poll horse-smart trainers and the consensus builds that Old Guy #2 needs to rethink. Owners are also telling me that some Canadian horses have clearly not read those rosy descriptions in the literature of the breed. "Docile but spirited." "People horses."

A researcher at the University of Guelph tells me her Canadian horse has Houdini's flair for escaping his stall so he can wreak havoc in her tack room. She warns me that Canadians are "too smart": They have to be kept busy. Another owner, one new to horses, tells me that a year of working with a pair of Canadians in driving competition has left him with the strong impression that Canadians are scamps. Bright, mischievous, inclined to take advantage.

There is also the testimony of Terry Veevers, a long-time trainer of Canadian horses on his farm near Guelph, Ontario. He schools Canadians for a replica pioneer town in Williamsburg, Virginia, where they want quiet, quiet horses. Sometimes *le cheval canadien* is perfect for the job. But not always.

"The literature says they're hardy and tough, and that's true," says Veevers. "But that's because they're stubborn. You push them and they'll push back." He cites a horse he's working with now, one called Dalton. A nice horse, road safe, with good conformation and lots of stamina. But occasionally he'll hear a noise in the bush and want to climb into another horse's lap.

Veevers finds that many owners of Canadian horses are also first-time owners, or people content to have a horse as a pet. It's when you *work* with them, he says, that you discover their strong dispositions. The training of a Canadian horse, he says, has to be smooth. They will, he repeats, push back. Yet nostalgia is turning more people towards the breed. People like the fact that its roots date back to the 1600s. Economics figures too: The high cost of feed and horse care has forced people to cut back on the number of horses they own. The Canadian can fill many bills: pull your carriage in competition, be ridden under saddle, pull skids of logs in winter.

Day by day, my "Buying a Horse" file grows thicker. I call principals in the Canadian Horse Breeders' Association (CHBA) all over Ontario and Quebec, put ads on the Internet at equisearch.com and haynet.com. Were I to place a classified ad in a newspaper, it might read: "Looking for a Canadian horse. Gelding. Sturdy. 16 hands. Generous. Sweet-tempered. Black."

Pat Garland, an Ottawa-area horsewoman long active in the Ontario wing of the CHBA, has just sold five Canadian horses and warns me it's getting hard to find them. "The momentum is building," she says. "It's going to get crazy. Demand far exceeds supply." Horse numbers, in general, after declining in North America early in the 20th century, began to rise again in the late 1960s. After losing his job on the farm pulling ploughs and hay wagons, the horse found new work in sport, on the trail, at the rodeo. It has now become fashionable to own a horse.

But many owners ride infrequently. Horses lend elegance to the landscape, but sometimes their only job is to eat grass and grow fat. A 1996 census revealed that the United States is home to seven million horses, up 20 per cent in the past ten years. But the lament of a piece in *The Economist* a few years later was that horses had become "living lawn ornaments for the five-acre rancher with an office job . . ."

"Everybody's raising them and nobody's riding them," said a horse dealer in Sheridan, Wyoming. The manager at the auction yard in Billings, Montana, agreed: "I've seen many a six- or seven-year-old horse come through here that's never had a saddle on him."

The Canadian horse, because rare, may be especially prone to that fate. And I doubt it makes for happy horses, since my overwhelming impression is that Canadians like to work and are easily bored. Sometimes they're bought on a whim. The reader of a magazine article on the breed may be swept into a purchase, nudged by that quiet patriotism Canadians are known for. (I once saw a cartoon: A young woman asks a farmer standing next to a black horse, "But how can you be sure he's a Canadian?" The horse has a quizzical look on his face and a star—a white mark on the horse's forehead—the precise shape of a maple leaf.) The Canadian horse, truly a heritage horse, appeals to those keen to own a living, breathing piece of the nation's history.

But where is the horse meant for me and how will I recognize him when I see him? I've bought and sold cars, even a house or two; those purchases revealed my essential caution. My partner, Ulrike, and I house-hunted with clipboards in hand, queried prospective neighbours, hired house inspectors; we bought successive Toyota Corollas only after poring over their track record in consumer magazines. But buying a horse left me longing for guides. Whom do I trust? *What* do I trust? My eye? What eye? Instinct?

My horse-buying file would eventually grow as thick as my wrist. It would house one pad of yellow lined paper, every page exhausted with my scribble; one lone classifieds page torn from a homespun horse magazine and pitching, in a typo-filled entry, an 11-year-old black Canadian gelding—a "versitile horse suitable for competitve rider." There were thick and thin gatherings of odd-sized paper, all stapled according to some long forgotten organizing principle; faxed copies of horse registration papers fading to grey; an e-mail from New Brunswick.

The file is home to all manner of horses not bought, directions not taken to far-flung farms and stables, reminders on Post-it notes to bring stuff on scouting missions: a tailor's tape measure to size a horse's girth, my cassette recorder, my old 35mm camera, a rented video recorder. To browse the file is to remember the kind of excitement a fisherman feels in spring the first time he drops his lure in the water. And while I had plenty of bites, for a long time I caught nothing. Promising tips fizzled; a line on a horse would lead nowhere.

The file records the waves of disappointment I felt then. I was told about a horse southwest of Montreal, a four-year-old gelding named Ebano. The trainer sounded right, as did the horse. I got directions, made plans to see him, but two days before the appointed time a lady from Vermont snapped him up.

"It wasn't meant to be," my horse-wise cousin Kathi Bayly consoled, sounding like Omar Sharif in the film *Lawrence of Arabia*. Sharif shrugs his shoulders and says, "It is written," when the sight of a riderless camel at dawn signals that a comrade has fallen off during a nocturnal desert crossing. That Lawrence went back and retrieved the sun-dried warrior; this Lawrence cursed his luck and went back to the phones and the classifieds.

The variables in the horse-buying business seemed dizzying: The marketplace itself puts pressure on the buyer to act quickly, but time and distance and my cautious nature all slowed the process.

April 2, 1999

I am learning (I think) to trust my instincts. I am gravitating towards the small breeders and owners. This morning I talked to a woman on a breeding farm with some 200 horses and felt uneasy, worried that she was a McBreeder, her farm an assembly line. A woman with only a few horses seemed to me warm and true. I tell myself, You're buying the horse, not the owner. But the owner's voice nevertheless seems to guide me.

I'm learning code:

*He would be a challenge.* You better wear a hard hat 'cause you're going for a ride.

*He is a very sweet horse.* We've spoiled him rotten so now he noses around in strangers' pockets for treats.

*He's a very versatile horse.* We've tried him at all manner of disciplines and he shows no talent for any of them.

*He's an ambitious horse.* He has a will of his own and you better have too.

*Easily jumps four feet.* We can't keep him in a paddock.

*Easy keeper.* He looks at a blade of grass and puts on 50 pounds.

April 3, 1999

Saw my first real Canadian today. A four-year-old 15.3-hand chestnut gelding named Ed. I liked his head, his calm and generosity, but not his bony bulk, high hip and overly large feet. To my untrained eye, a clunky horse. When he goes, Ed will miss his digs: a 300-acre farm at the end of a long, quiet road, with a stunning view of Lake Ontario. I took a video of young Ed and when I got it home and played it I could hear waterbirds calling to each other in the bay. I assured the owner, Nancy, that she lived in paradise.

Another horse for sale at the farm, Filon, a handsome three-year-old gelding with soft lines and greater spirit than Ed, had, I was told after remarking on them, chestnuts on his legs. Horse people know these as the hard crusty knobs on the inner side of the leg, but somehow I had missed the phrase and failed to notice that *all* horses have chestnuts. My equine education has far to go.

All winter long Nancy's Canadians stand outside, only sheltering among the cedars when the wind has bite. Sometimes, says Nancy, the snow lies an inch deep on their backs, but they seem happy to endure a little weather as the price of being free to roam the fields; her Arabs and Thoroughbreds, meanwhile, are given refuge in the barn.

I wondered about the impact of attending daily to these horses. Does affection for, or from, a horse derail her business sense? "Why,"

I asked her, "are you selling Filon, a horse you just bought a month ago?" Her reply sounded like a trainer's hard-won truth. "Everything is for sale." And yet I sensed her feeling for Ed. What was being showcased this grey hazy day on the flat brown earth outside her barn was not just the horse but this diminutive woman's life with horses. I liked the way she moved around them, trusted them, moved quietly yet assuredly in their midst. She was asking $5,000 for Ed. It seemed a lot. I had the feeling the fee reflected all the time Nancy had spent making him trusting and willing.

Each horse I visit on my journey tells me something about myself. On this visit, it was Ed's younger, more spirited stablemate I seemed to connect with. I liked Filon's curiosity. "He's more *there*," Nancy had said. I think I want that. I liked his elegant lines, his body's little shudders. At one point I rubbed his forehead and he swung away, then came back for more. I liked the edge, the complexity he seemed to represent. Ed was *too* quiet.

Janet Allen, a horsewoman in my area, told me on the phone about her Canadian, and how the horse looked after her on hunts. The mare would hear the sound of hooves on stones ahead and check herself. "They have a terrific sense of self-preservation," she observed, "and that means they're not as bold as you would sometimes like. But they're also extremely generous, and once they trust you they will do anything for you."

Janet has a soothing voice. I'm learning to trust my reading of a horse seller's voice on the phone. I'm starting to sniff the wind. A matter-of-fact voice or a genuine voice is nothing like slick or evasive. One day I grew annoyed as a breeder kept saying *Yes*sir to all my questions. I'm playing hunches now, though I'm not sure why. It never worked at the racetrack.

April 9, 1999
Seeing a horse in a handsome valley north of Toronto. The breeder's ambition is to cross Arabs and Canadians and produce "Arcadians."

She hoped they would have the calm nature yet doggedness of the Canadian, the speed and stamina of the Arab.

I had high hopes for the valley horse, for I'd come far, but the horse seemed small in every way. The trainer, a man of average build, rode him in a paddock for me and looked like a shepherd riding his Shetland. The three-year-old black horse seemed friendly enough and willing enough, but his trot looked choppy and stiff, the canter rudimentary and awkward. An honest horseman, the trainer was not about to praise the horse unduly, even with the owner standing within earshot. "What do you think of his conformation?" I had asked him beforehand, tossing the question into the round pen as the horse circled him, the owner on my flank. "It's OK," he said. "Not a world beater."

In the nearby paddock he rode him briefly, then dismounted and offered, "That's all he knows." Implicit: He doesn't know a lot. Still, he was young. A three-year-old. The trainer called him a baby. A kind horse, a people horse, he followed us around the paddock, nosing for carrots and hoping for sunflower seeds.

His owner told me that a few years ago her horses were daily escaping their paddock and going for jaunts down the road to greener grass, then returning by the same route. But the fence lines were all up in their own paddock. How were they getting out? One morning a friend hid in the bushes to see how they managed it, and he watched open-mouthed as one Canadian horse put his front hoof down on the fence and held it close to the ground while the others scampered over, then a compatriot did the same for him. This was either a genuine story about smart horses or a Lassie-like tale offered in the spirit of legend, I couldn't decide which.

Later, we sat in the woman's truck and she perused a great file folder full of photos. Black Canadians at shows, all oiled and muscled and looking splendid. It was hard to imagine that the fellow in the paddock, his heavy winter coat more brown than black, was a half-brother to these sleek black mares.

The innocent in these matters, but starting to know breeders, I mentioned the names of several other dealers. It was like putting a match to gasoline. That one brought her stud here and undercut my fee. That one kicks foals and his stable is like a pigsty. That one calls herself a trainer but she is, I assure you, a fraud. The woman did not pour vitriol on *all* horse dealers—she was quite kind in her assessment of one I had heard of in Quebec, north of Ottawa—but she was savage in her dismissal of others.

The horse world can seem small; the world of the Canadian horse like a village. Those who breed or train Canadian horses know their closest counterparts, and have had some encounter, pleasant or otherwise, with them. I have sought the advice of many who train and breed Canadian horses, and have been gratified by how helpful and forthcoming most people have been. It was like joining a little club and having old members go out of their way to welcome me. But the network is also scored by ancient grudges and silent partnerships. This breeder is OK, someone confides in me, his brother is not. This one is a purist who breeds chunky, drafty horses; this one has gone for pretty, fine-boned horses. Whatever happened to the middle ground? Whatever happened to discretion?

I feel raw and untutored as I go from farm to farm looking for my little horse of iron. Kathi says I should watch for the little light that will go on when I see the horse of my dreams. "We don't pay enough attention to those signals," she says. If I fail to heed the signal, blame those other sounds—the alarm bells—going off in my head.

Would I know a bowed tendon if I saw one? A capped hock or a cow hock? An enlarged fetlock? A parrot mouth? A bog spavin? A coon foot? A horse over at the knee? A windpuff? Once, in a library, I stumbled across a book of equine terms and pored over it, partly as an exercise in self-torment. There was a whole language I had to learn. Until then, you might have convinced me that a full latigo was a wrestling term, not a part of western tack. Morning Glory was not just a flower, but a horse who ran well in the forenoon and badly in the afternoon. I thought forging and cross-firing were, respectively, terms from the world of farriers and soldiers. In fact, they can also refer to variations on a theme of horses' front and rear feet making contact. Some horses are ewe-necked, goose-rumped, camped out. On every horse there exists, I was astonished to learn, a fly-shaker muscle. The mucous membranes of a healthy horse, I read elsewhere, should be moist and pink. Would I even recognize a horse who's in the pink? Dr. Jean Desrochers, a retired Quebec veterinarian once active in the Canadian horse breed, has written that a well-conditioned horse secretes a watery sweat that disappears promptly when he rests after exercise; a fat horse, on the other hand, produces a thick lather that takes longer to disappear. What's longer when I don't know shorter? Dr. Desrochers warns that a horse with his head low, who seems distant and who keeps himself at the end of his rope, may well be ill. The well-conditioned horse, at rest, will keep one hind leg semi-flexed. The horse's skin should be cool to the touch. His coat should be smooth, shiny and well-oiled. The eyes should sparkle. "Look for a kind eye," horsemen keep telling me.

In the Canadian horse, I am to look for certain traits established as intrinsic to the breed. Head square and short with fine short ears. Well-formed neck leading to a muscled body of medium length. Chest large and deep, breast large and well-muscled. The foot in proportion to the animal's weight: The heavier the horse, the bigger the foot should be. Hind legs straight and parallel, the stance square. Height from 14 to 16 hands. Colours black to dark brown, bay to chestnut. Weight is always a tricky thing to guess. Even height can be deceiving. The Canadian has little or no withers, and since that high point on the back is used to measure horse height, a Canadian is often taller than his official height would suggest.

The Quebec Ministry of Agriculture put out a film in 1992 called *The Conformation of Horses*. The screenplay's English translation is sometimes rocky, but I had no difficulty understanding this phrase:

"Buying a horse isn't a slight thing." The narrator urges the buyer to enter the transaction with eyes wide open and warns that "slight imperfections can have serious consequences."

"The head of the horse," we are told, "is the mirror of its temperament, intelligence and energy." A good head shows refinement and is "well attached to the neck." (I know what this means, but my literal self concocted a vision of screws coming loose and the horse's head slowly disengaging from the body . . .) Ideal is a neck at a 90-degree angle to the head. Speaking of degrees, the shoulder should be long and well-muscled and at 45 to 50 degrees off horizontal. That fine shoulder helps the horse extend his forelegs to lengthen stride and increase speed.

Another angle to consider is that of the pastern, that part of the horse's foot that corresponds to the human ankle. Ideal is one parallel to the angle of the shoulder, thus enabling the pastern to act as shock absorber. Straight shoulder plus upright pastern equals short stride and a bumpy ride on a less-than-fast horse. But an overly long pastern may break down under stress.

Look for strong, wide knees, properly aligned with the rest of the leg. Fetlocks should be wide, compact and oval in shape. Large, open nostrils facilitate breathing. A chest high, broad and deep allows more room inside the chest cavity for heart and lungs. The tail, held strong and stiff, is a sign of a lively temperament. Long backs are weak; short backs are stiff and uncomfortable. The feet are critical. Tiny feet on a large horse spell trouble. A large foot is preferable to a smaller one. Look for balance and symmetry, smooth lines that lead to both soundness and performance.

As buyer, the books say, look and listen. Put questions to the owner and hope for truthful answers. When was the horse last wormed? How does he respond to the farrier? Does he trailer well? Can you easily catch and halter him in the paddock? Is he quiet to work around and does he happily lift his feet to be cleaned? Is he head shy? What bit do you use—a simple snaffle or something more severe?

Has he ever had colic or been injured? Does he pick up the correct canter lead when moving in either direction? How is he with other horses? Is he road safe?

After looking at 10 or 15 horses, a blurring takes effect. One way to keep them separate in your head, I learned, is to have the seller send you a video of the horse being led and walked and ridden; that will spare you unnecessary travel and the seller wasted time. Once the field is narrowed, still photos offer another way of judging conformation. Here are things one should *not* see on the video: A bobbing head, one hip dropping or hiking, or short, stiff movements, all of which may point to lameness; front legs winging in exaggerated fashion to the outside or inside, possibly due to a conformation fault; ears flat back with the rider on, or tail swishing angrily.

Some horse buyers take the horse on a two- or three-week trial. If the horse who seemed agreeable at the seller's barn turns nasty at your barn, you bring him back. However, if the horse is injured in that time, compensation is tricky. In the world of horse buying it is *caveat emptor.*

Even experienced horse buyers go to sellers' barns with one or two horse-wise friends in tow. Some buyers have a vet draw a blood sample from a horse under consideration; the taking of the sample alone may deter unsavoury dealers from drugging horses. Let's say the horse's temperament veers sharply a few days later. If a second blood sample shows no drugs and the first one does, you have grounds to quash the deal.

And while it may be nice to know that the horse you're considering has won ribbons, that alone may mean nothing. As one owner pointed out in droll fashion, a Canadian horse may win "best of show" and the ribbon may be proudly displayed in the barn, but given the paucity of Canadian horses, the winning Canadian may have been the *only* entry.

I'm learning that like cars, horses depreciate. A horse reaches his maximum value between five and eight years of age. After that point, the horse loses value at the rate of 10 per cent a year. And a three-year-old Canadian is indeed just a baby horse. Depending on his bloodline, a three-year-old at 15.2 hands and 1,000 pounds can go to 16 hands and add several hundred pounds by the time he's five. The Ontario association that governs competitive trail riding and endurance riding (OCTRA, the Ontario Competitive Trail Riding Association) insists that horses under four are not eligible for the former, and horses under five may not enter the latter. You don't put babies in marathons. Only the track runs babies, and sometimes to death.

In my travels I learned that sometimes the seller speaks a kind of truth, but when you talk to someone who also knows the horse, a different shading on the facts emerges. One seller, for example, described his Canadian horse as "a gentle giant, a real pet." But the horse will also, the seller conceded, dip 10 feet sideways in a full gallop if he sees something that spooks him, like a hawk flying overhead. He is a horse who will jump an obstacle but only if the rider faces the jump bravely and confidently. This seemed an honest and plain-spoken portrait of the horse, one I rather liked when I saw him.

My own source, an old acquaintance who happened to have some direct experience of the horse, presented a different picture. At my mention of the horse's name, she just said, "Oh my." She called him an oddball. Not brave at jumps, apprehensive, especially in the beginning when the horse was in her schooling stable. "Smart, in his way," she proclaimed him, "but not really affectionate." Her advice: Get him on trial and don't pay the asking price.

Some owners of the Canadian horse use on their calling cards a 19th century lithograph of a Canadian. The horse is black and fine, not at all drafty. And yet some Canadians are as round as baby Percherons. When I look at the photographs in the old pedigree lines, it seems the horse is all over the map. Here a blocky stallion. There a reedy mare. I want to find the middle of those two extremes.

April 15, 1999

On the road in the Ottawa Valley, hunting for horses. First stop the home of Gail Mosher, a breeder of horses for the past 25 years, a farrier, a truck driver (18-wheelers) and mother of two.

Gail broke her neck barrel racing at the age of 19, though nothing in her gait offers a hint of that horrific accident. She lives in the hard country near Mountain, where some farms sprawl and others struggle, where grand houses with rainbow-shaped windows have sprouted down the road from trailer homes on crumbling concrete blocks. The Mosher farm lies somewhere between those two polarities.

An entrepreneurial sort by her own admission, Gail has three jobs at the moment: farrier, breeder and seller of Nikken products— "wellness technology" based on magnet therapy. Injuries to her neck and back from riding in western games at local fairs and from shoeing horses left her willing to try anything that worked. Magnets did.

Gail's farm is at the end of a long gravel driveway and there is no sign of horses. Only as you compass around the house do they come into view in their various paddocks. A few four- and five-year-old geldings here, several colts and fillies there; mare and weaned foal here, half a dozen brood mares over there.

It was the first order of business to meet the horses. The mares left the most powerful impression. I don't think I ever really understood the phrase "a kind eye" until I looked into the face of Gail's mare Classic. This mare and the others came to us, lowered their heads, sniffed me and blew out their warm, sweet exhalations. The mare was interested in the white steno pad I held in my hand; she nibbled at its edges and left some signature horse slobber in one corner. Classic was here.

The wind was high and cold that day, and sometimes sheet metal lying just outside the paddock would lift and ripple and send younger mares into a skittish half circle. The ice storm of 1998 had toppled outbuildings: Only downed beams and rippled metal remembered their locations. The wise old mares took note of the sound too, but they hung by us. And the more I scratched under Classic's chin and caressed her head, the more she groomed me, nuzzling my neck. Gail in her wellies, me in old running shoes, we moved around them and they circled us slowly, like fish in a school.

I thought of the 19th century lithograph of a Canadian horse. The horse is muscled, with a crimped mane and tail, the left foreleg and right hind raised to suggest motion. It's a picture of elegance. Classic, though rounder and carrying a foal, could make her own claim to that elegance.

Not everyone agrees on this point, but most people I talked to warned me against mares. Some can be simply too mare-ish, they said. Unpredictable, moody, so much so that both horse and rider become victim of her estrus cycles. But I was by degrees falling for that black horse from the lithograph, and so far, the mares, far more than the geldings and stallions, had the carriage, the personality I had in mind.

Big gorgeous Classic, her coat still furry from the winter but dappled and silky too, would put back her ears halfway, then immediately send them forward as Gail walked away. "Why are you leaving me?" said the first sign, one of displeasure. "Where are you going?" said the next, one of curiosity. And Classic would start to follow Gail.

Gail took me from horse to horse, telling each one's story. This one had been abused by a previous owner, who used a length of garden hose. This one had her jaw broken in a herd accident. As she walked, Gail described once buying a horse, on conformation alone, at 200 metres. A lifelong hemmer and hawer, I marvelled at such decision-making.

Gail's connection to the Canadian horse dates back to 1978, when Alec Hayward and Donnie Prosperine, both kingpins in the rescue of the Canadian horse breed, brought two mares and a stallion named Viger Duc over to her father-in-law's place. Gail was awestruck. "I had never seen horses so substantial with such a sweet temperament. They were so imposing but in a gentle way. Big gentle quiet horses. They reminded me a lot of my Sable Island pony." (In 1735, a resident of New France used Sable Island to graze his horses, so Gail's pony may well have had Canadian horse ancestors.)

As I drove down the road I kept coming back to Classic's kind eye. There was comfort there and I would want at least some of that quality in the horse out there, somewhere, destined for me.

April 14

Beckett's Creek Farm, northeast of Ottawa. Ray Lalonde, in his farmer coveralls, baseball cap and workboots, is offering a big strapping gelding, 16.1 hands or taller. The horse is eight and has spent most of his working life pulling sleighs and carriages, a job at which he excels.

He's a powerful, muscled horse and in better shape than any other horse I have seen this spring. But an air of suspicion governs him. I wanted to be precise about his height and brought into the saddling area a tall measuring stick. He got wide-eyed and shuddered when I placed it near him. Even letting him smell it failed to moderate his fear. "He's always been wide-eyed," Ray said.

Ray likes him. A willing horse with astonishing strength and stamina. He's cunning too, and manages to slip his halter, but only when no one's around. I didn't like his standoffishness, but he visibly calmed as we stood by him. He got curious about my notepad, but he wasn't nosing around for treats as horses do at farms where they enjoy pet status.

Out in the pasture, Ray's nephew, a chunky rodeo bronc rider, put the horse through his paces. He was no elegant mover. Suddenly, he looked huge. Gangly. Back in the stable was the horse I had really fallen for—another mare, this one called Midnight. Ray said an American had offered him U.S. $18,000 for that horse and he had declined. She was stunning, calm and sweet. The classic Canadian build, soft lines, long mane and tail, handsome head and that kind eye.

In mid-April I sat down with a woman long active in the tiny world of the Canadian horse. June Pelot lives at Clarence Creek, east of Ottawa. She's a 70-something mother of nine, including two adopted children. Her manner on the phone had been warm and welcoming, and so she was in person. She would laugh easily at some remembrance, lifting off the couch to show me a photo in one of several albums rich in horses and riders. I asked her how she got into horses, the Canadian breed in particular.

"I can remember as a young woman," she replied, "bawling on my pony's neck—I've forgotten why—and him pulling his neck around to try and comfort me. Horses kept me steady. They offered another dimension—beyond family." I liked that phrase, *another dimension*.

Though city-born and raised, she was always crazy about horses and purchased her first one without telling her parents. In 1979, June and her husband, Lloyd, bought 50 acres and built the house next door and, later, the one they live in now. A horse, they thought, would be a welcome addition and a useful tax deduction. Pretty soon the horses were Canadian horses, and both Pelots became active in the Ontario wing of the Canadian Horse Breeders' Association and in the Pony Club. They ran summer riding camps and the back forty was home to several dozen horses and ponies.

June's horse Tarka, a 14.2-hand gelding—"a little horse with a big jump," she calls him—made a name for himself at Ottawa-area shows as a jumper and eventer. After raising a slew of Canadian horses, most of them from Alec Hayward's farm, June Pelot has come to certain conclusions about the breed. They are people horses and outdoor horses, she says. It's almost an act of cruelty to stable them. "They like to be outside, to see people, hear dogs barking. Put them in a stall and they weave and crib."

They are also tough horses. "I remember one time one of our Canadians got his foot caught in a fence. I called the vet and he complained that the only time he ever sees Canadian horses is to stitch them up." Part lament, part compliment, the vet's comment reflected the ruggedness of the Canadian.

Pelot's phrase—"The breed is the breed"—puts her on the side of tradition in the great debate that seems to divide the world of Canadian horse breeders. "The Canadian horse," she says, "is a compact horse. Give him tall legs, make him 16 hands or higher, and he ceases to be a Canadian."

Pelot believes he is the ideal family horse, one who loves to work—and eat. "They're easy keepers," says Pelot, "but the problem is keeping the weight off them. They like their food." And like Terry Veevers, she talks about their wilfulness. "Almost all of them have a stubborn streak," she tells me. "It's a benchmark of the breed. I look for it." When I tell June what another owner told me, that the Canadian is a careful horse with a pronounced sense of self-preservation, she snaps her fingers, points at me and says "Bingo!"

I was clearer about the horse I had in mind. But well into April, the month of rain, I was still making calls, still casting about for my little horse of iron. Meanwhile, I was probing deeper into the history of the breed and looking for answers to a conundrum: Why would a heritage horse of such proven value twice face near extinction in the 20th century? The answers, it seemed, lay in the 19th century, when the Canadian horse enjoyed both its greatest glory and the worst sort of neglect.

THE CANADIAN HORSE.

# CHAPTER 3

# THE GREAT SELL-OFF

1800S

*However prized the Canadian horse was south of the border, few on this side realized that this precious resource needed to be protected. Instead, breeders sought to improve it by bringing in other strains, some of them dubious. And when we weren't fiddling with our heritage horses, we were giving them away for a song.*

IT IS CURIOUS THAT SO FEW PEOPLE in this country know about our own national horse, one whose contribution to North American breeding stock in the 19th century may rank second only to the Thoroughbred. Why this gap in our knowledge? When Americans discovered Canadian horses in the 1800s, they saw their value and took them south in great numbers: Canadians became celebrated as pacers and trotters, as

Above: Classic 19th-century lithograph of the Canadian horse.

roadsters and warhorses, and as superb breeding stock.

But at home, the Canadian people looked their own gift horse in the mouth, crossing their horses with various others to "improve" the breed. By the time of Confederation, 1867, the drain on good purebred Canadian horses had reached the critical point. That year, many authorities were lamenting that no quality horses remained in even remote parts of Lower Canada. The great sell-off was well under way.

Twelve years later, the principal of the Montreal Veterinary College remarked that "in the province of Quebec, we are assured by those best qualified to give an opinion, that our horses are steadily but surely degenerating. The question is often asked; why? and the reply is always the same; the country is overrun by cheap mongrel stallions."

The demise of the Canadian horse was fuelled by several powerful forces: poverty in this country, civil war south of the border, and the strange dictates of fashion. Let's examine the last item first. The defeat of the French on the Plains of Abraham in 1759 seemed to open the floodgates as the victorious English opted for favourite breeds from home. *Le cheval canadien* was no longer the only game in town. A kind of free trade in horses ensued. Horse traders in New York and New England, in Michigan and Illinois recognized the quality of Canadian horses and bred them with their own horses to improve local stock. Farmers in Upper Canada and the Maritimes also looked to Lower Canada for horses. But the fact remains that most Canadian horsemen never really appreciated the home breed, one practically chiseled from granite and after two centuries superbly adapted to the Canadian climate.

However prized the breed was south of the border, few on this side realized that this precious resource needed to be nurtured and protected. Instead, breeders sought to improve it by bringing in other horses, other strains, some of them dubious choices. And when we weren't fiddling with our heritage horses, we were giving them away for a song.

The defeat of the French seemed to create a first: a market beyond New France for French horses. Among the early customers, around 1765, was a young Benedict Arnold, who used to trade cheese, stockings and other goods in the St. Lawrence Valley for horses. Another horse dealer from New York State would go to Montreal, buy up to 75 horses at a time and then drive them down Lake Champlain on the ice before shipping them to the West Indies. A great many Canadian horses were sent to the Caribbean to work on sugar plantations, their bloodlines tossed into the equine mix and no doubt to the good.

Yet another market formed after the American Revolution of 1776 when Loyalists fled to Upper Canada and bought so many horses that the Canadian became their foundation stock and could be found all over what would become Ontario until the middle of the 19th century. Between 1800 and 1810, horses in great numbers moved from the St. Lawrence River on the Quebec side to farmers in northern New England, especially western Vermont. The dealers were called "horse-jockies" or, as one historian put it, "contemptible wretches." Canadians were bred to whatever horses were there and the result, by the 1820s and 1830s, was a breed prized by stagecoach operators between Boston and Portland for its strength and endurance.

The market south of the border kept growing, especially after the War of 1812. Special horse markets were set up at both Quebec and Montreal; in the latter city, reports historian Robert Leslie Jones, "a specialized horse market known sometimes as the 'the Tattersall's of Montreal' was established in a hotel-yard in the centre of the city." The farmers of Lower Canada raised more and more horses, specifically to sell them, especially when a wheat failure in 1815 left them with little else to sell. In Boston and New York, fast Canadian trotters could fetch up to $700.

By 1840, French farmers were no longer racing their horses on glare ice in friendly competition with neighbours. This practice dated back to the 1700s, when parishioners would race home from Mass

for sport. By the mid-19th century, the *habitants* were actually training their horses with an eye to selling them to Americans.

The farmers of Lower Canada, inadvertently, were creating
future world-class pacers and trotters. Their ancestors, out of need or
a pure sense of fun, had for centuries been making their horses into
superb athletes. The earliest settlers had travelled between Montreal
and Quebec on sleighs drawn by dogs. By the 1700s, when horse
numbers began to increase exponentially, the horse allowed what must
have seemed quick access to far-flung neighbours. *Habitants* thought
nothing of travelling 150 kilometres in a single day over ice.

Racing from church was considered great sport. Drivers would
even handicap each other, swapping children and adults from carriage
to carriage to even the odds, as in modern Thoroughbred racing when
a superior horse often must carry more weight than lesser charges.

Ice races, quite famous in the 19th century, were held at Quebec
City, Trois-Rivières, Montreal and Missisquoi Bay. As a result of such
races, two of the best known Canadian trotters, Lady Moscow and
St. Lawrence, were acquired by Americans. So important were the
ice races that farmers began to import new breeds into the country
with an eye to breeding for victory on the frozen courses. New breeds
were formed, such as the Canadian pacer (a blend of the Narragansett
pacer of Rhode Island and the old pacing strains of the Canadian
horse). George Barnard, a horse dealer and breeder in Sherbrooke
during the mid-19th century, remembered his grandfather taking
Rhode Island pacers "to the French Country about and beyond
Quebec, where they were readily sold, or exchanged for the stout
native work horses."

Barnard was then *the* authority on the old Canadian horse. He
observed that *habitants* of the mid-1800s, especially, valued the pacers for racing on the ice: The country of the seigneuries, he said, "is
. . . well peppered with pacing horses: I say *peppered*, for their presence forms the *seasoning* of their owners' life throughout the long cold
winters."

Thoroughbreds were also crossed with French-Canadian horses. In Lower Canada and the northern parts of the United States, they called them "Frenchers" and, around Montreal, "St. Lawrences": horses combining great speed with power. They were usually the product of a Thoroughbred sire and a Canadian dam, but not always. One, called Conqueror, was named best horse in Canada on three occasions. The Frenchers became best known as roadsters, and their dams contributed mightily to the makeup of the American trotter.

Stories told about the Canadian often painted him in quiet heroic pose, a horse you could count on. One story has it that a butcher in Quebec City had extended an overly long line of credit to a customer. At closing time one day, the butcher learned that the gentleman had boarded a steamship for Montreal with all his earthly possessions. When he rushed to the dock, the butcher saw the man on the upper decks saucily bidding him adieu. Whereupon the butcher hitched up his delivery cart to his Canadian horse, the one he had used on his rounds earlier in the day, and that night covered the 185 miles non-stop to Montreal and beat the steamer. He had gone the distance in less than 12 hours: better than 15 miles an hour.

Despite his many qualities, the *marche donc* dwindled in numbers. As early as 1835 some observers were lamenting that all this crossbreeding was making it hard to find purebred Canadian horses around Montreal. Robert Leslie Jones refers to the "mongrelization" of the breed as a result of "weedy and vicious horses brought in by American dealers." That process happened with alarming speed in Prince Edward Island and Nova Scotia where the Canadian existed in smaller numbers. There the "improving" of Canadians was causing the breed to disappear. In New Brunswick, only among the Acadians were Canadian horses still to be found in the late 1840s.

Jones, who wrote an extraordinarily comprehensive essay on the Canadian horse in 1947, makes an interesting point: Because Quebec farmers were not in the habit of gelding their stallions, the choice for potential buyers of breeding stallions was great. And owing to their great numbers, the studs were cheap. In fact, so many stallions went south of the border that it had what Jones calls "a deleterious effect" on the breed.

He also talks about the prepotency of Canadian sires—their ability to pass on special characteristics to their offspring. Sires of 14 hands bred to common mares of 15 hands produced horses of 15.2 and 16 hands. The author of a book on horse breeding in 1845, George Barnard remarked that "the loss of the coarser marks of the parents in these crosses is sometimes astonishing." In Vermont, New Hampshire, in New Jersey and northern New York, the Canadian horse was much prized as breeding stock. The infusion of blood from these little horses of iron gave stamina and character to their offspring and produced wonderful road horses.

The horse authorities of the mid-1800s fell over themselves praising the Canadian horse. Frank Forester's *Horse and Horsemanship of the United States and British Provinces of North America*, published in 1857, paints a precise and effusive picture of the breed:

> His crest is lofty, and his demeanour proud and coura-
> geous. His breast is full and broad; his shoulder strong,
> though somewhat inclined to be heavy; his back broad,
> and his croup round, fleshy and muscular . . . His legs
> and feet are admirable; the bone large and flat, and the
> sinews big, and nervous as steel springs. His feet seem
> almost unconscious of disease. His fetlocks are shaggy,
> his mane voluminous and massive, not seldom, if
> untrained, falling on both sides of his neck, and his tail
> abundant, both having a peculiar *crimpled* wave . . . the
> like of which I never saw in any horse which had not
> some strain of this blood.
>
> He cannot be called a speedy horse in his pure
> state; but he is emphatically a quick one, an indefa-
> tiguable [*sic*] undaunted traveller, with the greatest
> endurance, day in and day out, allowing him to go on

at his own pace, say from six to eight miles the hour,
with the horse's load behind him, of any animal I have
ever driven. He is extremely hardy, will thrive on any
thing, or almost on nothing; is docile, though high-spirited, remarkably sure-footed on the worst ground . . .

As a farm-horse and ordinary farmer's roadster,
there is no honester or better animal; and, as one to
cross with other breeds . . . he has hardly an equal.

Other historical accounts similarly extolled the Canadian horse's merits. Etienne Michel Faillon, a 19th century priest, described the
Canadian horse as "small but robust, hocks of steel, thick mane floating in the wind, bright and lively eyes, pricking its sensitive ears at
the least noise, going along day and night with the same courage . . .
spirited, good, gentle, affectionate, following his road with the finest
instinct to come surely home to his own stable."

There is a saying among horse people: "No foot, no horse." Foot
problems among horses are endemic in the 20th century, especially
as breeders and buyers bow to fashion and let practical considerations
slide. A striking aspect of the literature on the Canadian horse, especially from the 19th century when roadsters came into vogue, is the
extent to which the Canadian horse was prized for his feet. Even
then, it seems, horsemen worried about their horses' hooves. Here
is *The Home, Farm and Business Cyclopedia* of 1883:

No race of horses has sounder and more powerful
limbs and none can equal the Canadian as to feet—
these being tough, hard, iron-like and free from disease even under the most unfavorable circumstances.

Henry William Herbert, in his book, *Hints to Horse-Keepers*, published in 1859, pointed out what he perceived to be flaws in the
Canadian. He found them low and heavy at the withers, and lamented

their thick necks, straight shoulders and long backs. But he had far more praise than complaint. He liked their "small clear eye" and their "courageous aspect." And he, too, remarked on their feet:

> . . . the soundest, most undeniable, flat-boned legs that are to be found in any race of horses not thoroughbred, and the toughest, hardest and most iron-like feet that are to be found in any race whatsoever. In fact, immunity from diseases of the legs and feet, under the most unfavorable circumstances—when ill-groomed, ill-shod and subject to every trial and hardship—appears to be the distinguishing mark of the French Canadian horse.

Herbert, too, was struck by the Canadian horse's great heart and work ethic. "Their excellence," he wrote, "is universally acknowledged."

Robert Leslie Jones called the Canadian horse at this point, the middle 1800s, "indubitably among the best in North America." William Evans, another agricultural authority of the time, echoed prevailing Canadian and American opinion when he wrote that the Canadian horse "when of sufficient size, cannot be excelled for agricultural purposes by any horse we have ever seen on this continent." Evans called the Canadian horse the breed of choice for farmers in this country.

Observers in Nova Scotia likewise praised the Canadian horse. Writing in the *Colonial Farmer* of March 1843, Titus Smith said Canadians "make excellent horses for steep hills, bad roads and scanty pastures."

No surprise, the Canadian found favour with the North West Mounted Police and the military. The mounted units of the Montreal and Calgary police forces still use them.

I mentioned earlier that poverty contributed mightily to the crash in the Canadian horse population. One can hardly blame farmers for selling whatever they produce on the farm to eke out a living. And 19th century farmers in Quebec were hard put. If it wasn't declining prices, it was weather or insects or blight. But in selling or trading their horses, farmers in Quebec rarely perceived the transaction as a fire sale. Impecunious though they might have been, they saw themselves as good and wise judges of horseflesh. Observers saw it differently.

An Englishman named John Lambert who was visiting Quebec in 1806 very much admired the Canadian horse—a "fine little horse"—and he was somewhat horrified that horse trading with Americans was woefully unbalanced. Canadian horsemen, he noted, "are very fond of a horse which runs with a quick shuffling pace, and the Americans bring in with them a parcel of rickety animals which possess that accomplishment." The Canadian horse, bought for 10 or 12 pounds in Canada, would fetch three to four times that in Boston and New York. "The Canadians," wrote Lambert, "are reckoned very adroit at a bargain, and even fond of overreaching; but they sink in comparison with an American horse-dealer."

It may have seemed in hindsight that Canadian horse traders lost their shirts. In fact, though, the pacers were quicker on ice: The farmers of Quebec were simply trying to win some races, and hoped to improve their own stock by bringing in new blood. And if, indeed, the farmer made a poor bargain, perhaps he was in no position to haggle. Margaret Atwood, the eminent Canadian writer, early in her career revealed an abiding interest in Canadian history. Her book, *Days of the Rebels 1815–1840*, published in 1977, shows much evidence of her trademark wit as she paints the rebels in all their secret-society silliness. But she also paints a picture of reeling Lower Canada and helped me understand some of the economics behind the great sell-off of horses.

Atwood points out that the British takeover of Lower Canada darkened prospects for the French through the 1800s. The soil on their St. Lawrence Valley farms soon grew exhausted from overcultivation as the land was overworked and subdivided among families. British and American land speculators drove up the price of good land.

Immigrant ships brought Irish and Scots, and worse, cholera. In 1832, an epidemic ripped through Montreal and Quebec, killing thousands. The 1830s meant hard times for the French as insect plagues and floods ruined harvests. The poverty that ensued, with francophone beggars in the streets looking on as the British prospered, only fanned the flames of Louis-Joseph Papineau's *patriote* movement. Small wonder that amid such hardship the *habitants* sold their one possession still commanding a price: their Canadian horses.

Canadian horses turned up all over the continent, as some 500,000 Quebecers in the mid- to late-1800s sought new beginnings to the south and west, often taking their best horses with them or selling them off before departing. Ramsay Cook, the distinguished Canadian historian, called the diaspora of francophones "a national hemmorhage." Cook made the comment during a public lecture in Toronto in January 2000 at the Art Gallery of Ontario, then featuring an exhibition of paintings by Cornelius Krieghoff (in which the Canadian horse figured prominently). Francophones of the day, he said, feared that their new English masters would restrict their freedoms of language and religion and so they fled. "Today," said Cook, "we would call it ethnic cleansing."

Cook seemed especially interested in the Canadian horse; he kept using the phrase "these wonderful horses" during his lecture. (So keen on the Canadian horse did Cook seem that later, when he took questions from the audience, I asked him to explain his affection. His response suggested that he loves the idea of the heritage horse more than the horse in the flesh. "The horse," said this man who grew up on a farm in Saskatchewan, "is the only animal I'm afraid of.") Up on a stage, and referring to slides of Krieghoff paintings from the mid-1800s projected behind him onto a screen, Cook demonstrated the dramatic differences between the horses and carriages native to Quebec and the ones favoured by the English. The English gentry rode in sleighs with thin wrought-iron runners pulled by tall, thin, tiny-footed Hackneys. The French farmers stuck with their plain sleds with wooden runners pulled by their burly little horses of iron.

The *berlines*, though, tended to create *cahots*, or bumps in the road—skiers would call them moguls—which the *berlines* had no trouble navigating but which resulted in woefully bumpy rides for the delicate English sleighs. The British ordered the *habitants* to switch over to their style of sleigh. The French, of course, refused.

But they could see the writing on the wall.

Some *habitants* emigrated to the Red River Valley in Manitoba. Others set down new roots in New England and elsewhere in the United States, and they, too, took their horses with them. In Michigan, the Canadian horse population tended to stay in the hands of old French settlers around Detroit where locals called the Canadian "a poor man's horse." In 1872, an observer in Detroit complained of the horses that "they receive literally no care whatever, and roam in bands, scouring along the roads with the speed of liberty, and often making the night hideous with the uproar."

In the 19th century, the Canadian horse also spread into the Indian country of the upper Mississippi Valley and the Canadian northwest, where the breed mixed with the bronco of the southwestern plains. Many escaped and ran free with the mustangs of the plains.

My own first ride on a young Canadian horse early in the spring of 1999 had some of that same sense of abandon and high adrenalin. I would remember every moment of that ride, brief though it was.

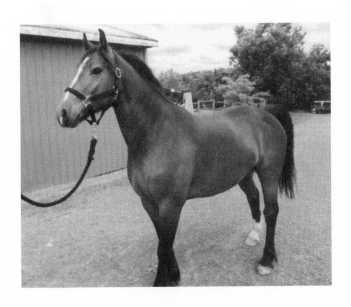

# RIDING HIGH ON A LITTLE HORSE

---

### SAROMA FARM, MAY 1999

*He went into the trot easily enough, then the head dropped, and the next instant I was*

*airborne . . . From the ground I was afforded a wonderful view of a spirited horse, his*

*black tail high, sprinting across the wide field, through the gate and into a grove of trees.*

MY BODY IS SORE IN FOUR different places. On my left hip is a bruise the size of a grapefruit, with a long red contusion where my upper thigh struck the ground and scraped as I skidded to a halt. An angry black edging is today filling in around the red. All very colourful. My inner left thigh hurts. One foot. The right elbow.

After a mostly sleepless night, I awoke this morning feeling overwhelmed by my first ride on a Canadian horse. For 10 years I've ridden what cousin Kathi calls "packers"—horses who admirably carry

Above: The young, untrained Saroma Dark Fox Dali.

---

on and do their jobs despite the shortcomings of their riders. I had ridden many horses: school horses at Wilmarny Farm, highly trained cutting horses and reformed mustangs in Wyoming and Alberta, a fine polo pony in Vermont, agreeable equine mutts that friends loaned willy-nilly to their horseless pals for trail rides. But always they were schooled horses. I had never ridden a totally green horse ("rude and green," Kathi called the combination) and I had never been thrown. Only one horse, a complicated mare at Wilmarny called Cassie, ever tried. Until yesterday.

May 4, 1999

Alec Hayward, that patriarch of the breed, had seen a bay in Jérôme Aumond's herd up near Maniwaki, Quebec, a few hours due north of Ottawa, that he thought might suit me. We made arrangements to see him together. I would drive to Alec's house near North Gower, south of Ottawa, and we would head north from there.

"Look for the house with the 1928 Essex in the front yard," Alec had told me on the phone. The voice had struck me as Ottawa Valley Irish, but it seems there's Scottish and English layered in as well. He had, I noted, small eyes that squint into the sun, an ample belly and a handsome white beard that complements his hair.

He carried with him that day a maple cane, yet he didn't limp and he never leaned on it. On its handle was a silver snap. When you flipped the snap aside, out came a hard metal measuring tape for determining the height of a horse. Alec had hurt his back in a riding accident many years beforehand—coming off a Morgan, he said. But there was something quite youthful about the man. He sported denim jeans and shirt and topped it all with an Australian outback hat he had bargained for at some county fair. I had the sense that Alec Hayward would haggle over the price of breakfast in a restaurant.

I had called him a month beforehand, introduced myself and my project and told him I would be grateful if he would keep an eye out. He's a virtual broker, constantly marrying riders and Canadian horses. Sometimes he gets a finder's fee, but typically no money passes hands. When I called him back early in May he said he might have something for me to look at.

A bay, he said. Fifteen hands, five years old. A real eye-catcher. Top shape. Broke to harness and saddle. The seller had gone over to Belgians. Has more money, said Alec, than brains. Jérôme Aumond was acting as agent. "I like Jérôme," Alec said. "He's dedicated to the breed, not the wallet."

All this Alec told me on the phone a few days before Dali put me in orbit.

The horse's actual name is Saroma Dark Fox Dali; his sire is Hobbyhorse Larry's Dark Fox. It seemed to me that a horse named after a wild painter, and whose dad was called Larry, just might be the ticket. The signs looked auspicious. The August 1996 issue of *Le cheval canadien*, I had earlier noticed, showed Larry winning a mittful of prizes at a horse show.

Dali's father's sire, La Gorgendière Fox Larry, is part of the line of horses that came from an experimental farm at Deschambault, the last government-sponsored program that tried to rescue the Canadian horse when its future looked bleak. Deschambault was also the scene of a cavalry battle near the Plains of Abraham, where Dali's ancestors fought with the French against the English. So Dali came with a dash of history.

Dali was a registered horse, 93.8 per cent purebred Canadian. He looked, on paper at least, the most interesting of any horse I had seen in my quest. The full name of a registered Canadian horse tells his history. Saroma Dark Fox Dali tells me that Jérôme and Sara of Ferme Saroma (Saroma Farm) owned the horse's dam, Ranch-L Nicot Ukraine, at the time of foaling; that his sire is Hobbyhorse Larry's Dark Fox; and the *D* tells the year of his birth (1994), when the names of all registered Canadian horses had to start with that letter.

It's strange, but of the dozen or so horses I have seen in my travels, none grabbed me enough to want to ride them. I brought my chaps, boots and helmet on each of these forays, but I either dismissed the horse as too tall or chunky, too small or otherwise inappropriate. Or perhaps I thought I would reconsider and come back accompanied by a rider with greater skill than I possess. This one, Dali, perhaps because he was so far from home and a second trip seemed prohibitive, merited me getting on. There were, I admit, warning signs. Jérôme had trouble putting the bit in place. The horse bent around and cast a wide and suspicious eye at the western saddle. And when Jérôme mounted him just outside the barn, Dali headed back inside and only a quick turn by Jérôme avoided a nasty encounter between his head (he wore no helmet) and the barn's low roof.

Out in the sprawling field, the horse's canter seemed tentative. Even steering him was not easy. Jérôme trotted him when I asked him to, and in hindsight it seemed significant that he trotted him *towards* the barn first. Coincidence? Or a smart move on a barn-sour horse.

Dali, a powerfully built bay, 15 hands tall and close to 1,200 pounds, seemed the right size for the job. The horse of my dreams was a few inches taller and maybe leaner, but he seemed a better bet for long rides than those 16-hand stretch Canadians I had been seeing.

In Jérôme's hands, he struck me as raw but agreeable enough. No swishing of the tail. Easy trot. Ears forward. I got on him and we walked a bit. He would do little dances now and again, and though steering was indeed a challenge, I was managing all right. It was when I asked him to trot, away from the barn, that the speed of this little film picked up considerably. He went into the trot easily enough, then the head dropped, and the next instant I was airborne. It was probably my loud and quite absurdly timed mid-air "whoah" that spooked him and sent him tearing off into the next paddock.

From the ground I was afforded a wonderful view of a spirited horse, his black tail high, sprinting across the wide field, through the gate and into a grove of trees. Bereft of his rider, he was no longer the confused young horse trying to read aids but a fast lone horse with a little taste of freedom. He repeatedly tried bucking off the saddle and I thought I read in his antics a little smugness.

In minutes Jérôme and a crew of young lads were in a powder-blue truck moving along the dusty two-lane track that led to the next paddock. It looked like an ambulance in some foreign land where there is no money to paint red crosses on the sides of the truck. The scene offered no sense of either urgency or emergency, for the truck moved awfully slowly, as if gas was a concern; it all seemed, but only in retrospect, quite comical.

Numb, but somehow propelled, I walked in slow wincing pursuit of the truck. In the far field and after some 10 minutes of chasing, the crew finally cornered Dali, Jérôme using a bucket of grain as bribe to get him in hand. Jérôme is a swarthy man with an agreeable manner and a nice sense of mischief ("Any vices?" I had asked him in French beforehand during lunch, referring, of course, to the horse I had come to see, and he replied that while the horse had none, he himself had plenty.) Jérôme now rode the horse back to me.

By this point Dali was quite wet from his exertions and wide-eyed. The notion of me getting back on him clearly troubled us both. Jérôme made a circling motion with his right hand, then flipped it palm-side up while nodding his head to me, a gesture that said, "Shall we try once more?" Even while my body moved forward, a voice in my brain was loudly urging hesitation. Dali skitted a little under that hot sun and eased away from my boot as I went to mount him. I paused again, talked to him some more, stroked his side and finally decided it was time to get back on him. Pure instinct guided me, and I remember all this as if it were a dream.

The ride back was fine. The gates, entering the near paddock and leaving it, gave him pause. Me too. I had a vision of me, one foot caught in the stirrup, striking the posts while being dragged like bloody bait behind a speedboat. They would come for me in a flatbed truck, my parts to be reassembled later by forensic anatomists—a term project for some med student. "Killed by Dali, darling," one droll student would say to the other. "Not that Salvador fellow, but Dark Fox Dali, that famous horse."

"You know," Alec said to me as I dragged my bruised body up the hill towards the car at Jérôme's farm and folded my chaps into the trunk, "I'm not a fan of this arrangement of meeting a strange horse and five minutes later taking him for a ride."

The words "Thanks for telling me now" formed in my brain.

When I told all this to cousin Kathi, who has had horses in her life for 25 years and ponies for a decade beforehand, she laughed most heartily. Not *at* me, she insisted, but with me. Getting my feet wet, really wet, at the age of 50, I took her back to when she was a girl making similar mistakes and, later, when she and her husband, Dick, began to shape a life around horses. They now have five, and with Kathi coaching and Dick riding at up to the intermediate level, they are a superb eventing team.

A young raw horse, she said, needs to have absolute confidence in his rider. By being asked to trot away from the barn and towards a gate that frightened him, he felt I was taking him into danger. "I know better than you do," the horse was saying, so the head went down and the back end snapped me skyward. As gravity pulled me hard back to earth I caught a peripheral view of the back hooves finishing their kick and a quick horse accelerating. I thought of something Tom Dorrance, an old gentler in Oregon, once said. As a boy riding along fences looking for breaks in the line he felt it important to get on with his horse, because an unhorsed rider on a sprawling western ranch faced a long walk home in good weather. In winter, should a blizzard flare, he faced death.

All the way home that day, my car hugging the road along the canyon walls of the Gatineau River, I thought of where I wanted to be on the scale of risk and safety. A bombproof horse was not what I wanted, but neither did I want a crazy horse. Where did Dali fit?

I hoped he occupied the middle, but I was not at all sure that the buck had stopped with Dali.

The second horse of the day, one I also had some hope for, was a 10-year-old called Xector. He was a 16-hand chestnut, quite a beauty actually, but he had the lean build of a Thoroughbred and he looked least like a Canadian of any I had seen. Only the mane and high cheekbones spoke of his traditional bloodline.

Worst of all, he would not be caught in the paddock. He had bonded with a little Appaloosa, and had taught his little buddy to evade capture as well. But there was little game in his avoidance. Fear bordering on panic got him out of corners. He would as soon run you over as let you grab his halter.

It took half an hour to herd him into the barn and then into a stall. "You never did ask me what I want for him," the owner called out to me as she and Alec and I played tag with Xector and the Appie. "I know," I shouted, "but I assume the price is going down by the minute!"

In the stall, Xector circled and eyed us warily. Even when Alec offered him a treat, he sniffed it cautiously and started back. The original owner, whom I had tracked down in Quebec before this visit, had called him on the phone "a safety horse," an honest horse but not a leader. He had been used as a carriage horse but had been sold eight months beforehand and changed hands three or four times. What baggage did he carry now? Had he been beaten? Had he landed with someone who actually feared him?

I never rode him. His owner said he was a joy to hack with and a fabulous jumper. Still, all else aside, I thought him too tall for the long ride. I wished him well and headed home.

Alec Hayward liked Dali. It was a blessing, an imprimatur. I didn't much enjoy hitting the ground not two minutes into the first ride, and buying him was far from my mind as I drove home with Alec.

But I had to admire the spirit that informed Dali's buck, and the more distance I put between me and that horse, the more he seemed to call out to me. I kept replaying the film in my mind, not of me sailing through the air, but of him racing to the far gate, eating up the ground and occasionally pausing in mid-air to buck some more.

"I like Dali," Alec said as we followed the meandering line of the river home. "He's a lovely little bay. I like his characteristics, his conformation. When he walks, one foot goes in a bit but that's because one foot is worn at an angle and all he needs is a little trim to get the foot back out. He's well set up. He stands straight. He's well balanced."

I was intrigued by this horse, intrigued enough to learn more about his sire. Hobbyhorse Larry's Dark Fox, I later learned, had been bred on the farm of Gladys Mackey Beattie, an anglophone Quebecer who had written *The Canadian Horse: A Pictorial History* in the early 1980s. The horse was later leased by Suzanne Spierenburg, a rider in Rocky Mountain House, Alberta. Now a major breeder of Canadian horses, with 23, she had Larry from 1996 through 1998.

And she rode the stallion for several years in the Battle of the Breeds at Spruce Meadows in Calgary, a world-class equestrian facility. The Battle of the Breeds is pure entertainment. Held during intermissions in elite show-jumping competitions, it features horses large and small, from Percherons to ponies, in competition. Imagine a draft horse going over jumps or barrel racing and you get the idea. But it's also an opportunity for breeders to show off their horses, and competitors take the event very seriously.

At first glance, Hobbyhorse Larry's Dark Fox seemed a most unlikely entry. Here is Spierenburg's sketch of him: "Quite a horse, a neat horse with a lot of drive. Real personality. All stud. If there was a mare in the country, he'd know about it. He wasn't laid back at all, very flighty and energetic. A high-maintenance horse and very smart. He was a worrier. He'd pace in his stall and I used to joke that if someone put him in a lowland stall he'd dig his way to China."

Fox, as Spierenburg called him (though she also called him Larry when he acted up), turned out to be a gifted and keen jumper. And all that pacing and tearing around paddocks meant he was in superb shape. He was a little tucked up, stood 15.2 hands and weighed about 1,200 pounds. "He had not been ridden since he was five," Spierenburg said, recalling her first ride on him when he was 12. "He was real feisty, and Alfred Cartier, who owned him then, led me on that horse all over his farm."

But she liked him, took him home and for three years took lessons on him with a local eventer, Trish Dahms, who competed for Canada in the Pan-Am Games at Winnipeg in 1999 and narrowly missed going to the Sydney Olympics in the summer of 2000. "He loved jumping," said Spierenburg, "as much as he loved mares. But he would rush the jumps and we had to use a gag snaffle he was so keen. He was just an awesome jumper."

On the other hand, he had no manners. Spierenburg would have to keep him to the perimeter at shows because he would lunge at mares. And she had to park him alone in a paddock, for she was certain he would kill any gelding put out with him. Yet he was playful. He'd play ball with buckets, he was never mean with his rider, he eventually did learn his manners, and the more she rode him the better he got.

For two years running, he was the best jumper in the Battle of the Breeds, and would have won a third year had he not knocked down an optional fence, a so-called "joker" fence, that Spierenburg elected to try. He was also a fine barrel racer, though his dressage, which had showed promise during training, collapsed under the stress and distractions of competition.

Though Fox represented his breed ably in that competition, he was, by Spierenburg's own admission, not a typical Canadian horse. "A lot of people who are green about horses have bought the hype about the Canadian as a laid-back horse. Well, Canadians are horses and they can spook and buck like any other horse. But most

Canadians are, in fact, quiet. We took a Canadian horse from the Henryville line to the Battle of the Breeds, and in one event the rider is supposed to pull a balloon towards the horse. The balloon had a happy face on it and it was making most of those horses crazy. That Henryville horse just ate grass; he barely looked up. Nothing bothered him." Last Spierenburg heard, Fox was doing not much of anything, neither bred nor ridden. "A waste of a good horse," Spierenburg lamented.

The odds were that Dali was at least a little like his dad, maybe a lot. But perhaps he took after his mother, Ranch-L Nicot Ukraine. Or maybe he had in him some of his granddam on his father's side, Ducat Major Nancy, out of the Henryville line.

There are eight major bloodlines in the Canadian horse stud book, each with its own folklore. Henryville horses are said to be quiet, Fox horses spirited, Lou horses cantankerous, and those who own Viger or Royal or Becancour, Pitro or La Gorgendière Major horses have no doubt heard other labels for these lines. But my sense is that the sire is only one component in the shaping of a Canadian horse; the dam, early training, even fate, all come into play. I was keenly curious to know Dali's progenitors, but eventually I would come to the conclusion that genealogy took me only partway to understanding him.

He had had almost nothing by way of training under saddle. And I had ridden him carelessly. Take away all that, school him, win his confidence and underneath, perhaps, lay an honest horse who was very much there, as that owner near Belleville had put it. More there than any horse I had seen in my journeys.

Perhaps Dali would not be a typical Canadian, not so docile and sweet-tempered, but he might be more athletic than most. Besides, it was foolish and misleading to burden one horse as the flagcarrier for a breed. Dali was Dali, and for reasons I did not immediately fathom, his name lodged in my brain.

I thought of that old rhyme.

*One white sock buy a horse,*
*Two white socks try a horse,*
*Three white socks look well about him,*
*Four white socks do without him.*

Dali had one white sock.

It looked as if Dali was fated to fall into the hands of a man who had much to learn about handling horses. But there are far worse fates. The Canadian horse, I am afraid, made a very good warhorse and many wars had use of him. Dali's ancestors and thousands of their kin fought in the American Civil War, a cruel and bloody carnage that cut a great swath through what remained of Canada's little iron horses in the latter stages of the 19th century.

Above: *A Mobile Veterinary Unit in France*, 1919.

CHAPTER 5

# THE CANADIAN HORSE AS WARHORSE

---

AUGUST 1864

*A Union artilleryman described how horses were not simply struck down by random fire,*
*but were actual targets. He remarked on the "peculiar dull thud" that a bullet*
*made when it entered the fleshy part of a horse, "sounding much as a pebble does*
*when thrown into mud."*

FOR ALL HIS VERSATILITY AS PLOUGH HORSE and carriage horse and
Sunday riding horse, and for all his high regard as a generally peace-
ful, good-natured horse, the Canadian was bred and built for war.
The burly horses sent by the Sun King were descended from
Norman warhorses, chargers capable of carrying the 220-kilogram
load of a knight and his armour into battle. The Canadian horse's

story, like that of many many horses through time, is steeped in blood and carnage.

If the Canadian line came perilously close to ending as the 20th century dawned, war played a part. Even before 1850 there began a steady flow of Canadian horses south across the border. The price of horses in the United States rose following the Mexican War—one made famous by the battle at Alamo, Texas, in 1836—and steadily climbed as the century wore on. The American market for horses kept expanding and sales of Canadian horses surged. One observer remarked, in 1848, on "the high prices paid for the pure breed of Canadian horses, by strangers, at Montreal." The horse dealers would eventually go beyond Montreal to the places known for their concentrations of purebreds—L'Islet and Beauce.

Dealers could have been buying for the coach trade, for racing stock, or for quartermasters. The seller never asked the fate of his horses; some dealers never cared, and the ones who did perhaps refrained from imagining the miseries of conscripted horses. As for the horses themselves, they never volunteered for war as men did, never knew the risks as men did. They simply did men's bidding, and as flighty and fearful as some horses are, nothing in their experience could have prepared them for what lay ahead.

As Civil War loomed in the United States, a Cavalry Bureau was formed in Washington to inspect all cavalry units and to coordinate the purchase and supply of horses. A large cavalry depot also took shape at Giesboro, near Washington.

The Union Army was initially low on cavalry but soon found more horses and the means to train them. The Canadian horse was an obviously close and valuable resource. The New Hampshire cavalry units, for example, were mounted almost exclusively on Morgans and Canadians. The First Massachusetts Cavalry, reads that unit's own historical record, "was fortunate to be mounted on horses brought in from Canada. These horses, known as Canucks, were ideal for cavalry service. They were small and tough and accustomed to variable weather and little food." The record goes on to say that of the original issue of Canadians to the 750-strong regiment in 1861, only one was left in 1864: That horse was stolen from his owner at a river crossing in Virginia.

The First Regiment of Massachusetts Volunteer Cavalry, as it was formally known, gathered men from existing state military organizations: the Boston Dragoons, the Boston Lancers, the Waltham Dragoons, the Springfield Horseguards. All these Yankees, some of them Harvard grads, would ride into war on Canadian horses.

The hell that marked their training offered only a taste of what was to come. Men and horses engaged in drills on a sandy island off South Carolina where temperatures reached 110 degrees in the shade. Flies and biting insects compounded their misery. As skirmishes with the Rebels led to battles, many of the horses succumbed to bullets and disease. Horses often lacked shelter, they stood on picket lines in mud up to their knees, and were often kept saddled for days on end.

Letters from soldiers, like the one from Charles Francis Adams Jr. of the First Massachusetts Cavalry to his father on June 19, 1863, contain grim accounts of actual battle. Valor came salted with confusion and cowardice. The letter reads:

> We were engaged at Aldie's Gap day before yester-
> day, and very roughly used . . . My poor men were
> just slaughtered and all we could do was stand still
> and be shot down . . . The men fell right and left
> and the horses were shot through and through . . .
> the 4th New York on our right gave way without a
> fight or an instant's resistance, and in a second the
> rebs were riding yelling and slashing among us . . .
> I lost thirty-two as good men and horses as can be
> found in the cavalry corps. They seemed to pick out
> my best and truest men, my pets and favorites . . .

No one knows how many Canadian horses were bought for use in the war, but one estimate suggests the four-year struggle consumed millions of horses. Given the hard economic times in Lower Canada, and the desperate need for horses south of the border, the number of Canadian horses sold off must have been substantial. Cavalry officers went through mounts at the rate of one every two months; the poor creatures forced to pull artillery were used up at an especially fierce rate.

A Union artilleryman in the Army of the Potomac named John D. Billings described how horses were not simply struck down by random fire, but were actual targets. The custom was to park the horses near the heavy guns in case the latter needed to be moved quickly, but this often left the horses without cover. Here, in part, is Billings's wrenching account of a battle at Reams Station, Virginia, in August 1864:

> The 57 horses belonging to my company stood out in bold relief, a sightly target for the Rebel sharp-shooters who, from a wood and cornfield in our front, improved their opportunity to the full. Their object was to kill off our horses, and then by charging, take the guns if possible.

Billings records how the horses would stand and receive five or more bullets before finally succumbing. He remarked on the "peculiar dull thud" that a bullet made when it entered the fleshy part of a horse, "sounding much as a pebble does when thrown into mud." A bullet striking the bone of a horse's leg, on the other hand, "made a hollow snapping sound and took him off his feet." Sometimes a bullet would enter a horse's neck and he would try to shake it off, "as if pestered by a fly." Horses would fall, then rise again, sometimes on three legs. Only 4 of the 57 survived the day.

As the supply of horses dwindled, prices soared and every available source of horseflesh was scoured. In 1863, in Mississippi, you could buy a horse, on average, for $364. By 1865, the going rate in South Carolina was between $1,500 and $2,500 in Confederate currency.

Cavalrymen who lost their horses to death or injury would be reassigned to an infantry command. They railed against having to march through mud. One trooper lamented that "the penitentiary could not be more loathsome" than having to join an infantry or artillery unit. The solution, for some unhorsed cavalrymen, was to steal a horse, further aggravating the supply problem. An English observer called Confederate cavalry in 1863 "the most incorrigible horse-stealer[s] in the world."

Scholars of the Civil War have remarked that despite the terrible losses, the horse was actually much underused in the war, especially by the South which had a clear early advantage in horsemanship and never capitalized on it. General William Tecumseh Sherman very much feared cavalry power in the south, where hunting and riding and militia work informed a gentleman's life. He called Confederate cavalry "brave, fine riders, bold to rashness . . . and they are the most dangerous set of men that this war has turned loose upon the world."

One reason the South never really unleashed all that power, aside from a failure to concentrate it or use it effectively, was the more mundane one: They simply ran out of horses. By July 1863, a Southern quartermaster was pleading for 8,000 to 10,000 horses to replace those killed or unfit for service. One cavalry unit had only 1,970 horses for 2,873 men: 31 per cent of cavalrymen had no mounts.

"It would be facile," wrote J. M. Brereton, the author of *The Horse in War*, "to claim that the outcome of the Civil War was decided by horseflesh; but the want of it was certainly a contributory factor."

The North, at least in the beginning, had few serviceable mounts other than draft horses used in farm work and no real tradition of hunting on horseback. The South, on the other hand, had Kentucky, West Virginia and parts of Tennessee and therefore an abundance of horses noted for their speed and stamina. And since the Canadian horse had already come this way in great numbers, I have to believe that Canadian blood suffused many of these Southern horses.

General Robert E. Lee's famous horse, Traveler, for example, was said to be half Thoroughbred, but he also carried the blood of Black Hawk, one of the great Morgan sires. And the Morgan, as we shall see, carried a great deal of Canadian blood.

In 1860, the U.S. Army had only five cavalry regiments. By the end of the war, the North had 80,000 horsemen in the field; the South half that number. In *A Stillness at Appomattox*, which won its author the Pulitzer Prize in 1954, Bruce Catton notes that by the end of the war the Union cavalry had gotten far better and the Rebel riders were running out of horses. A Confederate officer confessed glumly that Sheridan's cavalrymen nowadays "were more to be feared than their infantry—better soldiers all through." Everyone, it seemed, wanted to join the cavalry. But the romance of the cavalry charge, men shouting fierce war cries with sabres raised, unfolded quite gruesomely in actual fact.

Only in the last 450 yards did the cavalry gallop, lest the horses be spent before battle. They would walk forward at 100 yards a minute, 200 yards at the trot and the rest at the gallop. A cavalry unit 1,500 yards from an enemy infantry unit might use all three gaits, taking 3 minutes and 24 seconds to reach the foot soldiers. In that time, a line of infantry arrayed against several lines of cavalry could fire "a total of 644 rounds of bone-breaking conical bullets into the charging mass." Not to mention the artillery, which could unleash at least seven rounds.

A Confederate observer recounted the folly of one such cavalry charge:

> ". . . the cavalry came thundering by, but a deadly volley stopped their wild career. Some in front, unhurt, galloped off, on their way, but just behind them horses and riders went down in a tangled heap. The rear,

unable to check themselves, plunged on, in, over, upon the bleeding pile, roaring, shrieking, struggling mass of men and horses, crushed, wounded and dying. It was a sickening sight, the worst I had ever seen then, and for a moment I felt a twinge of regret that I had ordered that little line to that bloody work."

The infantry would form hollow squares, with the front rank placing the butts of their guns against their knees so that charging horses could not miss the glint of steel. The cavalry would try to whip their horses and so trample the square, but "the horses had more sense than that," as one observer wryly put it. "My men," wrote Confederate Colonel John S. Mosby, "were as little impressed by a body of cavalry charging them with sabers as though they had been armed with cornstalks."

More successful were cavalry charges against other cavalry units. But unless one side managed to surprise the other, the result was more likely a draw. And so cavalry evolved into mounted infantry, riding to a battle and there fighting on foot. One man in four would be assigned to hold the horses while his three compatriots advanced in a line on foot with rifles. The cavalry thus became a skirmishing force. Their key role was to make long-distance raids to destroy communications lines, railroads or supply depots.

Certain names crop up in any consideration of the most successful raids: General Nathan Bedford Forrest in July 1862 led 1,400 Confederate cavalry 90 miles behind the front line and cut the railway at Murfreesboro in Tennessee. General Sherman, during his advance upon Atlanta in 1864, was forced to use 80,000 of his 180,000 men defending lines of communications against Forrest's raiders, and another 15,000 men in hunting the raiders down. On the Union side, General Benjamin Grierson led cavalry 400 miles south in 16 days and cut supply lines to Vicksburg in Mississippi. Along the way, he took 1,000 horses and mules. Given the short supply, that was a major coup.

But there were disasters too. General George Stoneman's campaign at Chancellorsville in Virginia had accomplished nothing but paid a staggering price—the loss of 7,000 horses. Another foray by General Judson Kilpatrick had caused the loss of a thousand horses. The scale of these losses is worth pondering. The lament has often been made of the First World War that the brightest and best of an entire generation were lost to posterity, and that the 20th century might have unfolded in a very different way had we kept those minds and bodies. Surely the horse world suffers as well when the losses mount as they did in the Civil War.

When we glorify certain individual horses from that war, it marks a kind of denial that horses were slaughtered in the volume and manner they were. We shine the light on bronze equestrian statues, not on piles of bones. Robert E. Lee's Traveler, for example, the 16-hand, iron-grey gelding, was deemed worthy of his own biography (or, more precisely, a kind of autobiography, for its conceit was to be written from the horse's perspective and in his words). Traveler was said to be calm under fire, and despite four years of active service—he fought at Second Bull Run, Sharpsburg, Chancellorsville and Gettysburg, among others—he was never wounded. After the war, the retired general took Traveler to his farm in Lexington, Kentucky, where the horse was Lee's "only companion; I may say, my only pleasure."

Another horse, called Dick Turpin, and ridden by Henry Kyd Douglas, one of General Stonewall Jackson's staff, clearly saved his rider's life. Turpin describes how the horse had already taken a flesh wound to the leg when a rifle bullet struck his lower jaw. "He gave a weird cry of pain," Douglas wrote, "and sprang into the air, then he reared straight up and, throwing his head back in agony, struck me in the face and knocked me from the saddle." Though blood was pouring from the wound, the horse let his rider remount and took him in a gallop through the enemy line, up a steep ravine and back to safety.

"I took the bit gently from his mouth," Turpin recalled, "and when he lifted up his head in pain and tried to rub it against me in mute appeal for help, it seemed to me that tears were gathering in his eyes: but it may be they were those in my own." Dick Turpin died of lockjaw two days later.

Only in 1942 did the American government abolish cavalry units, so that well into the 20th century horses continued to serve on battlefields. Even after the advent of machine guns capable of firing 800 rounds a minute and accurately striking targets more than a mile away, a man on a horse was still seen as a great weapon by military thinkers. One British cavalry manual in 1907 was still extolling "the speed of the horse, the magnetism of the charge, and the terror of cold steel."

But when the Canadian horse went into battle in the 20th century, in South Africa and Europe, he had as much to fear from his own handlers as from enemy bullets. A great many Canadian horses were shipped off to South Africa to fight in the Boer War at the end of the 19th century. And here again, they distinguished themselves by adapting easily to the profound change in climate and by resisting the so-called African Horse Sickness that killed many European horses.

Colonel Soame Jenyns told the British Lords Committee on Horse Supply that "the Canadians made first-rate troop horses, very fairly bred, capital hacks, a little straight in the shoulder, which is of course objectionable, but wonderfully good sound horses, admirable animals."

But the numbers of horses lost in that war defies belief. Very few were actually killed in battle; misuse, abuse and recklessness by their own riders and commanding officers meant that of 520,000 horses taken from Britain and the Commonwealth, 350,000 died. In one account that defines the level of horsemanship some mounted infantrymen took into that war, one British mounted infantryman asked his commanding officer which he should feed his horse—mutton or beef?

The 9th Lancers from Britain started the campaign with 518 horses; a year later 36 were left. The Queen's Bays started with 775 troop horses and lost 748 to disease and deprivation.

The Boer War saw conventional cavalry tactics give way to raiding. Lord Kitchener complained bitterly that the Boers "are always running away on their little ponies." U.S. cavalry officers used to utter the same complaint about Plains warriors on their rugged little horses. Kitchener finally concluded that massive infantry columns would never win on open, rolling terrain. Thus he substantially increased his complement of cavalry and by May 1901 one-third of his 240,000 men were mounted. Night raids by the British became common, or long night marches that would put them within striking distance of Boer camps at dawn.

Still, Arthur Conan Doyle, who served as a physician in the Boer War and who wrote *The War in South Africa*, spoke disparagingly of "the great horse question": the inability of the British to use horses wisely. Despite "having the horses of the world on which to draw," the British commanders imported unfit horses and failed to learn the obvious lesson: It is better to give 1,000 men two horses each, and so let them reach the enemy, than give 2,000 men one horse each, with which they can never attain their objective." The eminently successful Mongol raiders of the 12th and 13th centuries, who rode with a personal string of four horses each, could have told them that.

At the Toronto Reference Library there is a remarkable book called *The Canadian Rangers: Canada in the South African War, 1901–1902*. It's actually a scrapbook of newspaper clippings pasted onto the pages of an old mining engineering yearbook. The book contains the dispatches of John Innes, a *Mail and Empire* correspondent who was given the rank of private and a feisty, 16-hand, Roman-nosed horse (not likely a Canadian) called Jerry. The writing is graphic and blunt, yet surprisingly evocative and even lyrical, given the conditions and haste in which the pieces were written. The long yellow-brown columns of print, the paper slowly atrophying from its own acid, powerfully convey the harsh and stunning landscape, the inanity of war, and, through it all, the life of a horse in war.

It seems that a Canadian major named Merritt had convinced

Lord Kitchener that pack horses, fitted with a Western-Canadian rope hitch that kept the load absolutely rigid, could spare the cavalry having to carry 35 or 45 pounds of gear, including blankets and food. The commanding officer was much impressed, but the military was slow to adjust.

Here is Innes writing a little later:

> When we finally lined up by troops, the entire half regiment stood and grinned at itself. You never saw such a sight as our horses presented with all their paraphernalia aboard . . . Jerry looked like a four-legged Christmas tree, and seemed to know it, and was ashamed . . . a pity that the enemy did not run across us in force that day, for I think they would have killed themselves laughing, and thus saved us the trouble of a lot of fighting.

Innes, who also provided fine sketches with his long dispatches, records the burning heat, the choking dust, the locust swarms—"the whirring of their wings was like the rushing of wind through the trees"—and the dangerous night rides. He recalled a line from a song he had heard in Toronto—"Sit back, hold tight, Mary's going to sing"—and used to say it in his head on those terrible dashes through the darkness.

Jerry, with whom Innes had reached a happy accord, was later shot by an inspecting officer "who succeeded in stirring up the vials of his equine wrath" and who declared the horse unfit for duty. His replacement was an awful mare (he called her a night mare) named Skate with a pounding trot; Innes begins to ponder the quality of the horses in his regiment, how some were excellent and others were clearly "riff-raff."

Innes's view of Skate changes and affection takes root. He describes staying up almost till daylight hunting for "little tufts of grass that were half moist." Then he took some oats in his hand, wet them with a few mouthfuls of water he had saved from his canteen "and tried to get the poor brute to nibble at it."

The First World War, the last war in which the Canadian horse played a meaningful role, was as terrible for the horse as any in history. It's unclear how many of the breed actually served in that war, but I do know that some 1.5 million horses of all breeds served as cavalry alone, with countless more deployed in hauling guns and supplies. An estimated 500,000 horses died between 1914 and 1918.

A poem called "Dumb Heroes," written by Captain T. A. Girling of the Canadian Army Veterinary Corps near Ypres, France in 1916, includes this verse:

> *It's the daily work of the horses,*
> *And they answer the spur and the rein,*
> *With quickened breaths mid the toll of death*
> *In the mud and the holes and the rain.*

A history of the Canadian Army Veterinary Corps was published in 1999, and it makes at times for grim reading. It seems that the first horses dispatched from Canada in the fall of 1914 fared well during the 12-day ocean voyage, with up to 973 horses packed on to a single ship and close to 8,000 in total. But their tribulations began the moment they disembarked at Plymouth. The book's author, Captain Cecil French, paints the scene upon arrival at Salisbury Plain:

> . . . owing to lack of head ropes, halters and picketing gear, the animals had to be tied up to trees and vehicles by any odd piece of rope or strap that could be found. Then began a series of trials that would have disheartened any but the most resolute. Complete absence of shelter, almost continuous rain, and a biting wind that swept down from the neighboring hills, all

conduced to bring about a most deplorable situation.
The animals were soon standing in a veritable sea of
mud and every time one raised its foot it sank deeper
and deeper into the mire . . .

Many horses succumbed to gangrenous dermatitis and had to be
destroyed. The few blankets at hand were soon plastered with mud and
the hay was blown away in the wind. On the battlegrounds of France,
horses were clipped against mange but then fell prey to pneumonia.
They died of shrapnel wounds, drowned in mud or perished for lack
of food and water. During the bitter cold of the winter of 1917,
reports Captain French, and even when hay rations were available,
horses ate their own blankets in a desperate attempt to produce body
heat. In some units, 75 per cent of blankets were lost this way. Men
sleeping in barns without straw or fires often gave their own blankets
to their horses, only to find the precious cover gone next morning.

The end of the war should have offered some respite to surviving horses. It did not. With few exceptions, horses from Canada sent
to war did not come back. It was feared that returning horses would
bring disease with them, and so surviving horses were sold, sometimes to butchers in war-ravaged places desperate for food.

It's clear from Captain French's book that many members of the
veterinary corps did all they could to alleviate the suffering of horses. But
among the appendices in the book is a sobering one below a sketch of a
horse, with a small star on his forehead, just above the eyes. The caption
below reads: "Point of aim for pistol shot to humanely destroy a horse."

Below the caption is a brief text of instruction: "The proper
method to follow is to hold the horse by the head-rope with the left
hand then bring the right hand up pointing the revolver about one
foot from the head. When releasing the trigger aim slightly upwards
at the centre of the forehead well above the level of the eyes, just
below where the lowest hairs of the forelock grow. See that no one
stands directly behind the horse. One shot should be sufficient."

CHAPTER 6

# COMING TO BLUE HAVEN

---

JUNE 1999

*I have begun, eerily, to dream about Dali. Not so much dream as spend wakeful hours at
night trying to decipher his mind. Gilles talks with great animation about how
exhilarating it is to learn over time what makes a particular horse tick. You hope you
find the key, that there is a key.*

EARLY IN THE SPRING OF 1998, while we were still living in Camden East,
northwest of Kingston, I went to a horse auction at Tom Harrison's
quonset hut just outside the village. My quest for a Canadian horse was
still a year away. I had been warned off buying horses at auction, but I
was warming to the idea of owning a horse and I was curious to take
in the atmosphere of a sale. Ulrike shook a finger at me as I left.

Above: Gilles Dupuis, Dali and Barb Wills.

---

She has seen me return from auctions with chickens (*before* we had built a pen), paintings of religious scenes in chipped and gilded frames and other castoff items bought on a whim or because I pitied the aged seller watching once cherished possessions pawed over on a lawn.

I did, in fact, see a horse there I liked, a tall, black quarter horse. I struck up a conversation with a horse trainer, a francophone cowboy in a ball cap named Gilles Dupuis. His lean wife, Barb Wills, in form-fitting jeans and western boots, joined us, and I asked them to take me on a tour of the barn out back where the horses awaited their fates. I wanted to know more about horse conformation, and we went from horse to horse looking for obvious faults.

Gilles admires Tom Dorrance and Ray Hunt and the "willing communication" school of horsemanship, the horse whisperer kind whereby horses are trained through gentle persuasion and never by force. When stumped by a horse, Gilles phones his mentors. I had no doubt he was a gentle hand with horses, but he was, by his own admission, a convert to that approach.

When he had a hard question for me—about Monty Roberts, say, whose entrepreneurial side seemed to gall Gilles—he would lean his head back and look down his nose at me. Suddenly this short man seemed bigger, tougher. Like a bantam rooster who had sworn off aggression but still walked the barnyard with a hint of his old swagger.

Barb seemed more inclined to diplomacy. Vibrant and keen, she saw Monty Roberts as a missionary of the gentle way with horses. And if the message had made him wealthy, well, so be it. The message mattered more than the man.

At the end of that day, I was more intent on getting a horse. Not that black horse, but maybe a horse from Blue Haven barn where Gilles and Barb start horses and give lessons. I took from Barb a hand-drawn map and a phone number, but the family move to the city, a wrenching one after 17 years of living in the country, delayed my dream of buying a horse. Barb's map lived atop my computer's hard drive and there gathered dust. Other papers succumbed to my rare purges, but not that folded map ripped from a steno pad.

A year or more later, I was consulting, as I have so many times in recent months, cousin Kathi on a horse matter. With patience and the occasional dart, she has entertained my childlike inquiries. I take satisfaction in knowing that while she has offered me the benefit of her long experience, I have also made her laugh. "I dined out," she told me, "on that story you told me about going to a farm and not being able to catch the horse you were supposed to test-ride. That was a good one."

When I also told her that my long day of driving into Quebec early in May had netted me a hard fall from a young horse, one I was seriously considering buying, she stopped laughing long enough to urge me to reconsider. But when I dug in my heels, she had, as always, good advice: I needed a trainer, someone to school the horse and teach him manners. After huddling with a friend, she came up with the name Barb Wills. Why did I know that name? The map, now lodged underneath my computer, poked out its head.

Some unseen hand was putting things in place. It happened that a slot would open at Barb and Gilles's barn, just 10 minutes from our house in Kingston, early in June. It happened that their stable is only minutes from another stable, the one that Dali could conceivably call home at the end of summer after his first round of schooling. I had made inquiries, discovered Lakehead Stables, and felt sure that this modest facility with an outdoor ring and lots of hacking, and run by a family of avid horsepeople named Grooms, would be ideal.

After months of uncertainty, a plan was taking shape. I had gone to bed the night that Dali dumped me, sore and unable to sleep on that bruised side. The next day, however, I ignored the pain and heeded an instinct—one of Kathi's little bells—that told me I had my horse.

May 7, 1999

I have struck an accord with Jérôme Aumond. I am to take Dali for a month, and if I like him at the end of that time I buy him. The horse will be vetted en route to Blue Haven and if he fails that check, we return him to Jérôme's farm.

Now there is the matter of trailering. After calling around, I settle on a hauler named Bob Tremain, who has raised Canadians. "What are you vetting him for?" he asks me on the phone. "There won't be anything wrong with that horse. They're tough as nails those Canadians." I reply that should the horse develop lameness *and* have to be sent back, we need a baseline. That horse, starting June 3, is my responsibility. And if he does go back I want him going back in the same, or better, condition.

As well, he is coming to a new barn where they will want to know if his shots are all up to date. Has he been wormed? Had shots against flu, eastern and western encephalitis, rabies and Potomac fever (a sometimes fatal disease thought to be carried by snails) and rabies? Has he had a Coggins test, to show he has not been exposed to equine sleeping sickness?

At the barn, assuming I keep Dali, we'll have to make decisions about shoeing, conditioning, food and supplements. If the deciding starts now, so does the education. Of Larry and this horse, son of Larry.

May 13, 1999

Sunday afternoon, in the tea room of the Waring House Inn at Picton, I read from my book *Wild About Horses* to a small but attentive crowd. Bookstores organize these events to boost sales and the cause of literacy; writers, glad of a free meal and an audience, generally leap at them.

Afterwards, a woman and her daughter approach me. She once operated a riding school near the village of Wilton, near our old place in Camden East. At one point, Mary Ann Barrett had 30 horses; now she has one, a still fit 28-year-old chestnut mare. I mentioned in the course of my reading that I would shortly buy a horse and she says she has stuff to give me if I'm interested.

A few weeks later I drop by her place. The legacy of her years in horses is a garage full of old trunks. When she opens them, there emerges a piquant smell, a blend of must and horse and dust. It's a strong scent but not altogether unpleasant.

I am glad to get all she gives me, and not just for reasons of economy. Some of the items come with a little history. Mary Ann had spent some time in England in the early 1970s (riding royal horses), and one of the heavy horse blankets she gives me is made of jute. Its heady aroma reminds me of the dusty old potato sacks my grandfather used to store his spuds in. Mary Ann good-naturedly praises the blanket, saying that despite its age, it still bears the mark of its original quality.

I take away two sturdy rubber pails with bits of old hay glued to the rims, a little red hoof pick, an old but still serviceable halter, a light cotton turnout blanket in excellent condition, several brushes, a salt-lick holder, a haynet and a blacksmith's apron. I am further invited to return when I know what bit I need, for the trunks are thick with them, along with surcingles, old buggy harnesses, stirrups and bridles.

"We'll have to have a bee one day, my daughter and I, and clean up all this old tack. Have a yard sale," she mutters into the trunk. Somehow I doubt she ever will.

I give her a copy of *Wild About Horses* by way of thanks, but Mary Ann's generosity only really becomes clear later when I learn the price of all she has given me. "Thanks for giving me a leg up," I write inside the book. I have the feeling it gave her pleasure to see this horse paraphernalia having a second life.

A woman who exudes both calm and enthusiasm, Mary Ann is like some riding instructors I know. A missionary doting on a convert, she loves to see a fresh case of horse fever. When I tell her that the horse I am about to buy had bucked me off within minutes of getting on him, she counters with her own story of falling off the same horse 18 times in succession. She was training for eventing competition and a certain combination of jumps was confounding her horse. The horse eventually got the combination; Mary Ann had a broken finger to show for her determination. My bruise from a single dumping, which I have been describing in glorious detail to all who would listen, suddenly seemed paltry. I feel like a boy proud of his new-found rock until someone tells him about boulders.

## June 2, 1999

I'm getting little surges of adrenalin in anticipation. We pick up the horse in the wee hours tomorrow morning.

Gail Mosher tells me today that the Fox line is noted as a fiery line and that a friend of hers had a Fox stallion "with a little screw loose." On the other hand, it seems reckless to dismiss a horse based solely on his pedigree. Individual members of a bloodline may subscribe to that line's reputation or deviate from it. This is what I tell myself.

Gail says she does something with any horse she's looking to buy: She pushes just lightly on his forehead, and if he resists a little but tucks in his head, then he's displaying a willingness to learn. If he pushes back, this is a reason not to buy that horse. Maybe I'll try it with Dali.

## June 7, 1999

I am hearing horror stories about horse transport. Riders breaking arms and legs leading recalcitrant horses into trailers. Horses rearing in panic and cutting their heads open on the hard metal of trailer tops. Buy protective boots for the horse's legs, urges a friend, for their shoes wreak havoc on ligaments. Buy headgear, says another. No one mentions actual accidents on the road, but I am familiar with one that almost claimed the life of Big Ben, the Canadian show jumper. That, too, would be on my mind as I drive with a professional horse mover to get Dali. Four hours there. Four longer hours back.

Actual transport, it transpires, is a breeze. It is the transporter who gives grief.

Truck-drivin' Bob is a thickset man with a slow, awkward gait, courtesy of two back operations after falls from horses. He treats his Chevy truck with its rebuilt engine, new windshield and overhauled transmission—details that come unbidden and early—better than he does me.

Bob smokes Export "A" Mild cigarettes, the blood-red package never long from his hands. Every five minutes he sets a match to one. The more he smokes, the farther down my window goes. But even the gale-force winds that swirl around the truck cab fail to douse the flame of his lighter. Practice has made perfect his technique of cupping the hands to torch the tobacco. To his complaint of the cold I reply, "I need my air, Bob." I want him to understand that I am gagging on the acrid smoke. But my need pales beside his, and the more he smokes the colder the cab gets.

We leave his house near Gananoque before 2 a.m. and drive through hard rain all night. Dawn breaks as we motor due north along the canyonesque Gatineau River. I had given us what I thought was plenty of time to make a 10 a.m. vet appointment in Kemptville. Trucker Bob, cousin Kathi and others had all offered the same advice: "Don't be late for Larry." As in Larry Butler, DVM.

Kathi calls him a thorough and exacting vet, the best man for the job. I have the sense that he does not suffer fools gladly, or anyone foolish enough to be late. Somehow, the night, and a few missed turns here and there, swallow time and we arrive at the Ottawa Valley Large Animal Clinic with about ten minutes to spare.

Some four hours beforehand, I caught my first sight of Dali since the day he sent me sailing. He stood in an open stall in Jérôme's barn, sporting a brand-new blue halter. Only later did I learn of the tradition in horse buying of the seller handing off the chosen in a new halter. Jérôme made some joke about it being election day in Ontario and the prospects of Tory victory. I replied that Tory blue is not my favourite color; besides, I had bought Dali a leather breakaway halter, one that I have been told is more forgiving of a worried horse in a trailer. I had also bought a head bumper, a bonnet that goes over the horse's head and guards against injuries from rearing.

I never put it on Dali, and not because the thing looks like an old-time leather hockey helmet. Dali approached Bob's blue two-horse trailer, took a few seconds to ponder it, then willingly followed Jérôme up the ramp. He had run a little yellow rope around the horse's neck and through the middle ring on the halter, so that the little pressure he exerted on Dali forced his head down. Not up, where horses go when they're wary and wide-eyed.

"I've been transporting horses for 10 years," Bob said through the haze as we hit the road, "but you learn something new every day." Get a horse to lower his head and the whole body relaxes. Bob would take Jérôme's little trick home with him.

Bob drove big rigs for a decade before starting to move horses, so he knows the business. He drives more slowly once Dali is aboard, especially on curves, and he assures me that he would feel it were the horse to slip or thrash. I wonder how he can differentiate between that and the normal bumps of the road, but he is keenly confident that he can. I believe him. His wife is an eventer who once rode back in the trailer with an injured horse, and she told him the road feels smoother back there. Dali is no doubt focused on his haynet and the carrots I have placed there.

Bob spoke of the several Canadian horses he has owned. "Don't know what you're vetting that horse for," he repeated. "Larry's not going to find anything wrong with that horse."

Dali comes off the trailer extremely agitated at finding himself in new surroundings. Where the hell, he seems to be saying, did home go to? "*Doucement,*" I say to him, "Easy boy," as he skips and prances and eyes the horses in nearby paddocks, calling out his supremacy. I feel like a ribbon on the tail of a kite. It is all I can do to hold on to him.

But, by degrees, after much walking and circling, he discovers the grass. He tears at it as if he's never eaten anything so delicious, or as if he's really really irked. He rips and tears, rips and tears. Where-the-hell-is-home? Where-the-hell-is-home?

Every few minutes his head comes up and he scolds a horse leaving another trailer. Bob had warned me that the vet check would require much running alongside the horse, and I try a little of that, but the change in my pocket spooks him. We go back to walking and manic grazing.

Everything is new to him. Everything is a threat to his safety.

Only later, when Dr. Butler has finished his examination, do I appreciate how well Dali has handled the whole experience. The horse who came off that trailer seemed to me too much horse, too much, at least, for me. But he came down. He had sense. And he is even more handsome than I remember him. He has lost most of his winter coat and his skin glistens in the sun. The ears are alert and constantly taking readings. When he is calmer, I try Gail Mosher's little trick. I push slightly on his forehead and he yields. Later, with the lead rope, I pull down with the same polite tug, and, again, he complies.

Dali enters the examining room—the size of a one-car garage with black cork footing—well enough. But we have to wait there 15 minutes for the vet to appear. Dali clearly wants to leave and makes motions to follow Bob every time he dekes out for a smoke. But we do more circles and the *doucements* work some magic. In the examining room, Dali does some examining of his own. He sniffs the stall ties, the plastic garbage pail, his own manure, and lets the horses next door know that he is a horse to be reckoned with. We toy with the idea of attaching him to the cross-ties, but he looks so shocked at the prospect that we abandon it. I hold him by his lead rope and talk to him while the vet sweeps over his body like a house inspector looking for the flaw, the tiny do-not-buy sign buried in the bone, the tendon, the psyche.

I use the time to admire his head, as delicate as his body is burly. A star and a stripe run almost all the way down to his nostrils, the left nostril linked to a distinctive pink mark that reminds me of a heart-shaped leaf, complete with stem. There is a small rosette at eye level, a cowlick at his neck. And not only is the right hind lower leg white, but that hoof is white as well. The markings strike me as distinctive, even unusual.

The vet check—a few dozen flexion tests, palpation, taking pulse and respiration, examining vision, gums and mouth—goes along swimmingly. The vet in the blue coveralls has the easy manner of a cocky mechanic, talking to Dali all the while and thanking him for his good manners. This is a vet used to dealing with high-strung Thoroughbreds, and so the little dance that Dali sometimes breaks into is of no consequence. "Appears to have a good quiet attitude," the vet writes in his report. News to me, and welcome.

Outside, Doc Butler looks on as I repeatedly run alongside Dali, away for 30 or 40 metres, then back. The running is a breeze for Dali; I am fairly spent by the end of the exercise, meant, I presume, to check for lameness or injury.

"I can't find anything wrong with this horse," Dr. Butler finally says. "But there is a little tenderness in that right front leg. It's probably of no consequence and if you were just to use him for hacking, I'd see no need for X-ray. But since you aim to use him for distance riding, it might be worth a look."

Sure enough, the X-rays reveal two fracture lines on the medial splint bone. In his office, Dr. Butler points to the X-rays, hung up, as if to dry, on the wall of fluourescent light. Then he turns to a plastic model of a horse's leg to show me precisely where the problem lies. The splint bones are little buttressing bones that run along each side of the far bigger cannon bone. Nothing in Dali's walk or trot signalled the hairline fractures, but there they are. The X-rays tell the tale and show a callus the size of an almond on the inside of the leg.

My heart sinks. There looms the prospect of a long sad ride back to Messines, breathing despair and Bob's Exports, "my" horse a reject. But good news follows the bad. One Larry to another, Dr. Butler suggests that I keep the horse and simply re-X-ray in four to six weeks' time. The fracture lines, he says, are healing nicely, and with rest, splint boots to protect him during turnout, and DMSO ointment applied everyday to the callus, Dali would likely be fine.

In the roller-coaster ride I am on, I have just experienced my first sudden dip and rise. We hit the road again, this time heading for Blue Haven, the stable that Dali would call home for the next three months. He went on and off the trailer like he had been doing it all his life.

Barb Wills and Gilles Dupuis, who will teach Dali his manners, each welcome him when we pull into their yard at midafternoon. I have been travelling now for more than 12 hours straight, but there is pride and adrenalin coursing in me as Dali steps down. Gilles, used to training and showing trim Appaloosas and quarter horses, sorely laments Dali's thick neck. Calls him a tank. Barb, though, loves his little ears and pronounces him as cute as a button.

Wrenched from the comfort of the familiar, she warns me, some horses take weeks to adjust. They go off their feed and suffer stress-induced weight loss. I privately worry that Dali will kick his stall, never having been in one before. But in minutes, after greeting the grey next door, he settles down to a lunch of hay and a good drink. Here is more evidence of inner calm and native intelligence. He is still green: Putting a halter on him is an adventure that sees Barb circling and circling in the stall, always a little behind the merry-go-round.

Both Barb and Gilles remark on the discolouration at the corners of his mouth where the skin has turned light brown. "Someone's been pulling on that mouth with a bit," Gilles says. "He's very protective of his mouth," and thus Dali's disinclination even to be haltered, let alone bridled in days to come.

Gilles puts his back to the horse, lightly grips Dali's head, and tucks one finger into the corner of the horse's mouth. Dali opens his mouth wide, disapproving but not objecting entirely. Eventually, he gets to like it, and Gilles begins to work the horse's mouth and gums. The sturdy bay lowers his head farther and almost closes his eyes. "He'll be asleep in a minute," Barb laughs.

And so it goes at Blue Haven. They put in time with each horse, earn that horse's trust.

Blue Haven sits atop a hill at the end of a little crescent, a most unlikely dead end to a little urban circle of wide brick houses with neat flower beds and careful lawns. A dense line of trees on the horizon creates the illusion that Kingston is a distant city, not minutes away.

The 12-horse barn and ample arena are clad in a sturdy blue aluminum. Gilles, who once worked in construction, built both the facility and the house down the hill. He wishes they had more than the seven acres they have, but its privacy is unassailed. The place has a welcoming air, and all manner of people consider it a drop-in centre. A welcome mat with a horse in profile hangs outside the barn door, and so neighbourhood kids wheel around the circular driveway on their bikes, come to catch a glimpse of the latest foal. A dog chanced by one day and Gilles partnered the lucky stray with a girl down the road. Neighbours come to rest their elbows on a fence and watch Gilles or Barb ride, to gossip, to hang out. Two laid-back cops who came to horses after retiring from the force make visits often, their aim to tease Gilles, who seems to love the attention.

"What mischief are you guys up to today?" I asked them one day, the three of them leaning into the bed of Gilles's red truck, as if answers lay there amid the bits of straw and sawdust. In the background was a new garage, which Gilles had erected in a day. He possesses remarkable energy, but he always pauses to enjoy the company of these horse-mad men.

"We're trying to convince Gilles to come with us to a new strip club in Gananoque," said one, though I was sure he said this in jest.

"No one would pay to watch Gilles take his clothes off," I offered, adding my little stick to the burning pyre they were building around Gilles's feet. All duly guffawed.

What Blue Haven will try to teach me in the day-to-day handling of my horse is attention to detail. It starts with running a clean barn. Gilles can be talking about this or that horse and suddenly he has a wide broom in his hand. Horse hair, detritus from hooves and manes, or heavier fare barely land before the broom comes into play. Gilles likes his concrete floors pristine. He becomes annoyed when horses release in the cross-ties (Dali and a big dark bay called Prime Time are repeat offenders), and when Dali delivers, I quickly find a shovel and broom.

One day well into our time at Blue Haven, after a morning rain when Dali had been rolling in the mud, I groomed him, as I had always done, in the cross-ties at the west end of the barn. Would you mind, asked Gilles, grooming him near the ring? He explained that the dust coming off Dali might clog up his stable fan and was already turning Daisy's bed into a dustbowl. Fat, friendly Daisy, another castoff dog adopted by Gilles, resides by day in an open cupboard only feet from a horse in cross-ties.

Barb later referred to Dali's banishment as "another one of Gilles's dust-fits." But he takes the same meticulousness to his horses. He notices small changes. A swelling here. A chipped hoof. A turn in a horse's mood.

Like Barb, he is practically beyond being ruffled by a horse. The more a green horse bucks or acts up, the more he is inclined to laugh. There exists in his diminutive but powerful frame a wealth of knowledge about horses, and when he starts one of his little lectures,

which invariably begin, "Let me tell you something, my friend . . ."
I listen.

The day after Dali's arrival at Blue Haven, I brought Ulrike to the
barn so that she too could admire "my" horse. Turned loose in the
ring, Dali looked, to my great surprise, secure and happy. He reared
a little, playfully, rolled numerous times and neighed greetings to the
other horses back in the stable. I liked the lightness of his trot, how
curious he was about everything. Gilles and Barb each worked with
him, using techniques close to Monty Roberts's to get the horse to
come to them. They never looked directly at him, for that would
have been taken as aggression. They would snake a line towards him,
and if that caused him to veer, they would turn away and back up.
If he abided their coming, they would continue on. Eventually, Barb
or Gilles would get close enough to pet him, his reward for standing. And then would follow that bit of magic that Monty calls join-
up: Gilles walking away, seemingly disinterested, and Dali following
at his shoulder.

I will become a part of these training sessions too. Just holding
him by a lead rope for the 90 minutes we spent in Kemptville, I
began to feel that I was becoming a small anchor for him. Life for
horses is often a series of storms, and they always look to safe haven.
Blue Haven will be that, I hope, for the dark bay horse called Dali.

June 7, 1999

Dali gets what might be his first bath by garden hose. Gilles
approaches him with the nozzle, pressing on casually as the horse
backs and backs, snorting fear. The cold of the water must have felt
wonderful in that oppressive heat. Yet Dali clearly fears the green
snake that spits rain. He rails against it, then stands for it, then
retreats. Finally, he stops in one corner of the ring, caught between
trusting and running. Every time he budges, Gilles says "No-no, no-
no," and the horse stands. Not happily, but he stands.

"He's becoming a real pet," says Barb. Local kids chancing by the fence line earlier drew Dali closer for a look-see. At one point today, he pored over me with his nose. Hmm, he seemed to say, I remember you.

Gilles likes his big round eye. Barb likes his willingness to learn. I like the way he scooted from the barn after the bath, longing for the sand and the roll we all knew was imminent. Dali's roll is total and blissful. He works his back, the better to have it scratched, into the dirt, and paws the air with his legs before rolling onto one side, driving his head forward with a jerk and popping back up on all fours. Then comes a final, whole-body shake that engulfs him briefly in a dusty fog before he walks off, pleased with his watusi and better armed against the flies.

June 9, 1999

I'm working with a quiet mare in the ring alongside Barb and Dali. A useful precursor to riding, ground work is aimed at teaching a horse to yield to pressure. The horse wears a halter and is attached to a lead rope. One exercise is to pull the horse towards you using the slightest pressure on the rope, then send him back again, first by *asking* (waving the rope delicately in your hand like a metronome), then by *telling* (tossing lines of energy with your arms, like an airport ground crew backing up a plane), or, if necessary, by *demanding* (tapping the horse's chest with the rope).

Pressure from the side is applied in the same way. You can push the horse away with your hands, but eventually even pointing to his flank will cause him to move. These are lessons in subtlety.

The difference between the two horses is plain. Dali, smart, sensitive, not-quite-sure-about-all-this-touch-business, reads signs early and moves aside or back as asked. The mare, equally new to all this, tends to wait for the third degree.

Gilles takes over the mare to drive home a point: You need, he says, to be more the pilot of any horse-human ship. He would stop the mare short by lifting his left hand, and his third degree was a far more meaningful slap against her chest with the rope. Gilles is a gentler but he means business; I think he has a point. Dali would see my little rope taps against his chest as weakness. On the other hand, my strong sense is that fighting with him would be a huge mistake.

The mare seems so slight and sleepy alongside Dali's imposing yet vibrant bulk. *Small* does not describe him; *substantial* does. Barb later runs an empty dog food bag across his head and body, a desensitization process aimed at protecting both horse and rider against the inevitable day when a garbage bag blows across our path on the trail. Dali does not much like it, and various muscles—at the neck, shoulder, flank—shudder as the bag makes its rounds. It's the same flexion that horses use to evict flies. "What's that? What's that? What's that?" his body parts say. But he does not flee, does not panic.

Cecily Ross, in her piece in *Harrowsmith* magazine back in the early 1990s, observed a Canadian horse called Jake at Upper Canada Village and remarked that he possessed "the fiery bearing of a French war horse, but he is as sensible as a pair of English walking shoes." I hope Dali can strike the same balance.

In the wake of some unpleasantness the other day with the farrier during a hoof trimming, he does lift his feet so Barb can pick them clean. The left hind requires some patience but it does finally come up. Later, in the cross-ties, he seems to enjoy being groomed. I don a plastic glove and put on the DMSO, happy to be working on my horse.

June 11, 1999

"You see that," says Gilles. "That's attitude. We'll deal with that." He had been walking Dali around the ring, the lead rope loose, his back to the horse, not a care in the world. Then Gilles would stop, without warning, and Dali would brake a millisecond later. It was a remarkable display of the horse reading the human.

But now and again Dali would balk at this game, shake his head and flow out around and to the right of Gilles. And Gilles would shake his own head, stud-style, and run straight into Dali's face, causing Dali to retreat. Then the game would recommence, and Dali would listen anew, completely in tune with Gilles. It was a pantomine that spoke of the horse's disposition, intelligence and focus.

The last part of the lesson had Barb laying a saddle pad over Dali, which sent him scurrying for a minute or so. But then he came down again. He's fiery at times, but he responds to smart handling. "He'll be a dream to ride," says Barb. "A pet." Gilles isn't so sure. I wonder if both are not right: Perhaps our rides will echo that first encounter. I anticipate bad beginnings, better ends.

I think he's a horse you have to be confident with. He needs assurance and firm handling, but my sense is that if I escalate, I will quickly have too much horse on my hands. He will no longer be Dali-ghtful.

June 14, 1999

I have begun to consider the matter of the saddle. Which one? How to marry horse and saddle? New saddle or used?

While saddle-hunting, I encounter on the phone a woman in Hawkestone, near Barrie, Ontario. Lyn Hart runs a tack shop and rides a 16.2-hand Canadian mare in the hunt. Her horse, she says, is cranky when being tacked up, then settles down nicely. "She's very careful," says Lyn, "always looking. I'd buy another in a heartbeat."

Lyn ran a riding school for 17 years and has ridden a lot of Thoroughbreds. What she likes about her Canadian is how she checks out situations first, then proceeds. Lyn's Thoroughbreds would often blithely advance, get frightened, then panic; her black mare is more cautious, but she will "go all day and part of the next." Her mare seems typical of the breed. All that time their ancestors spent free-ranging has made Canadian horses wary of noises in the bush. Such alertness likely saved those ancestral horses from predators countless times.

It is, perhaps, why Dali can seem so nervous about things new to him: garden hose, fly spray, dog food bag. Once he sees they pose no threat, he settles.

I have begun, eerily, to dream about him. Not so much dream as spend wakeful hours at night trying to decipher his mind. Gilles talks with great animation about how exhilarating it is to learn over time what makes a particular horse tick. You hope you find the key, that there is one.

June 14, 1999

I ask Barb today what she *really* thinks of Dali. The last session had been marred somewhat by his shenanigans over a truck delivering bedding for stalls. But ever cheerful, ever the optimist, she sings the horse's praises: Smart. Sensible. A teenager but a solid citizen in the making.

"You are the pilot," she says once more. He is a horse in need of guidance, and he responds well to Gilles's firm but never harsh hand. Barb, in a kind way, says I am not to be discouraged by one sour moment. He does not bolt and never stays upset for long. And while she was saying this, Dali was burying his head at her belt. "Look how he's changed," she says, "just in the short while he's been here."

It struck me how much she talks to him, rewards every obedient step, refuses to be frazzled by his little tantrums. That disposition of his, that spirit, will, I hope, serve him well on the long trail.

Frank Prosperine called this evening. He remembered Dali's grandsire, La Gorgendière Fox Larry, though they just called him Larry. Donnie Prosperine, Frank's father, had bought the chestnut stud at the Deschambault sale in 1981. Larry stood out, a handsome horse with four white stockings—"real flashy," said Frank. A purist about the breed, Frank called him "a decent size." He means by that not bigger, but smaller. Frank laments the way some breeders are creating taller, finer horses. "How can you call a 17-hand horse 'the little horse of iron'?" he mocks.

An official at the sale linked Larry's comparative diminutiveness (14.2 to 14.3 hands) to the fact that he had not nursed well as a colt. The other Canadians at the sale that day towered over him.

Frank remembered Larry as a "real good looker and mover," but they had to shift him to another farm because he would not settle down in the presence of other studs. Once removed though, he calmed and showed good manners.

June 15, 1999

I got a little nicker from Dali today when I went to the stable to groom him. "Always a good sign," says Barb. Before grooming, his head went low to my belt; he likes contact now, and in the stall comes to the halter when it's held out for him.

But he's still skittish. When I scraped my boots across the concrete while he was in the cross-ties, he shivered at the sound. And lifting his feet is still an adventure: There is a deft touch required to get a green horse to lift his feet and I have yet to master it.

Gilles advised me to pinch the chestnut inside the front legs. It works with Dali, but sometimes you have to wait. Today he lifted the right front easily, but the left front caused some confusion. At least he showed willingness; you could see it in the way he wanted to lift the other foot. Eventually it came.

The back legs are harder. Here the trick is to massage at the hock, then squeeze the back of the hock where it forms a little egg. When the foot comes up you grab it, tip it up, then ease the whole lower leg onto your thigh and go back a bit, never out to the side. Massage the hock some more, then clean the foot. Massage again and lower the foot, swinging it in small circles before easing it down. Eventually, hoof cleaning becomes an easy part of grooming.

Unless I take the time to perfect this ritual, I may find myself flying through the back end of Gilles's barn, courtesy of Dali's great stifle. That's the joint where his hind leg meets his body, between the femur and the tibia, and its breadth and coiled power invariably invite comparison with my own muscles. I end up feeling small.

"He's a nervous horse," says Gilles. "A very nervous horse. And sometimes it takes a long time to get that out of them."

I doubt that Barb would say he's nervous. She'd say skittish. She often laughs at, marvels at, his exuberance. The other day she brought him in from his turnout in the ring because he was roaring around with such vigour. She feared for the state of that hairline fracture.

Barb is an articulate woman who can talk about connecting with the horse spiritually without making it sound like nonsense. She refers to the horse's basic needs: safety, comfort, food—and play. And she believes fervently, as I do, that if you get the horse on your side, win his trust, he will look after you and be generous in a way that a horse disciplined into submission never will.

She's going slowly with Dali, but I can tell she's getting impatient to get up on him. She put a bit in his mouth the other day, and at first his long pink/grey tongue snaked out and over it, but eventually he forgot it was there and left it where it was supposed to go.

We've already put the saddle pad on. Next will come the surcingle, then saddle, then rider.

Kathi has warned that it's tricky matching horse and saddle. She and Dick had a terrible time, despite hiring a saddle master to come and fit their horses, using all sorts of gadgets.

Paul Morgan, an Ottawa-area saddler I know with connections to Ian Millar and thus my acquaintance with him, calls those who make too much of saddle fitting "equine evangelists." He told me Ian has always used the same saddles, simply using saddle pads to compensate for the variously sized horses. All very old school now.

Now there are fitters who make rounds to barns with their fancy gear. Paul concedes that saddling can get complicated, but it need not be so. You have to fit the rider to the saddle, and the saddle to the horse, and, yes, the horse can muscle up or down, lose or gain weight. Still, there are ways of adjusting the saddle. Foam inserts are one option; wool or synthetic packing is another.

But which saddle? Hunter or eventer or close contact, Steuben or Passier or Crosby, new or used?

## June 16, 1999

A good day in the ring. I played gentler, this time with better luck. Dali listened. He did not get stroppy. Even leading him on his left side, which unnerves him, did not cause him too much discomfort.

Lifting the feet to clean the hooves, though, is still a sore point. Today, he got sufficiently riled that we aimed for a lesser achievement and simply tried lifting the feet and letting them down slowly. The hind feet, especially, are sensitive.

As for bridling, I aim by practice to make it perfect. For this, too, is not something I have done a lot of. We also put fly spray on today, and, as before, it caused him grief. Though I wish he were calmer about these matters, I am coming to admire the fact that the fretting never lasts. It's as if he has to make a point about everything.

"Just go about your business," counselled Barb, "as if you've done this a hundred times before." And it worked.

## June 17, 1999

During grooming today Dali jumped, as if a cougar had landed on his back. I surprised myself with my own reflexes, and leapt back several feet in a hurry. Barb, as she always does in such circumstances, leaned back and laughed. What likely spooked Dali was the sound of the cat bounding off the side of the barn.

"It sure got all of him," said Barb.

Even catching him in the stall was difficult today. A full meal of hay lay on the stall floor, and it was a pretty easy choice for the horse. My halter or his hay? He would swing his end around and point his nose in the corner. I wasn't about to chase him, but neither was I giving up. Eventually, when he had decided I wasn't going away, he acquiesced.

I feel like a rank amateur at such moments. The first time I got the halter on, I missed his nose and had to retry. Maybe at some point Dali begins to feel sorry for my bumbling.

And still, cleaning those hooves of his, especially the hind ones, gives me pause. He may swing one in a lazy circle when I let it go, like a baseball player arcing his bat while waiting for the pitch. I would rather not be the ball on the end of Dali's home-run swing. I had never been afraid of a horse before, never been thrown from one. But then, I had always ridden certain kinds of horses.

Chris Irwin, the author of *Horses Don't Lie*, is an equestrian coach often described as Canada's Monty Roberts. During a clinic, he once referred to school horses "as the most desensitized horses on the planet." We later met at an Irish pub in Kingston and he talked about how school horses imbue riders with a sometimes dangerous overconfidence. The rider begins to think that all horses are as predictable as the bombproof, kidproof ones at his local stable. The rider flatters himself into thinking that his assigned horse's obedience owes something to the rider's acquired skills. The rider thinks he's actually a rider.

Chris wore an amused smile as I described my first ride on Dali.

"I never bothered to read the horses at my stable," I told him. "I was too focused on my seat, my hands, my leg. I simply wanted to know which button I pushed to get the canter." Dali has enforced the single greatest change in what I meekly call my horsemanship: I no longer simply act around horses, I also react. Dali is teaching me to use my eyes and all my senses. He is, above all, teaching me patience.

Kathi, as always, has decided opinions about Dali's foot phobia. She tries always to see the conundrum from the horse's perspective: We have here a horse suddenly being handled a great deal after five years of almost no handling; and the handler is more rookie than not. When you lift a horse's feet, you take away his ability to flee, his primary defence. Why should Dali trust you with something he holds sacred: his own safety?

A food reward, says Kathi, will overcome that obstacle of the feet. He lifts one foot, he gets a wee bit of carrot. Most horses, she says, are bribable. Dick actually rides with a fanny pack loaded with horse kibble, and he will periodically, in the course of a ride, especially to reward special accomplishment, reach in to that pack. The horses know the routine and crane their necks around. Happy horses.

June 23, 1999

The American author and horsewoman Maxine Kumin talks about "the dailiness" of horses: the acts of feeding and grooming and care that become, owing to the grace of the animal, less like work and more like sustaining rituals. *Dailiness* is an apt phrase.

But I would coin another. Dali-ness. I might define it these days as a little explosion in the face of fly-spray, a saddle pad, a garden hose. The tremors warn of an earthquake that, so far, anyway, has failed to arrive. But those tectonic plates keep shifting.

Barb, wisely, refuses to take them seriously and laughs out loud at them. There's a certain bravado about Dali, and to take his antics too seriously is to play his game. I hope I am right when I say I see trust building in him.

The other day, Barb, for the first time, put him in the long-lines—30-foot reins drawn past the bit, along his body and back to the handler. The aim is to teach Dali something about stopping and turning according to light pressure on the mouth. This upset him mildly at first but he quickly settled down. All according to his pattern. At first we did our passes up and down the ring with me at his head holding a loose lead rope, "to give him moral support," explained Barb.

Then I unhooked the lead line and he was on his own. He made a beeline for me, seeking to bury his head in my chest. "Dali, it's very nice you've bonded with Larry," said Barb, "but we have work to do."

He was quick to learn this lesson of the long-lines and his manners were fine. The real work will be at his mouth. He still refuses to carry the bit properly, with his tongue under the snaffle. He manages to snake his tongue over the bit and it waggles constantly outside, like some errant pink banana. We want him to accept the bit and stop worrying about the bar.

During the lesson, the lines occasionally find their way under his feet. Barb lifts his front foot to bring the line out; when it happens again I try to raise the front hoof but fail. We choose not to press the matter; I simply pull the line forward. A lone Greek chorus is heard to object. "You guys, taking the easy way out," says Gilles, leaning on the Dutch door and looking into the covered arena. We have not noticed him there and his voice is disapproving. But I understand Barb's thinking: Dali has done well today, so let us not force an argument about something we can work on later.

The feet, the mouth: Those are still issues.

Other little tests are going well. He comes willingly now to be haltered, loves to stand by the door and have his forehead scratched, and abides the fly spray.

The other day I groomed him and then took him into the ring to put the spray on, forgetting that there is almost always another horse either in the ring or just outside the open door. Sure enough, in mid-spray a tall chestnut ambled in. Thankfully, Dali and he are pals and I was able to usher him back into his stall. But had they been fractious . . .

A phrase Gail Mosher once uttered came to me. She had delivered two horses to buyers in Manitoba, and worried, upon arrival, that they lacked the necessary horsemanship. "They seemed to have no idea," said Gail, "of the nose horses have for trouble." How a fence can snare a gelding's leg, how a paddock may fail to contain a certain mare, how a stallion can wage war.

Gail warned them that the stud on their farm must be kept out of earshot and eyesight of any young colt. "That stallion," she told them, "will go through, over or under that fence, and when he gets to that colt he will not just kick him or intimidate him, he will beat him into a bloody pulp." She feared her message was taken as exaggeration, despite their assurance that the two horses would be kept apart.

*My Friend Flicka*, that 1950s television series I used to watch as a boy, never prepared me for such harsh equine truths. Four decades later, My Friend Dali is teaching me that the real world of horses is more complicated, and yet more compelling, than I ever imagined.

Go back a hundred years from Flicka in black and white and you will find yourself at perhaps the high point in the history of the Canadian horse, when Quebec alone boasted a staggering number of Canadians—some 150,000. But so rapid was the breed's decline that were it not for the efforts of certain champions of the breed in the late 19th and early 20th centuries, there would today be no heritage horses in Canada.

# CHAPTER 7

# ON THE BRINK OF DISASTER

DESCHAMBAULT, QUEBEC, 1981

*The age of cutbacks was upon us and an obscure breed of horse seemed an obvious, even glaring, extra in tight times. The small remaining herd of Canadian horses at the Deschambault Research Station were all sold . . .*

IN THE LOWER CANADA OF THE MID-1800S, the focal point of community life was the livery stable. More important than the church or town hall, the hotel or saloon, and far more entertaining than the theatre, the stable was a place where you swung deals, met friends, traded gossip. The stable owner would fix your wagon and know where to procure horses at the best price. His assessment of a horse's value was deemed to be the one of record.

Above: Horse show at Deschambault, Quebec, 1940s.

In the horse-centred society that was then Lower Canada, the veterinarian ranked with the doctor. The blacksmith, wheelwright, coach-builder, saddler and harness-maker all did a brisk business. In the cities and towns of Quebec, the clip-clop of hooves on cobblestone, the rattle of wheels over roads and the tinkle of bells on bridles—the general din of horse-drawn traffic—would have created a level of noise on a par with today's urban environment.

A world without horses seemed unthinkable, and even well into the next century the horse still powered farms, moved families and their goods, and continued to figure in the minds of generals. In 1921, the horse population in Canada would reach its peak: 3.6 million. The late 19th century should have been a heyday for the Canadian horse. But by the late 1800s and early 1900s, as we have already seen, the demands of war, the mechanization of farms and other circumstances combined with devastating effect. The Canadian horse was almost completely wiped out.

Historian Robert Leslie Jones argued that the breed actually disappeared as a distinct race towards the end of the 19th century. He was incredulous that this could happen, for he was certain that this one breed had enriched the horse population over a massive geography: The Maritime provinces, New York, Michigan, Illinois and, even more so, Ontario and New England had all seen a great infusion of Canadian horse blood. Only the Thoroughbred, he insisted, made a greater contribution towards developing the leading American horses of the 19th century.

Somehow, the Canadian horse's contribution fell from view. This is the most striking thing about the history of this horse: how pre-eminent the creature once seemed and how quickly he lost that status. "These once-famous horses," who had played a key role in the formation of other celebrated breeds, the Morgan, the Standardbred, the American Saddlebred and the Tennessee Walking Horse, were, by 1880, says Jones, "seldom mentioned."

And the first to forget these heritage horses were people in the horses' own homeland. The Quebec Board of Agriculture, formed in 1852, began to encourage the use of imported breeds and even denied the Canadian horse a place at fairs and exhibitions. Familiarity had indeed bred contempt. The horse's stock fell and the Canadian was shipped off in great numbers to fight in the American Civil War or crossbred with imported horses.

At crossbreeding farms established 90 miles south of Quebec City, the stated aim was to breed a larger version of the Canadian horse for heavy farm work. Meanwhile, a steady stream of these "fine little horses" continued south and to other parts of the world. But the stream was finally drying up.

When the alarm bells at last sounded, the authorities bickered over how to proceed. Some experts argued for importing European horses to cross with the mongrel horses who remained. Others, and they would win the day, believed it was possible to revive the race by carefully selecting and breeding the best of the horses remaining in Canada. The leader in that undertaking was a veterinarian in the federal Department of Agriculture, Dr. Joseph-Alphonse Couture.

Photos of him reveal a serious, intense-looking man with a great walrus moustache. He had, said one historian, a distant look: "He was a thinker." An admirer of the little horse of iron, he was also a patriot. At the age of 16 he had enrolled in the Canadian army and fought against the Fenians, Irish-Americans who conducted raids into Canada in the late 1860s as part of a campaign to secure Irish independence from Britain.

Dr. Couture's lobbying led to a law prohibiting further exports of Canadian horses and to the establishment in 1886 of a commission to form a French-Canadian Stud Book. The Canadian Horse Breeders' Association was formed in 1895 to give greater impetus to that effort. The first horse to enter the stud book was one called—let the clarion of horns sound—Lion du Canada.

The horse was owned by one Edouard-André Barnard, an agronomist and a Quebec patriot whose father had been arrested and jailed during the 1837 rebellions in Quebec led by Louis-Joseph Papineau. Yves Bernatchez, a lawyer in modern-day Deschambault and a keen reader of Canadian-horse history (his great-grandfather helped create that first stud book) calls Barnard "the real father of the breed."

Barnard, in his later years (he died in 1898) wore a white beard down to his chest and is remembered as a man of rare character. As deputy minister of agriculture in Quebec and as one who farmed, himself, he saw that the Canadian horse was disappearing and simply had to be protected. Barnard, with help from wealthy friends, made money available to launch the stud book.

The keepers of the book did a good job for four or five years, but then the commission let standards slip, allowing into the registry horses that should have been denied for reasons of conformation or genealogy. A new commission was thus formed after association members huddled with Dr. J. G. Rutherford, Veterinary Director General.

Dr. Rutherford, like Couture, championed the breed. He praised *le cheval canadien* before a standing committee of the House of Commons in 1909. "Taking him altogether, he was a remarkable little horse, eminently suited for the needs of the habitant, well capable of performing the light agricultural work of the small Canadian farm under the old regime and equally well adapted to the roads of Quebec . . . [and] capable of negotiating deep pitch holes and deeper snow drifts, which would bring to grief many animals of more weight and greater pretensions."

Dr. Rutherford lamented the "mongrelization" of the breed, which he dated from about 1880. He called it a short-sighted and "very grave mistake" to allow stallions of various breeds to intermingle with the Canadian. Clearly, he aimed to do something about it, but not by lowering stud book standards, which had been set high in order to restore the breed.

Those standards, he feared, were badly in need of "stiffening" by 1907. Dr. Rutherford despaired of restoring the race to its original condition, but he did believe that a new breed could be established, one that would have most of the old breed's traits while perhaps even improving on the original. By intelligent selection and careful mating, he sought to create within a few generations "a fixed type" capable of perpetuating itself.

In 1907, the commission examined 1,937 horses, accepting only 644. Between 1907 and 1912, and after widening the search to include Ontario, Manitoba and the Gaspésie, the commission registered 1,555 more horses, including 242 horses whose lines led back to the old stud books. This would suggest that the breed did not entirely disappear, as Jones believed. If the Canadian-horse line was indeed reconstituted, into the mix was tossed 15 per cent of certified stock.

Here is what the inspectors wanted to see: a horse between 900 and 1,100 pounds, short head and fine muzzle; great width between the eyes, eyes bright and spirited, ears alert, neck strong and well-arched, and mounted high on a well-sloped shoulder, body long and deep and rounded, with a muscled rump and a tail set quite high. The chest was to be wide and deep and hang quite a bit over the muscled front legs. Mane and tail were to be long and exceptionally wavy.

In 1909, of the 2,528 studs and mares presented for registration, only 134 stallions and 835 mares were selected. Some 345 other horses in the stud book of 1886 were tossed out. This would have been a bitter pill to swallow for the many owners who thought their horses were purebreds. On the other hand, some bona fide purebreds were doubtless left off the list because their paddocks were too remote and beyond the reach of inspectors. Many fine horses in Quebec, the Atlantic provinces, Ontario, western Canada and the United States were thus lost forever to the registry.

Still, gains were made. By 1905 the Canadian horse had regained its place at Quebec fairs and the Royal Agricultural Winter Fair in Toronto. The first exhibition of pureblood Canadian horses took place at St-Jean d'Iberville in 1908 and was considered a great success. In an effort to boost the profile of the Canadian horse, the federal government had organized this first of three *"grandes expositions."* The display of 42 stallions and 88 mares drew 20,000 visitors over the course of three days. Similar exhibitions followed at St-Hyacinthe in 1909, and Trois-Rivières in 1910.

The formation of Canadian Horse Breeding Syndicates, the first one dating from 1932, was aimed at producing consistently high-quality stock. And by 1942 there were 16 of them. But the federal government's greatest contribution to the Canadian horse was to form a breeding program at Cap Rouge Experimental Station in 1913, using land leased from the Seminary of Quebec. They started with a mere 20 horses at a place that had figured in the very early days of Canada's history. The explorer Jacques Cartier had passed a hard winter at Cap Rouge, just upriver from what is now the site of Quebec City, in 1541.

Cap Rouge was the first of several government-run operations aimed at securing a future for the Canadian horse. Other places—St. Joachim, Ste-Anne de la Pocatière, Deschambault—would become signposts in the 20th century history of the Canadian horse, as both the federal and provincial governments tried desperately to find meaningful work for our heritage horse.

In 1919, the breeding operation shifted to the St. Joachim Farm, some 500 acres 25 miles east of Quebec City. The intent was to continue on a larger scale the work begun at Cap Rouge. During its years in operation, the farm stabled anywhere from 65 horses to just over 100. Clearly the operation enjoyed enough funding to dress up the place for photographers. Old photos show horses in white halters attended by grooms in white suits, even white hats. During the entire 21 years of the St. Joachim Farm's operation, horses were always wintered outside in single-boarded, open-front sheds facing south. Not one horse suffered anything more serious than a cold.

J. R. Pelletier, superintendent of another experimental station at Ste-Anne de la Pocatière—the last gasp of federal involvement in the breed—wrote a report in 1943 looking back on the previous two decades of government work on the breed, and in it he echoes a recurring theme in the literature: The Canadian horse, pound for pound, is one of the strongest on the planet. Pelletier also pays moving tribute to Dr. Gustave Langelier, former superintendent of the Cap Rouge Experimental Station and officer-in-charge of the St. Joachim Farm from its early days until his retirement in 1933. He was, says Pelletier, "a devoted lover of the French Canadian horse."

Langelier was an entrepreneurial sort who had bred with distinction Ayrshire cattle and Clydesdale horses. His fanatical record-keeping may explain his success in animal husbandry. One of his cows set a record for milk production; one of his horses merited Langelier a gold medal when the stud was named best Clydesdale stallion in the world. Keen to have him working on the side of the Canadian horse, the federal government purchased his farm at Cap Rouge and made him director of the breeding station.

Langelier started with 38 lines in his attempt to standardize and elevate the breed. He would eventually fix on Albert de Cap Rouge as *the* foundation sire. And he took some pleasure in seeing a team of Canadian horses beat the then celebrated Black Horse Ale Percherons at the Toronto Exhibition, forerunner to the Canadian National Exhibition. "Though there are no records to prove it," Langelier once wrote, "[the French-Canadian horse] could probably develop and keep on developing more power per hundred pounds of his weight than any other member of the equine family."

Langelier's colleague and farm foreman at St. Joachim, George Atkins, was the uncle of Alec Hayward, a principal in the breed's revival in the late 1970s. Atkins apparently brought the first Canadian horse to that farm. He could, at one time, identify from memory just over 100 horses at St. Joachim. He loved the breed and he loved his horses, Langelier observed, "and he always handled them in the most gentle way on fair grounds as well as in routine activities of the farm." Discontinued as part of war effort cutbacks, the national campaign to save the Canadian horse become a provincial matter in 1940 and the horses at St. Joachim were sold at auction. The experimental station at Ste-Anne de la Pocatière remained as a small federal breeding operation—seven mares and one stallion. By then, two trends had become apparent: Horses were no longer needed in war, and farms in Quebec were becoming increasingly mechanized.

A small, provincially run stud farm of 15 horses was set up in the fall of 1940 at the village of Deschambault, about 65 kilometres southwest of Quebec City. Private breeders continued to produce Canadians, but with declining interest. Registrations of purebred Canadian horses fell dramatically in the late 1940s and early 1950s. In 1947 a mere 28 were registered; in 1951, only 15. Government breeders at Deschambault kept on producing heavier horses for farm work at a time when machines were truly replacing the horse. Worse, Quebecers had for centuries seen the horse in purely practical terms; the notion of the pleasure horse, the trail horse, of hunters and jumpers, was a long way off. The future of the Canadian horse had never looked more bleak.

Breeders went from pillar to post. First they sought to produce bigger and less spirited animals, with the average weighing, in 1978, some 1,450 pounds. Then came a plan to produce hunters and jumpers, and though the Canadians made excellent jumpers, this course of action was also soon abandoned. Other breeders continued to produce the old type of Canadian, typified by the quiet Henryville line. Still others crossed Canadian studs with mares from other breeds, and though the offspring made fine eventers, this program was likewise dashed.

Cut in two by the small highway that runs alongside the St. Lawrence River, the experimental farm at Deschambault still exists, a tall fleur-de-lys presiding over neat buildings with green metal siding and white roofs. In the old days, cattle occupied the river side, Canadian horses the high side. Chemin Atkins, leading down to the river, commemorates one man's contribution and a time when the fields were dotted with black heritage horses.

But in 1981, Deschambault Research Station, as it came to be known, ceased its involvement with the Canadian horse. It seemed that government intervention had staved off the breed's extinction, but the outlook for the Canadian horse now looked every bit as bleak as it had at the turn of the century. The age of cutbacks was upon us and an obscure breed of horse seemed an obvious, even glaring, extra in tight times. The provincial government offered handsome financial incentives to private breeders to keep the line going, leaving the marketplace and the fates to determine whether the Canadian horse had a future or merely a glorious past.

Deschambault's small remaining herd—17 mares, 14 fillies, 6 colts and 7 stallions—were all sold on November 21 of that year, some individuals for as much as $7,200. But some of them were very big, at 16 hands or more and 1,600 pounds! Among the group was Hobbyhorse Larry's Dark Fox—Dali's spirited sire.

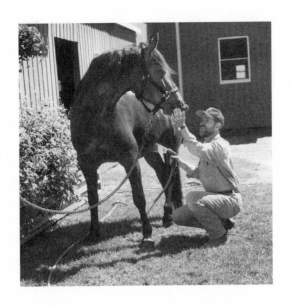

CHAPTER 8

# "*HE* WON'T BLOW OVER IN A STIFF BREEZE . . ."

BLUE HAVEN FARM, JULY 1999

*Damn those feet. They truly make me nervous. It's not a pleasant feeling, knowing that the first horse ever to put a little fear in you is the horse you're bent on buying. Every day I learn something new about this horse: hints of his quality, his stubbornness, his bullying side.*

"IS OWNING A HORSE LIKE OWNING A DOG?" someone asked me the other day. I replied that dogs are essentially subservient, eager to please, and take immense joy in small pleasures—a walk in the park, food dropped from a table, seeing their masters come home. The horse has a far more princely bearing. We groom *them*, after all. I groom my dog, too, but rarely; I groom Dali every time I ride him.

Above: Bath time at Blue Haven, Dali and the author.

But today, June 24, Dali reminds me, in his desire to be touched, of our dog, Dusty. After I groom him, doctor that shin and give him some carrots, he comes to me at the stall door. For some reason, I start talking to him in French and he responds with acute interest. His head comes up from the stall floor where he has been trolling for hay bits, and he looks me in the eye. I begin to scratch him under the chin and his head falls lower and lower, his eyes get heavy.

The horse has come so far in three weeks. He's still not keen to have his mouth touched, but touch elsewhere has become a pleasure. He willingly drops his head into the halter, and I hope the feet will soon fall into line.

Yesterday, Barb encountered rudeness in the cross-ties while picking up Dali's hind feet. Gilles stepped in, but he too had trouble. I was impressed with the dogged calm Gilles took to resolving the problem. He drew a rope around the troublesome right hind hoof (the pastern showed earlier evidence of injury, maybe an encounter with a fence, and perhaps the reason for the sensitivity). Gilles then used the rope to lift the foot, from the side and then from behind, keeping the pressure on until Dali relaxed. Gilles repeated the exercise several times.

When Dali threatened a kick, Gilles gave him a little jab to the belly with his fist, a firm and instant response to Dali's naughtiness. After more rope work and some reassuring massages to the hocks, Dali was lifting the back foot on command, five and six times in 30 seconds.

"He's not a nasty horse," says Gilles. "He's just not confident about keeping his balance on three legs." Sometimes Gilles will work with horses in the ring, using a rope to hold up one leg and only giving it back when the horse goes soft. The horse learns not to worry when one foot comes up and to keep his balance when it does.

Gilles thinks I am inclined to coddle the horse. He watched me massaging Dali's mouth and said a bit scornfully, "Pretty soon you'll have him in your living room." My sense of the horse is that he needs comforting and confidence-building and, when required, a firm hand.

Horses love ritual, but so do I. Is that why I feel much calmer around him, more inclined to chat with him? Are the routines of grooming and riding and hot-walking becoming physical mantras for us both? Dali visibly responds to my voice, and to my manner when it's relaxed.

The bit, though, continues to confound him and he often slips his tongue over the snaffle. Driving with the long-lines, on the other hand, unfolded even more smoothly than it did the first time. Gilles, mounted on another horse, even "ponied" him a bit—walked along-side him. No problem.

When Barb drove him past me in the long-lines, he looked over to me as if to say, "Get me outta this thing, will ya?" Barb noticed the beseeching look and laughed. I took solace in the fact that it was to me he looked for relief.

June 26, 1999

"Sometimes a problem in a horse gets worse before it gets better," Gilles says. Dali continues the testiness over having his back feet, and especially the right hind, picked up.

"Before we leave here," I told Gilles as he ponied Dali around on a tall quarter horse named Duke, "I really want that horse to be calm about having his feet picked up. I don't want to be fighting him every time I clean his hooves."

"Well, you better start working on it then," replies Gilles, who then himself goes to work in the ring. He ties a rope around the right hind hoof at the pastern, and pulls back hard from some 15 feet behind. What Gilles is asking the horse to do, and Dali has difficulty understanding this as anything but torment, is to back up. To teach him that he can do it with three legs (the fourth up in the air). To build confidence that when someone lifts a foot, the horse will not topple.

Dali just wants that rope off, and he kicks and kicks. Hard, snappy kicks, one after the other, kicks that would shatter a thigh bone or the boards in a stall. Fearsome, fearsome kicks. It takes about seven minutes for Dali to understand that Gilles is asking for reverse, and there are times when he turns his head right around and looks at Gilles as if to say, "Cowboy, have you completely lost your mind?"

My own response is tangled. I want Dali and me to stop fretting about his hooves, but if this is the cure, I am alarmed by it, awestruck by the power in those kicks and worried that Dali will hurt himself in some way. Mostly, I want this session over.

When it does end, Dali backs up easily on three legs when asked, and even—after the rope is taken off—when his tail is tugged. Then Gilles steps in and, one after the other, lifts all his feet. Then he asks me to get back there, gently rub the hock and lift that troublesome hoof. The hoof comes up and for perhaps the first time there were no warning roundhouse swings, no testiness, no sullen hard drop. Dali's foot touches the sand like a feather.

June 29, 1999

Gilles comments again on Dali's attitude. He has learned the basics of the long-lines, but I gather from what Barb and Gilles have said, his work ethic leaves something to be desired.

"Every horse in this stable likes to go to work," says Gilles, the sweat running down his brow this steamy day in June. "He should be the same."

Barb is gentle with Dali, rewarding him for every good turn with her voice and hand, and he responds. Her language is soft and salted with the little French she knows. Gilles is more demanding. Gilles takes him right to the end of his patience, to the point that Barb is saying aloud what I am thinking: "Gilles, he's had enough for today."

Long-lining is hard work, and after Barb schools him, her neck is glistening. Then Gilles steps in for more long-lining, and now everyone—horse and both trainers—is hot and wet. I think to come forward and give the horse his reward: a hosing down outside the barn. But no, Gilles wants more.

He asks the horse to back up. To stand still while Gilles, with his back to the horse, slowly, methodically, arranges the long lines. More backing up. More tack adjustment. I want this foot back. Now that one. Now stand still. Now back up. And on it goes. It seems almost cruel, yet Dali is completely in synch with Gilles's demands. "He's paying attention all right," says Barb.

Dali, Gilles would say, is a horse whose respect you must earn. And respect starts on the ground.

July 2, 1999

Another hard day at Dali's feet. The left hind will not be lifted and when it comes up, so does the roundhouse swing and, something new and more menacing, the turn of the hind end. I back out and Gilles steps in. He urges me not to bail out so easily and quickly, to stand my ground and stay close to the horse. Close, ironically, is the safest place to be when a horse thinks about kicking.

Damn those feet. They truly make me nervous. It's not a pleasant feeling, knowing that the first horse ever to put a little fear in you is the horse you're bent on buying. Every day I learn something new about this horse: hints of his quality, his stubbornness, his bullying side.

Gilles massages the right hind hock, but Dali refuses to let that hoof be lifted and swings around menacingly. Now comes what horse people call a correction. Gilles undoes the cross-ties and gives Dali a sharp crack with the end of the rope under the belly. This sends Dali swirling around, his head raised high in agitation. Later I ask Gilles why he effected his correction on the end of a tether and not in the cross-ties.

Barb answers that one: "If his head goes up and he breaks those chains, then he has that knowledge—that the cross-ties can be defeated—and that horse will never again be safe in cross-ties."

The discipline has dramatic effect. Gilles has only to point to that front left foot and it comes up. He teaches the horse to stand stock-still, to lift each foot on command. If Dali is indeed a bully, and it seems he has that in him, he is by no means beyond redemption. He is like a choirboy as each foot comes up in turn.

But then, we've been in this place before, confident that the foot problem has finally been licked. And it's come back. I think I have to move around Dali with a quiet confidence and give him time to respond. But when he digs in those mighty heels of his, I have to as well. Years in the company of smart trainers has taught me the wisdom of proceeding this way, and the theory is well imprinted on my brain. The body, though, has yet to pick up the lesson, to move with the kind of confidence a horse can see and trust.

The bit continues to be a problem. Dali does not pack it properly, and until that tongue is neatly under the bit and not over it, we cannot really begin to ride him. Next Wednesday, we will have had him exactly five weeks and the vet in Kemptville had advised re-X-raying Dali in four to six weeks. We are growing impatient to get on him. If, and I dread the possibility, the shin has shown no sign of healing, then I must return him to Ferme Saroma and pay a great price. Hours lost, money spent, hopes dashed.

July 6, 1999

Dali meets me at the Dutch door of the ring. His mane is braided, giving him the look of a chunky Indian pony. I cannot say it suits him. He looks diminished. I should be more grateful: The braiding is Barb's attempt to keep his neck cool and staunch the flow of sweat.

The whole province is in the grip of a stultifying heat wave that sends me packing Monday to our cabin and the promise of many dunkings at the point. The cabin, a square-timbered house first erected by pioneers in 1830, is quiet and removed. It's not on water but close enough.

Days and days of overwhelming heat and humidity have left us all a little faint. On Monday, the combined effect left Torontonians feeling like it was 113 degrees Fahrenheit. The air feels, and is, heavy and vile, inducing mild nausea when you step outside. Today, at least, there is a strong breeze. *Hot wind* is more like it. In such heat I long-lined Dali for the first time, under Barb's tutelage.

"I've noticed a real change in him the last two times in the long-lines," said Barb, clearly pleased at his progress. "His face has gone soft, and his ears, which before were always moving back and forth as he worried about his mouth, have kept forward. He's really begun to trust us."

My aim in long-lining him was to go lightly. On stops and reverses, especially, I was immediately to go soft in my hands after any successful maneuver, as a reward. "That's his paycheque," says Barb. And he earns his pay. Never once does he balk or press on unreasonably. He gets skittish when horses are brought into the arena, but settles in seconds. Even the bit is literally falling into place. He wore it in his stall for one or two days, happily eating with it parked in his mouth.

My bonus comes when he agreeably let me pick up all four feet. The clue that the feet would not be an issue comes when I take off his right splint boot and he raises the left front hoof. "Excuse me, did you want this, uh, hoof?" he seems to ask.

Dali is learning to be generous, learning to anticipate. Better yet, I trust him now. His skittishness has come down by more than half. "You're getting to be," Barb said to him today rather rhetorically, "a solid citizen."

There are times when I feel like I'm getting to be an old hand. As I approached the barn at Blue Haven later that day, I caught a whiff of that elixir: wood shavings, girths drying in the sun, old and young manure, horse leather, horse. It seemed entirely pleasant and familiar. Some of the horses nickered when I arrived, and I wish I had had the good grace to greet them back. Next time I will.

July 7, 1999

Dr. Mark Rutherford, the vet who years ago sent our poor sad projectile-vomiting young cat into the feline ether, took X-rays this morning at Blue Haven. As I did at Kemptville, I donned lead apron and oversized lead-lined plastic gloves and held each X-ray board behind Dali's splint bone. Now it's 2 p.m. and I'm waiting for the call.

"Your horse is fine," Mark might say. *Your* horse.

Or, "I don't have very good news about that horse." *That* horse.

Earlier, at the stable, on Mark's palpation of the injured area, there seemed to be no tenderness. No swelling. "Hot zones," as Mark called them, quickly reveal themselves. At the time, I was sufficiently encouraged by Mark's positive gut assessment to approve two other procedures. They would have to be done sooner or later: the so-called floating of the teeth and the removal of his wolf tooth.

The latter sits on my computer, the tooth looking almost like that of a human, a creamy light brown, with the root, or what Mark got of it, blood red and narrow at the end. Up in the small red hole Mark made in Dali's gums lies the rest of the root, where it will eventually atrophy.

Mark gave Dali a sedative and within 40 seconds the horse's head dipped noticeably, his great brown eyes grew heavy and he wobbled slightly on his feet. Throughout the procedure, which took about 20 minutes, I held Dali by the leather halter Mark put on him and felt the weight of his head leaning into my hands.

Floating is crude dentistry, what I imagined dentistry to be when I was a kid and screamed and bit so hard that the first dentist I ever faced simply gave up on me. Mark inserted a polyurethene gag into each side of Dali's mouth as he worked on it, a plain device to keep the horse's mouth open for entry. There followed a variety of rasping tools—long, silver-handled things with angled ends like some toothbrushes. The rasps are made of various titaniums and sandpaper-like materials, and Mark raked over the rows of teeth, top and bottom, until they were even.

The wolf tooth came out next. It was out before I knew it was out. I must have diverted my attention to my poor drugged horse, and during that time span, as if to spare me, Mark had dislodged the tooth. Earlier I had seen him tuck into the back of his pants a pair of pliers as long as his arm. My heart sank at the thought of it being used. It never was.

Later that afternoon, Mark's familiar green truck with its white divided canopy chock full of veterinary equipment pulls up outside my house in Kingston. He has the X-rays in his hand. "Looks pretty good," he says, which I welcome, though I was hoping for "wonderful" or "great news." Mark holds up the thin sheets of film to the sun and on some there is no line at all, just a cloudy grey that signals good solid bone. Only on one can you see a thin line, but even it is engulfed in cloud. Mark says if Dali was his horse and he was getting him in shape for endurance riding, he'd go a little slow for four to six weeks.

Turns out I have four to six weeks, and more. The splint was like a stoplight, a flashing cautionary orange. Suddenly the light had turned green. I would buy this horse.

July 14, 1999

Yesterday, for the first time since Dali bucked me off a few months ago, a rider got up on his back. And aside from one moment of skittishness, likely occasioned by geldings horsing around outside the ring, he was calm and even appeared to enjoy himself.

Like all else here, Barb and Gilles eased Dali into that first ride. Barb saddled him and left his halter on, then Gilles on Rocky chased him around the ring. The chase—it would become a precursor to every ride—is meant to tire Dali a little; the thinking is that if a young, raw horse is inclined to buck, let the buck occur during the chase and not with a rider up.

Dali seemed almost sleepy, and while he played the chase game nothing could induce him to buck. But when Gilles attempted to pony him, it took 10 minutes of dancing in circles, and much good and delicate maneuvering on the part of Gilles, to convince him to be led by a rope.

Finally, by talking softly to him, rubbing his head and asking firmly but never harshly to accept the rope, Dali fell in behind. Watching were friends of mine from Toronto, David and Claudine Carpenter. They left impressed equally by the calm and discipline of Gilles's horse, the skill of Gilles himself, and the way Dali responded.

When Barb entered the picture and flapped Dali's side with the stirrups, he danced sideways and it took another five minutes of steady desensitization to those stirrups flapping to get him back on side and ready to proceed. Gilles looked quite absurd, almost hammering the stirrup into the saddle as if this were part of everyday riding.

Implicit was a warning: how dangerous it is to go the other way—to pussyfoot around a horse. Ray Hunt, one of Gilles's mentors and a prominent American horse trainer who espouses the gentler way, does no such tiptoeing around his horses; he moves with an almost careless abandon, but he's had years to develop that pose. It masks a terrific attention to detail.

No doubt Hunt would have noticed, as Gilles did, the little kink in Dali's tail when, the stirrup flapping finally over, Barb slowly eased into the saddle and rode him behind Gilles and his horse. Gilles was referring to the way a nervous horse holds his tail ever so slightly aloft, not buried deeply in the croup. I learn something new every time I go to Blue Haven. This was yesterday's little lesson, and had I known about it and watched for Dali's stiff tail two months ago I would never have mounted him as I had done that first time.

Today, Dali is again ponied and then ridden by Barb. His tail was set a little high in the beginning, but chasing him beforehand failed to evoke anything close to a buck. And Barb was able to turn him easily, even coming close to spinning. He remains light in her hands.

His weight, though, has to come down. Barb felt his great girth as soon as she got on him. He will always be a big-boned horse, warned Gilles, and it will take many many days of hard riding, and a diet, to take that weight off. Maybe that's a good thing. It will take long hacks and much schooling to make him trim and keep him trim.

Meanwhile, after sending a fax to Jérôme yesterday confirming my intention to buy the horse, I learned this morning from Mark Rutherford that the X-rays were a few days late getting to Larry Butler and he has not had a chance to look at them. I had assumed that no news was good news.

"It's such a common injury," Mark had assured me. "I think as long as you don't ride him hard the next little while, he'll be fine." The palpation he had done on the sore area had revealed no sensitivity; that, he told me at the time, is as important as the finding on an X-ray.

Hope so.

July 19, 1999

I have a horse but cannot ride him. Not yet anyway. Barb will take on the task until she's confident about passing him over to me. But to keep in fair riding shape, I continue to take lessons at my old stable, Wilmarny Farm. My instructor—everyone calls her Tiny—gives me novice horses, the better to simulate the future with Dali. Tiny reminds me often that good days with horses will be followed by bad, that lessons you thought were learned can come undone.

The business of the famous "fx line" through the splint bone has similarly been a roller-coaster ride. Dr. Rutherford's pronouncement that the X-rays were "pretty good" was followed, several days later, by a fax from Dr. Butler's office. Each time I read the fax, I read something different. First it seemed cautionary, then reassuring.

On the one hand, it read, "The fx line through and around the splint bone has healed" and "Everything is progressing nicely."

On the other hand, there was "still a small sequestrum embedded in the callus that needs to solidify"; "the periosteal reaction on the outside of the callus needs to calm down and become less reactive;" and prior to the note about everything progressing nicely was that tiny lament: "Although slower than I would like to see it . . ."

Had we done the wrong thing by commencing the ground work? Should we even have begun to ride him? Should we have kept up the DMSO and not stopped it last week? The fax seemed to raise more questions than it answered.

I call the clinic and Larry Butler happens to pick up the phone. This time the message is clear: The actual words, the tone, all calm me. It was OK to have done the ground work with Dali. Riding him an hour four or five times a week is fine. Use the DMSO on alternate weeks. But the bottom line, I am heartened to hear, is "Your horse will be fine."

The vet's words amplify my sense of what owners go through when their horses, as Kathi puts it, "are up on blocks." Horses are such tough animals, yet their delicacy and vulnerability surprise and alarm me.

July 20, 1999

"Well, *he* won't blow over in a stiff breeze." They are Kathi's first words upon finally seeing for herself the sturdy Dark Fox Dali. She later calls him "a little pork chop," a reference to his bulk, but she seems certain he would lose some of that girth as I begin to work him.

He is what he is. A squarely built horse. And I liked what I heard in Kathi's response, which would, I knew, be honest. She saw, as others have, a kindness in his eye; she liked his big trot (though it was far bigger before Barb got on him). Dali struck Kathi as a sensible horse. "You'll have fun with him," she said, especially after he showed some skittishness when Barb trotted him.

Barb said later that riding him is like "sitting in a couch. He's really smooth in the trot." It made sense that a horse as big as a couch would offer the comfort of one.

"He eats like a pig," moans Gilles. "You put hay in his stall and there isn't a single bit left."

Pork chop. Couch. Pig. That's my boy.

July 21, 1999

Went to hear Chris Irwin, author of *Horses Don't Lie*, speak at a local bookstore last night. I kept thinking of Dali as the lanky gentler from Swift Current urged his audience to read their horses as closely as they would a worthy book.

He told me things I already knew, but I understood them with a new clarity. Horses, he said, need the comfort of the hierarchy. In a herd of 10, each horse has a number in that pecking order and knows his or her place. As a trainer, you want to act like you're *just* above your horse in that order. Trust and respect: That's what you want from your horse, who wants the same. It's when you act as though you're the number-one horse and treat your mount as though he's a 10 that problems arise; worse is to act as though you're 10 and he's number one.

Irwin is one of those rare gentlers who admits that horses occasionally need to be hit (though never more than the equivalent of a slap). It's when, where and why you administer discipline that matters, he says. Act like an assertive horse, says Irwin, not like a predator who has lost his temper.

His little tome offers clues to reading horse language. The way the horse holds his tail, the set of his hips, the movement of his ears, the look in his eye, the set of his mouth, the way he moves his feet: All can convey disrespect, fear, anger, anxiety, boredom, even blends of emotion. Irwin talked about a horse issuing calm defiance.

What, I wonder, is Dali conveying when we chase him before Barb rides him? I read confusion, even disappointment. I see him standing in the corner, looking out to Barb with his ears fixed on her but his whole body on high alert. I thought you were OK, I take him to say, but you're just like all the rest.

Must we chase him with such vigour?

"Don't underestimate this horse," Barb replies. "He's still honky [unpredictable and apt to run] at times. When we play this chase game with other horses around here, they act like barnyard pets. He's not there yet." The hind end he turns to her when she approaches him in the corner of the ring is indeed about disrespect, and I cannot blame Barb for taking some of the pepper out of him. But something else is going out of him too.

August 2, 1999

Tonight I drive over to Evergreen Farm, only a few kilometres east of Blue Haven, to watch a master German saddler in action.

Jochen Schleese, CMS, reads his calling card. Certified Master Saddler. In a forest-green golf shirt with his company's name over his heart, and wearing khaki shorts and good running shoes, he looks younger than I imagined. I expect a "master" to have white hair. He has trained for three years at Passier & Sohn in Germany, and in 1986 emigrated to Canada, the same year he was named official saddler to the 1986 World Dressage Championship.

Schleese's day began earlier in Perth, Ontario, where a dozen or so clients came to avail themselves of his services, like pilgrims to a prophet. Jochen pulls his green van into Evergreen's covered dressage ring and sets out his various tools on a table. There is a great metal contraption topped by a wheel, and into this thing go saddles new and old, upside down. I presume that the turning of the wheel at the top effects changes to the saddle's wooden or leather/wood tree.

There is a leather caliper that Jochen's agent, Margo McBurney, calls "the squeaky Italian thing." Jochen's assistant, Jens, who seems agreeable to my many questions, calls it a leather wire tracer. A milky rust colour, it is positioned atop the horse's back and can be adjusted since it's ribbed every few inches (black spidery lines mark the places) and can flare to the inside or outside as the horse's sloping body does the same. The tracer also houses a small level at its apex so that a plumb line can be determined. Matching rider, saddle and horse, I discover, is a bit like building a house. A discordant line anywhere will eventually come back to haunt you.

Finally, there is a truly bizarre device that looks for all the world like a miniature pipe organ when placed on the horse's back. The handsome grey in the cross-ties appears alarmed at seeing this thing placed where a rider and saddle would normally go. "Do you expect me to play that musical instrument?" his wide black eyes seem to say. The device looked like something that wacky Rube Goldberg might have invented, but its purpose quickly becomes plain.

By loosening wheels at the end of that rowed array of small black plastic pipes, the latter falls against the horse's shoulder and there stops. The wheels are then tightened and the pipe's positions secured so what you have when you flip over the device is a kind of topographical map of the horse's back. A lot less fancy than other methods in Jochen's armamentarium, but no doubt effective.

He also has a saddle pad laced with sensors and connected by technological wizardry to a computer screen. In a graphic, stride-by-stride way, a saddle's efficiency in evenly bearing the weight of the rider can thus be measured. Plaster moulds can also be taken of the horse's back.

The scene tonight in the dressage ring is all much ado about doing the best for the horse. I expected a long parade of dressage queens, come to buy $4,000 saddles. Some riders have indeed come for high-end tack, but I am pleased to see the great care taken by Jochen and Jens to restuff a rather plain, rather old English saddle.

I have been of two minds about getting "Schleesified," as a friend put it. The whole procedure seemed a bit precious: poring over saddles that cost as much as my horse, the $100 "barn call" fee paid by each person, even the very notion of "a saddle clinic." I was supposed to *pay* this saddler to come around and sell me a saddle?

And yet I liked his Teutonic fussiness, which my German-born wife, Ulrike, had introduced me to a long time ago. Insistence on high standards, though, is sometimes mistaken for imperiousness. A woman at the Evergreen Farm clinic said she was once told by Jochen, "Don't you *ever* put that saddle on that horse again." And yet his rumoured arrogance was nowhere apparent; only a businesslike manner freshened with occasional wit (to the dressage rider on an acerbic horse in a test ride, Jochen said, "I know you're taking your life in your hands, but could you try turning him to the right now?"). His catalogue boasts of his many prizes for entrepreneurial achievement, but it struck me that his vaulting ambition is not built on shortchanging his customers. He values his expertise and charges for it, and I respect that.

The saddle clinic was just one more lesson I tried to absorb, one more reminder that with horses and riders everything matters—not least the leather that lies between them. In the end I did not get Schleesified, but the used saddle I bought was a German-made Passier. *Gute Qualität*, as they say. My horse is worth it.

Barb has put about a dozen rides on Dali and, at my request, has modified her chase routine prior to riding him. She uses a long lunge whip to move him along, but the white plastic patch at the end that seemed to alarm Dali is gone. He dutifully goes into a trot or lope as she pursues him, but her pursuit has been reined in. It's now shorter and less vigorous. Dali ends by following Barb around the ring like the pal that he is.

Barb runs a cord from the side pull (a bitless bridle) at his head to a point on the saddle and asks him to walk or trot in circles. It's a bending exercise, and bending is coming more easily.

By degrees Dali grows more trim, which pleases me. But he also has a lazy streak, reflected in his slow-motion amble and the way Barb in the saddle has to keep after him in the trot. He doesn't know yet about work ethic. He does, though, know about blowing himself up while being girthed, and often has to be recinched several times before Barb finally gets on him.

Barb looks on this optimistically, as she always does. Easier to apply gas than brakes, she will say about Dali's trot when it descends into that hot-day shuffle of his. As for ballooning before girthing, she says, "He knows how to look after himself," and then she tells the story of another horse who never knew to protect himself in that way and panicked when he thought the girth was going to take his breath away. The story, which is also a parable about stupid trainers, has a sad and tragic ending.

August 4, 1999

The Chris Irwin clinic that Barb and Gilles and I took in last week near Ottawa has had a dramatic impact on Blue Haven. Today I walk into the arena and discover half of it effectively blocked off by a tall green portable fence, not unlike the one Chris uses. It isn't a true 50-foot round pen, says Gilles. More like a poor man's version.

Barb couldn't wait to try it. Inside the pen on Dali, she gradually increased his trot speed until he broke into a canter. This was a first. But it was a flighty one that saw him make for a corner and brake. He wasn't trying to ditch her, just expressing his discombobulation.

"He's not ready yet," said Barb. "Eventually he'll figure out that a slow lope is easier than a fast trot, and it'll come." But the bends, the turns on the forehand, the reverses and serpentines, are all coming along nicely.

"He's becoming a real sweetheart," I said aloud as I took off his tack later. Earlier, while I groomed him, I ran my hand over that old splint of his, feeling for heat. There was none. I ran my hand over his back hocks, down his belly, trying to memorize the way the muscles fold into each other. I wanted to imprint on my brain the lines of his body so I would know by look and feel an aberration when I saw it.

As I cupped my hand around that splint, Dali lay his head on mine. "That's not affection," I remember Chris Irwin saying, "that's domination." I lightly pushed Dali's head away.

His hooves, which had started to chip and crack, are much better since a recent trim by the farrier, but when I wondered aloud about putting hoof oil on them, cousin Kathi gave me a firm negative. Hoof oil, she says, is about soothing horse owners' anxieties about their horse's dry and chipping feet. Applying a petroleum product to hooves prevents them from breathing normally. When I told her that Barb has been sprinkling the shavings in Dali's stall with water, Kathi immediately cut in, "She's *smart*."

What I am learning, from both Barb and Kathi, is what time it takes to shape a good horse. The slow way is indeed the fast way. "I'm just establishing a line of communication with the horse in the round pen," Chris Irwin had said in the clinic, trying to dampen anyone's unrealistic expectations of quick and miraculous solutions to horse conundrums. "I want to establish the horse's focus, leading to trust and respect, and maybe willingness."

Natural horsemanship, he insisted, is not always about being gentle with a horse. "The most natural thing for a horse," he said into the microphone that day in Stittsville, "is to kick and bite another horse." When a young rider's horse, clearly full of himself, would not be haltered in the round pen, Chris slapped him firmly on the chest twice, and the horse shook his head as if to say "I needed that" and accepted the halter.

I took notes as Chris spoke, recording some of his aphorisms:

"You do not *teach* a horse how to do a flying change. The colt first released into the paddock knows it already."

"In dealing with a horse, you have to know when to retreat, when to stand your ground, when to push."

"The trainer should ask himself: Do I have the moral authority to ask that horse to face his fear?" To rush that fence, leap that creek, pass that plastic swirling in the wind.

"Establish communication on the ground and let it continue in the saddle."

"In the saddle, don't forget to breathe. Breathe exaggeratedly. Short choppy breaths will only make the horse anxious. When you breathe deeply, he hears and feels you. You'll relax, he'll relax."

He warned one rider, "The rest of these horses play checkers. Yours plays chess."

"Most riding," Chris had said, and it bore the ring of truth, "is about riders fixing problems of their own creation." By failing to cue the horse about an impending bend or transition, we make the move harder for the horse, and too often we reach for a bigger bit or stick. The problem is typically not recalcitrance on the horse's part, but pilot error.

August 5, 1999

Today I earn at least a little respect from Dali. Little by little, Barb is handing off the chores of bridling and saddling to me. I can hear Gilles laughing at my antics from the other side of the ring. When Dali ducks away, I take the whip as Barb has instructed me to do, and send him packing, round and round until my easing up causes him to stop and look at me. Then and only then can we do business.

Similarly, when I take the bridle off, he uses that opportunity to duck into a vacant stall, no doubt hoping for a treat. When I go after him, he presents his back end to me and I make him circle. When he pauses sideways to me and looks to be swinging away once more, I have had enough and tell him so. "Don't you even *think* about it," I tell him forcefully, and to my surprise, and maybe his, he stands stock-still and drops his head into the halter.

He was turned out this morning, but the thunder and lightning—Blue Haven sits high on a hill and gets lots of strikes—caused Barb to bring him and the others back in. Dali, maybe more than other horses, wants his turnout. It was clear when we tacked him up this morning he had plenty of vinegar.

Thanks to Chris's clinic, I may know better what my horse is saying than I did before and I delight in reading him now. "We look too much to the head. Look at the tail," Chris implored us. "It all starts there, in the hindquarters. Read your horse back to front."

That day, Chris went through some of the many signs and signals that horses flash. I could hear Dali's tail swishing as I brushed him earlier in the cross-ties, yet there were few flies about. Agitation. The head came up a few times. Worry. He even stomped his foot a time or two. Impatience. A butt turned to you is a clear sign of disrespect, as raw a message as a horse can deliver. A head lowered and raised in one motion to level is a bow, a sign of respect; a quick bow raised to high-headedness is a sign of fear. The tail held high and stiffly denotes confidence; a tail curling like the letter C denotes relaxation; a tail right between the legs signifies fear and should alert the trainer or rider to back off. A release of manure could mean you are literally scaring the shit out of him, or it could mean he's relaxing.

I find myself now talking differently to my horse, asking him to square up so that front and back hooves are more or less parallel, to sidle over, to move back. The talking calms the horse, gives him another means to understand. I want him to square up because Chris mentioned in his clinic that a horse not squared is prepared to flee or enter your space. It's not much to ask of a horse, to square up.

I am discovering with Dali that how you ask matters. Ask too boldly and you alarm him; ask resolutely and he usually says OK. But like a teenager, he will test and test. And always, he keeps score.

# CHAPTER 9

# HORSE RESCUE

1990S

*"Nous élevons pour nos enfants*
*les chevaux de nos pères."*
*("We raise for our children the horses of our fathers.")*
—*from a brochure issued by*
*L'Association québécoise du cheval canadien*

ONE MORNING IN MID-JUNE OF THE YEAR 2000, the clear sky a welcome sight, for spring had been famously wet and cold, I drove up
the north shore of the St. Lawrence River. It was to Deschambault
that I was drawn.

*Le cheval canadien* is still rooted in Quebec, on farms near villages

Above: Gilles Racette at his farm near Trottier Mills.

called St. Paulin and East Farnham and Trottier Mills, and others with odd names like St. Louis du Ha Ha and Pohenegamook, Shipshaw and Shigawake. Places near Quebec City also figure in the breed's history—Anse au Foulon, the little bay where that first herd of horses from France swam for shore in 1665, and Cap Rouge, Ste-Anne de la Pocatière, St. Joachim, Deschambault, La Gorgendière, all the sites of government farms where *le cheval canadien* was raised throughout the 20th century.

Dali's grandsire, La Gorgendière Fox Larry, was the last horse to be sold when the provincially run farm at Deschambault was closed in 1981. The last, remembers Gilles Racette, for a reason.

"He came out like a loony, crazy as all get out," says Racette, who was there. A Montreal police officer for 30 years, he calls himself retired. He wears his 55 years lightly, and his deep black eyes and imposing salt-and-pepper beard seem the perfect complement to his powerful hands, used to milk cows, haul hay, hold horses. His modest farm in the low green mountains southeast of Trois-Rivières has him up most days at dawn.

Louis Philippe Racette—a 20-year-old son of Gilles and his wife, Anne Bélanger—won the senior jumping division at the 1999 Quebec Games aboard their 15-hand chestnut Canadian stallion, Tonnerre. Clearly, the family knows a thing or two about horses.

And what Gilles remembers about Fox Larry is that this small, refined chestnut had a loose screw in his head. Gilles said he once had a Fox Lalou stallion who used to go after their kindly old Lab dog as if trying to kill him, and they eventually sent the stud back. He also remembers a Fox Larry mare who tried to kick and bite someone attempting to tattoo her, and even growled—a sound that in all his years with horses Gilles had never heard before. Many of the cross Canadians Gilles has encountered have come from the Fox and Lalou lines. On the other hand, he says, the Lalou stallion that replaced the menacing one was "a perfect gentleman" and the Fox Larry mare he owns now is "quiet, gentle and calm."

Yves Bernatchez, the Deschambault lawyer and Canadian-horse authority who was also at the auction, likes the Lalou line, but Fox Larry he remembers all too well. That horse, he said, was the only one at the auction with "a bad head." Yves meant what was inside.

I listened to Gilles Racette and Yves Bernatchez and André Auclair, another knowledgeable horseman and a breeder of Canadians. They all insisted that the breed is stronger than individuals in the breed. In every Canadian-horse line, good sense ultimately prevails.

Auclair is a believer in heritage lines (he has some 42 Canadian cows, more than 100 Chantecleer chickens, 40 or so Canadian horses, and he even plants heritage seeds in his vegetable garden). He runs a kind of Noah's ark on a valley farm at the bottom end of a quiet road near St. Paulin. There are, Auclair insists, no bad lines among Canadian horses, and if the Fox line runs hotter than the others, that only means Fox horses are better suited for competition. And there are many trainers and breeders who actually prefer the Fox line for its intelligence and spirit.

Still, the line hoists a red flag among most who know the breed. For four years, Gilles Racette owned the father of that line, Brio de la Victoire, a champion in the American western show ring and a horse he quite enjoyed. Even at the age of 27, that horse, Gilles recalls, was still spirited. Fox Larry, though, by every account I heard, was just plain crazy.

My journey into Canadian-horse country in the summer of 2000, then, was as much about the history of my horse as it was about the history of his breed. The trip had a loose feel and was marked by several serendipitous turns.

Jean-Paul Paré, who had overseen the breeding program at Deschambault in the late 1960s and early 1970s, had told me on the phone to look up Jean-Yves Vézina, once the farm foreman and now retired. A nice old man with lots of stories, said Jean-Paul. My notion was simple: See the farm, look up Monsieur Vézina.

Deschambault is one of the oldest villages in Quebec, and it so happens that the part of the village most steeped in history is also one of the quietest. My first evening, I went to the presbytery, a gathering of church and convent and other early 19th century stone buildings set high atop a cliff overlooking the St. Lawrence River. Much removed from the main road, with its gardens and benches and commanding view, it's a place well suited to the spiritual contemplation it was meant to foster. The eastern sky before me seemed immense, and the light spilling through the cloud banks at sunset had the kind of clarity I had seen in Krieghoff paintings. I was powerfully drawn to this place and once there had no desire to leave.

A plaque at the outlook informed that Le Seigneur Jacques-Alexis Fleury d'Eschambault lent his name to what was then a fortification here at the end of the 17th century. Navigators, the plaque added, feared the rapids below this vantage that could reach 10 metres high. The present seemed so peaceful; the past clearly reeked of violence. It struck me that the farther east you go up the St. Lawrence, the deeper into Canadian history you travel and the more the Canadian horse is intertwined with that past.

On a hunch, I decided to stay at Auberge Chemin du Roy, a splendid bed and breakfast some distance from the village off a road named after Louis XIV. The place was wildly Victorian, with silver domes and pink clapboard and a small waterfall to lull you to sleep at night. Another hunch drew me to a café in the village whose drawing card was its sculpted sign featuring a wooden horse in profile—clearly a Canadian horse—pulling a *calèche*.

At Le Café de la Galerie d'Art, a hole-in-the-wall bar, I told the *propriétaire*, in my simple French, that I was here to research a book on horses. And he ducked out, and from a holder outside the art gallery next door pulled a brochure rich in black Canadians. "Nous élevons pour nos enfants les chevaux de nos pères," read a quote set off from the text. "We raise for our children the horses of our fathers." It turned out that the building that housed both café and gallery is owned by the aforementioned Yves Bernatchez, long active in the Canadian Horse Breeders' Association. The barman called him on the phone and a rendezvous was arranged for next morning. *Par hasard*, I had landed on the doorstep of the one man who knows as much about the history of the breed as anyone.

A heavy-set man who was recovering from a heart attack just days before, Yves told me that where the presbytery now stands, French cavalry, on horses we now call Canadians, had centuries before rebuffed English troops in the first phase of the battle that would spell the end of French rule in Canada. The site of *le vieux presbytère* had stories to tell.

Bernatchez, too, had a tale to tell of La Gorgendière Alto Fox, the sire of Fox Larry, and he told it over coffee outside the café next morning. Monsieur Vézina even drove past at one point, and Yves waved to him, but I never did get to meet him. Alto Fox was a tall, black horse and there was consensus that he would make a wonderful jumper. His head—its shape, that is—was not very nice, but it was thought that careful breeding would correct that problem in generations to follow. It was the contents of the head that caused consternation.

Staff at Deschambault, including Monsieur Vézina, had had their fill of Alto Fox and intended him for a meat truck, until, that is, a government horseman, a friend of Yves, intervened. After a day or two of working with Alto Fox, he loudly proclaimed before a gathering of staff, as well as Quebec's minister of agriculture, that he had saved this horse and that he would make for a good line. Staff at Deschambault must have blinked in disbelief.

"He was not a nice horse," Bernatchez recalls in an understated way, and he would know, for Alto Fox had lived in his barn for a summer. But Alto Fox's sons, he said, were nicer than he was. One hopes.

The day of my first ride on Dali, the day he tossed me, I learned a lot, and not just about the unpredictability of a green horse. The man who led me to Dali, Alec Hayward, is one of the patriarchs of the

Canadian horse, a keeper of stories, and one who sang the breed's praises 20 years ago when the end of the line looked imminent.

If Alec Hayward seems to own the lore, it's because he lived it. Driving all the way up to Messines, Quebec, that day from Hayward's place near North Gower in the Ottawa Valley, I let the tape recorder run. Alec's father, I learned, once had a farm at Stoneham, north of Quebec City, where Canadian horses did it all: logging, riding, pulling carriages and cutters, ploughing. Alec pronounced the place Stone-*ham*, as in the meat, which rhymes with the way he says Mont-*calm*, the French commander at the siege of Quebec. Alec's uncle, George Atkins, spent his life working for the federal government's various farm enterprises to save the breed.

As we drove north into *Quee*-bec, as he calls it, though he's quite fluent in French, Alec remembered some of the Canadian horses in his early life. "We had a gelding named Barney, born in 1935," he said. "Barney was our play toy. I remember playing tag and getting under his stomach and putting my head out through his front legs so they couldn't tag me. If I was five, so was he. We also had a mare called Rainey, a gift from my uncle to my grandfather. Rainey was born in 1919. I remember driving her; she died at the age of 28. Everybody had Canadians in those days, though some didn't like them. They said they were too small. But you would see those horses pulling the mowing machine in the afternoon as proud as they had been pulling it in the morning.

"We loved their beauty, their temperament—very people-oriented," Alec said. "They never bite or kick. I never had a fear of horses. At our farm we had French-style windows and at mealtime the horse would stick his head in the window and we'd give him a piece of bread from the table."

For a time there were no Canadian horses in Alec's life. He and his wife, Jeanne, lived on a farm in New Zealand and he sold machinery, but by the late 1970s Alec and his friend Donnie Prosperine both felt it was time to get involved with Canadian horses. They weren't so much trying to rescue the breed, nothing so grand as that. It was more an instinctive gesture, like giving water to a thirsty man. Or credit where credit is due.

"I think it's unbelievable that no one knows anything about these horses," Donnie Prosperine once said. "This is our national horse, but you don't learn about them in any history books."

The breed was on the ropes, and confined to Quebec. Alec and Donnie simply wanted to raise a few Canadians, to keep the line going in Ontario. But the trick, they soon discovered, was to get these then rare horses out of Quebec.

"Donnie and I had quite an uphill battle to get the trust of these people," Alec recalls. There was a sense that the horse belonged to French Quebec and that any crossing the border would never come back. Eventually, in 1988, Donnie Prosperine won the respect and trust of the Canadian Horse Breeders' Association when he became a director, winning all 87 votes. In those days, the association membership was overwhelmingly dominated by francophone Quebecers. This has changed somewhat: Regional associations have since formed in Ontario and elsewhere in Canada as the breed set down new roots.

But in 1978, neither Hayward nor Prosperine could have foreseen brighter days for the breed. They searched in Quebec for almost two years and endured endless frustration. The few good horses they saw were not for sale and the poor ones they passed on. By now there were thought to be 300 or 400 purebred Canadians left.

Finally, a man called Léo Gourde called them in 1979. He led them to another fellow named Gérard Lemieux near Granby who had a stallion, Viger Duc. The horse had just won a championship in Montreal at the Velodrome and they went to see him. Alec, who admittedly has no great capacity for liquor, remembers that Gérard had offered him a glass of rye whiskey three-quarters full, then another. Soon he was showing Donnie and Alec old pictures of Canadians. By now it was 11 p.m. and Donnie, always in a hurry, was getting anxious to go.

Still, they did go into the stable to see the horses—the mares Windsor Rosine and Windsor Michette. Gérard asked Alec which he thought was the better mare; Alec picked Rosine. Gérard was perhaps testing this would-be buyer's horse sense, and it seems, in hindsight, that Alec had chosen wisely and passed a test. For some kind of door had opened.

Before they left, Donnie told Gérard he would buy the mares. Alec, though, told Gérard, "I can't afford your stallion. I'll tell you what I can give you for your stallion if you want to sit down and we'll be friends after my offer. I expect you to refuse it." Which Gérard did.

But some days later, Gérard called back. He'd had a change of heart and suddenly they had a deal. "The old lad," as Alec called Gérard, had only one bit of advice. "Don't disgrace your horse," he said, meaning that Alec should treat the stallion with the dignity that is his due. And Alec believes he did. "I put a stud fee of $300 but I would not breed the horse to a bag of bones. I've refused a stud fee more times than I've accepted. And I never sold a horse for less than meat prices; I'd sooner put a bullet in them."

Alec would not divulge, even to Jeanne or to Donnie, what he paid for Viger Duc. And he wasn't about to tell me either, even decades later. But those three horses marked a meaningful entry of the Canadian horse into Ontario, and from there to points west. Alec Hayward and Donnie Prosperine began to breed Canadian horses, and at one point they together owned 28. For the first time, the breed had champions beyond the Quebec border.

The Canadian horse appealed for all the same reasons he had in the 19th century. Here was a handsome, hardy, versatile horse, but the heritage aspect—the profound sense of history that came with every papered horse—finally began to hit home. In the 1980s, as the breed enjoyed a minor resurgence, Hayward was quoted in a national magazine: "I think Canada has finally discovered something that's uniquely ours. The clubs and organizations are waving the flag and people are starting to pay attention."

The passion that Prosperine and Hayward took to their breeding programs was soon felt by others. Gail Mosher became a convert. June Pelot. Ginny Dailley. Donna Hoffman. In time, so many anglophones in Ontario came to own Canadians that a wing of the Canadian Horse Breeders' Association was formed, and the national association's newsletter went bilingual.

But in horses, as in politics, the Quebec/Ontario border still has its invisible checkpoints. Old prejudices, old hostilities linger.

On the way to Ferme Saroma, I told Alec that I had heard two kinds of stories about horse dealers in Quebec. The one kind portrayed them as crooks. Other stories conveyed in them a sense of great warmth and congeniality, how you could not escape without a meal and a drink and maybe a night's lodging. Was there any truth in either story?

"You take the logical part of it, put them together and they're both right," said Alec. He mentions the name of a certain Quebec dealer, goes into a mild lather and slams the man as a low-life. But the rant has nothing to do with francophone or anglophone, it's got to do with unsettled scores and sour chemistry between two people who once were friends and who both claim allegiance to the same breed of horse.

At one point in our journey, we stopped for breakfast and, once more under way, I had to remind Alec to secure his seat belt. Turns out Alec is a contrarian: He had recently been stopped by the police for failing to buckle up. Naturally, he's fighting it in court.

He tells stories about leaving home at the age of 15, of sleeping in cars and finding jobs in construction. He's a man who has cut his own path in life. In 1999 he got embroiled in a legal battle with the Canadian Horse Breeders' Association over the registration of his horses. Alec sees the move as a retaliatory gesture delivered by petty empire builders jealous because so much media coverage of the Canadian horse, in magazines especially, cast him in a saviour's light.

He drops acidic little lines about the Ontario wing of the CHBA—how "they pulled a snooker around us and took control of the club . . ," and he longs for the old days, "when we had intelligent people in there." Gilles Racette sounds very like Alec when he talks about the Quebec scene, with "johnny-come-latelies passing themselves off as experts and trying to improve the breed."

It's hard to say whether Alec's innate belligerence occasioned the skirmish. He has strong opinions, especially when it comes to horses. He's the kind of man you'd rather not tangle with, but the kind of friend you'd want on your side. And clearly he thinks the world of Jérôme Aumond.

"Where we're going today," Alec had said in the car, "he's a separatist. He's also the salt of the earth. A few people I deal with I trust. Jérôme is one. He's dedicated to the breed and he's put out some damn fine specimens."

For all his praise of the Canadian horse, Alec also issued some warnings. He said Canadians retain the instincts of their ancestors who knew to run from leaves rustling in the forest. "You've got to treat them differently," he said. "You have to be patient with them. You can't beat them. If you do, they'll either kill you or you'll break their spirit. Or they'll wait. And they'll get you. They'll pick a moment. I know one old fellow who used to drag his Canadian mare around the field with a Belgian and beat the hell out of her. She got him one day. It was two hours before he got out of the stable. She was a lamb with everyone else."

Inspite of his hard edges, Alec Hayward has a soft spot for his Canadian horses. He seems genuinely sad that his mare, who has grown more protective with each foal born, two weeks earlier had given birth to a little filly who *hates* Alec. He had to give the foal medicine and now she won't go near him. "Normally," says Alec, "my foals can't get enough of me." This one sees him coming and heads the other way.

The fact that there are Canadian foals at all in the 21st century marks a victory. The seeds sown by Alec Hayward and others, starting in the late 1970s, had ridden the winds and taken root from one end of the country to the other. All those kids who rode Canadian horses in June Pelot's pony club near Ottawa knew what horse they wanted when they were older. Ginny Dailley's years of work celebrating the Canadian horse at African Lion Safari was paying dividends out her way west of Toronto.

Canadian horses boarded trailers in Quebec and Ontario bound for the prairies or the Maritimes, for now there were people who wanted to breed these horses and buy them. The daily press, horse publications and several national Canadian magazines—*Canadian Geographic, Canadian Living, Harrowsmith, The Beaver*—all published lengthy articles in the 1990s on this vulnerable heritage horse. The 20th century had not been kind to the breed, but as the new millennium dawned, it seemed that the little horse of iron once again had keen admirers.

Will Oddie, who operates a 960-acre organic farm 30 minutes northwest of Regina, read the *Harrowsmith* piece on the Canadian horse and something clicked.

On the phone he has one of those smooth, velvety voices that an old radio producer like me instinctively wants to put on the air. Will, now "fifty plus," had studied landscape architecture at the University of Guelph and practised in both Winnipeg and Regina. He still dabbles in it, but you can call him *farmer* now without straying too far from the truth. With his wife, Elaine McNeil, he runs the farm where he was raised.

There were always Percherons around, a few riding horses. Will's grandfather was a blacksmith. You get the sense that while he rides a fair bit, he rides without thinking too much about it. He makes jokes about the western saddle at least offering a pommel to hold on to when the horse bolts. But these days he has 19 Canadian horses on the property, and in Saskatchewan that ranks him among the biggest breeders of Canadians in the province.

In the summer of 1995, he noticed the name Alec Hayward in the *Harrowsmith* article, called him up and, with a friend, headed east—for all kinds of reasons. Will was heeding a patriotic twinge, he liked the notion of a multi-purpose horse and he had a horse-mad daughter. Alec was their broker then, just as Alec was mine. They went to see Frank Prosperine near Ottawa, and on the Quebec side Jérôme Aumond, Gilles Racette, Camille Loiselle, Gérard Lambert.

I was astonished to learn that one of the horses they came back with is a full sister to Dali—an eight-year-old chestnut mare named Bianca bought by Will's friend. Will described the horse thus: "Very broad, very patient, fairly headstrong too, but laid-back as you can get. Nothing fazes Bianca. She's close to bombproof. She has an Arabic look, with flared nostrils and a dished head, and a stripe right down to her nostrils." I imagine I could easily pick her out of a crowd as Dali's kin.

When I asked Will Oddie to pronounce on the characteristics of the breed and he grew cautious, my respect for him immediately went up another notch. It is, he implies, not that simple. "My fellow breeders say Canadians are laid-back," he says. "But I hate to make boasts of a quiet breed. I like Canadians, but these are generalities. People coming to our farm are suprised by how you can walk among the herd. They are more laid-back. I've seen Arabs, for example, prancing with their tails up. Canadians are cooler blooded than that."

Will's blacksmith grandfather would have appreciated what a farrier told Will a while back: that the Canadian horse is well put together and that the wall of their hooves is thicker than that of any horse he's seen. Another observer, a nationally certified driving instructor who had come to Regina to give a workshop, remarked of Canadian horses that "they seem to be fairly measured in how they take things on. 'Tell me right,' they seem to say, 'and I'll give it a try.'" That remark seemed, in the light of my experience with Dali, profoundly insightful.

For all the calm Canadians on his farm, Oddie will also tell you of a few young horses who are quite nervous. It would be dishonest, even reckless, to call them all quiet.

Oddie is charging $4,500 for his green Canadians, a hard sell in a province where young purebred Appaloosas and American saddlebreds can be had for $1,500. In both Saskatchewan and Manitoba, PMU (pregnant mare urine) farms produce an abundant supply of estrogen for pharmaceutical labs and a great many colts and fillies. And because some of his horses came from Alec Hayward's stable, he finds himself caught up in that messy lawyerly business about registration papers. There must be days when he wonders what he got into when a magazine article convinced him to head east on a horse quest. But not many, Will says. Not many.

Richard Johnson, a vet who lives in Mount Hope, Ontario, is another Canadian-horse owner whose interest in the breed was piqued by articles he read in the aforementioned magazines. Johnson had reached an age when he had both the time and the means to get back into horses. He had had ponies as a boy and later a quarter horse, but university seemed to end that connection to horses. Still, the interest "smouldered into adulthood" and the notion of owning a Canadian appealed to his sense of national pride.

In the winter of 1996, as I would in the spring of 1999, Johnson travelled to Ferme Saroma and Jérôme Aumond. He purchased a mare in foal called Saroma Surprise Etoile. The move made, he admitted, no sense. Lambert Rex Apollo later joined the herd, as did two unregistered Canadians named Diamond and Zircon, who were variously used to haul manure, cut hay, plough fields and walk in parades. Johnson says, "I have been bitten deeply by this horse bug, and hope the affliction will hold me for some time to come."

And he makes a useful point about the Canadian horse as a breed worth preserving and worth sharing. "In a world," he wrote in a Canadian-horse newsletter, "where grain varieties have been so highly modified as to hardly identify with their origin, there are people intensely dedicated to preserving those original qualities, not just for posterity, but as a source of genetic diversity which may be needed." He believes, for example, that it's possible both to advance the breed while preserving its salient features—"e.g., those wonderful feet."

Dan Wilson of Woodmount Farm, near Michael Lake, Vancouver Island, similarly felt the heritage tug in 1996 when he went back east to Quebec to buy some good breeding stock. "I like the way they move, and the way they keep," he once said. "And I was determined to start breeding them out here on the coast, because they're a part of Canadian history." Wilson and others formed the Canadian Horse Association of B.C. "I guess these horses say something about the Canadian character," says Wilson. "We're tough, but we're gentle. They make a good symbol, don't they?"

# CHAPTER 10

# THE EDUCATION OF SAROMA DARK FOX DALI

BLUE HAVEN FARM, SEPTEMBER 1999

*I flip through my "Buying a Horse" file, wondering if I have made the wrong choice.*
*Maybe I should have bought one of the pricier, fully trained horses on offer? Does there*
*exist such a thing as a fully trained horse?*

I RIDE DALI FOR THE FIRST TIME ON AUGUST 5, and not without trepidation. Barb rides him just before I do and complains that "he's not steering worth a damn." Then she nearly comes off when he scoots. Her body angle quickly reaches 45 or 50 degrees and she finds herself much behind the action of his run. She recovers quickly, laughs and says, "You want to go? Let's go!" and keeps up the canter that Dali has given her in the blink of an eye.

Above: Barb Wills on Dali in the ring at Blue Haven.

"There, you cantered and you didn't die!" she says, mocking him gently. He lopes effortlessly in his warm-up but he's not sure about higher speed with a rider up. The scoot was likely occasioned by a startle; the mare or her foal may have struck the barn wall outside. My chunk of a horse surprises me with his quickness.

I have waited a long time for this ride: 64 days. I led him off the trailer at Blue Haven the afternoon of June 3, and after all the ground work and several weeks of watching Barb ride him, I finally get my turn. It isn't at all like that afternoon at Ferme Saroma, though flashbacks come unbidden and I focus on taking deep breaths, not short choppy ones.

But if the ride wasn't as eventful as that first one, neither was it particularly elegant. The steering on Dali was leaden, uncertain and unpredictable and I was shocked by it; school horses have their faults, but at least they know about steering.

Since Dali wants away from the walls of the ring and into the centre, where perhaps he feels safer from whatever dangers lie on the other side, I have to apply my inside leg and not too much rein. When he scoots (I get the minor-league version of the one he gave Barb), my hands go high and Barb warns me to keep them down lest Dali become alarmed.

In a few minutes, I get the feel of him. Like Barb, and with her urging, I let the trot that evolves out of his scoot continue. And there I am, posting in a well-defined circle. I even manage to put a little life into his walk. But I am painfully aware of how little he knows. For Dali to stop scooting, to learn his transitions, for us to look anything like a team, will take many many miles.

"He would never buck you," Barb assures me from the ground, and I sense she's right. On the other hand, I will keep in mind something else she once said: "Never underestimate this horse."

August 7, 1999
Yesterday's ride in the arena felt more like the real thing. It hap-

pened that when I was in the saddle a deluge of rain came down on the roof, so loud that Barb had to come right to Dali's head before I could hear her instructions. We could have been standing inside a waterfall. Here, I thought, was a test of Dali's cool. The roar put him on high alert. "You're all right," I repeatedly assured him (and me) as we rode our circles and serpentines. "You're all right."

Earlier in the day I had ridden a 12-year-old mare named Duchess at Wilmarny and the memory of her neck was fresh in my mind as I compared hers to Dali's. She seemed scrawny and she's not a tiny horse.

But as wide and thick as he may appear, Dali has a wonderful trot. I think back to a trail ride a few weeks ago near Picton and to my assigned mount, a taut little quarter horse who rode like a wagon over a corduroy road. Riding Dali is like settling comfortably into a La-Z-Boy. And while the real test will come when I spend four to six hours in that chair, he doesn't *feel* particularly wide.

Yesterday, while riding Dali, Barb was remembering Dali's bucks when she first put that western saddle on him. "We had the stampede here," she said while trotting in a circle on the author of those mighty bucks.

More and more I miss him when a few days go by and I don't get to the stable. I think about riding him, and how to get through: to muster a brisker walk, a nicer downward transition. More and more I trust him.

When I sprinkle water on the shavings in his stall and wet his feet in the process, he delicately raises one hoof. Time was I would have ducked away, convinced he was set to strike. Now I know he's raising it as a tea-drinking matron would lift her little finger.

August 14, 1999

The next time I'm riding Dali and I ask him for a neck bend, and I see him blink as if to say, "Why should I?," I will have a fresh answer for him: "Because you are—it's official—*my* horse and I pay your room and board and much else."

On Friday the thirteenth I drive to Ferme Saroma to give Jérôme the full payment. He and his wife, Sara, have invited me to stay the night and participate that day in the parade that forms part of their regional agricultural fair. Theirs is a touching gesture to a virtual stranger. And I brought my sleeping bag, fully intending to spend the night. But an unexpected bout of shyness overcomes me.

As I start back home along the road that arcs past the very field where Dali took me for that ride, I feel a small pang of regret. I have the strange feeling that I have wrenched Dali from his home ground. Maybe that's why I have spurned Jérôme and Sara's hospitality: I feel the fifth wheel here, my French inadequate, my place on an old wagon pulled by black Canadian mares in a parade somehow unearned and silly.

"Un bon prix pour un bon cheval," I earlier told Jérôme as I paid the price of his, now my, registered Canadian gelding: $3,000. I was very pleased with my purchase.

Last week Barb intended to progress from the side pull to a bit. But the chosen bit happened to be in the house, and out of laziness and curiosity she placed in Dali's mouth a plain eggbutt snaffle—a classic gentle bit—and tried riding him. He packed it like an old pro.

We had surmised that his refusal to carry a bit easily beforehand owed something to nervousness aggravated by a sore mouth. Someone in his brief riding past had been "sawing" on him, a phrase that graphically captures the hard back-and-forth motion of the bit in a horse's mouth when the reins fall into the hands of a certain kind of rider or driver. The discolouration in the skin at the corners of Dali's mouth, which cleared in less than a week, provided clear evidence. What a great relief to see him carry the snaffle; I had feared we might be weeks or more clearing that hurdle. He continues to surprise me.

On the other hand, his left side, which used to be his "good" side, feels stiff. Dali resists bending while making counter-clockwise circles, and until that settles, Barb will keep schooling simple. Walks and trots only. She has suggested I not ride him until he's bending better. I was too happy about the bit even to think of complaining.

Soon I hope to stop borrowing Barb's western saddle and replace it with my own English saddle. A used one but a good one is what I have in mind, I tell Kathi, who spots a classified ad in the local paper. The owner, it transpires, lives just north of Blue Haven and has a Canadian horse of her own. Lift the saddle's panel and you see the inlaid stamp of G. Passier & Sohn, plus "Made in Germany" and "Hannover," along with a registration number. Jochen Schleese has clearly worked on the saddle for he has left his mark—a gold nameplate. The good thing about a Passier, says Kathi, is that the tree can be adjusted numerous times, unlike many other saddles.

I try the saddle at Wilmarny, testing it along with two others, one a newer Passier. My Passier is close in comfort to the newer one, but the third saddle feels as if it's fashioned from rock. The difference is remarkable.

I have determined that, failing any objection from Kathi, who will come to Blue Haven on Monday to see how it fits Dali, I will buy that saddle. The $550 fee includes leathers, a girth and two saddle pads. "Not a bargain," Tiny's mother, Maria, observes, "but still not a bad price."

The saddle has been sitting all weekend propped against my filing cabinet, and the rich aroma of supple leather and saddle soap wafts past me as I read in my rocker. My workshop downstairs, too, has begun to look like a tack shop. I must be a horse person.

August 16, 1999

Blue Haven is bedlam today, and the one who sails most calmly through it all is Dali. Workmen have arrived to replace a beam in the arena, solve a drainage problem and install new eavestroughing. This means hammering on the roof, a digger clawing at the earth, a gravel truck dropping a load of stone and Gilles in the arena on his tractor.

This is the day we have chosen for Kathi to eye the saddle on Dali. For some reason, she always wears sandals and shorts, not paddock boots and jeans, when she comes on these errands of mercy. But then, she could not have foreseen her involvement in the saddling of Lawrence. She could not have imagined wielding Barb's camera, taking shots of Dali with and without saddle, and of me in the saddle *sans* stirrups and helmet.

The saddle is to be sent to Herr Schleese for restuffing; the photos and primitive drawings I will do of the slope of Dali's back, using a flexible ruler called, for some reason, a French ruler, will help the saddler in his calculations.

Later, it strikes me that after all the parading around the grounds, looking for the perfect flat spot and the best angle for our snapshots amid all the construction, Dali has perhaps had enough. How will he handle the added burden of schooling?

Barb's expectations are meagre; she will work on steering, nothing more. She has seen green horses regress when the bit enters their world. "All that niceness," she says, "can sometimes disappear when you move from the sidepull to the bit." The strange thing is this: Dali actually gets better as the lesson continues. His walk is strong and purposeful, the trot easy, the canter rolling and smooth. "Excellent," says Barb at the end. "Excellent."

We joked that the noise and commotion of the day were like the desensitization process used on police horses. Dali is cool about everything. We moved him about on the grounds, asked him to stand against a certain wall, to stand square, not to eat, to back up, to stand still while Kathi photographed him from the back of Gilles's truck. All this he abided. And then schooled wonderfully.

Kathi declared in a note to me a few weeks back that I had a special horse, a rhetorical flourish I thought. I now prefer to believe that she meant it and that she is absolutely right. Dark Fox Dali, it seems to me, is indeed a special horse.

August 19, 1999

Took a break. Went to the cabin to paint walls. Barb reported that Tuesday, following a most agreeable Monday, featured leaden steering and abrupt stops. Not out of nastiness or stubbornness, she thought, more a matter of self-preservation. As if movement with a rider up was somehow dangerous to his being.

Today, Dali is once again a dream. Barb is using the inside leg to telegraph turns, and the outside leg, placed at the girth, to bring the shoulder around. She uses the trick of placing your belly button in the direction you want to go, and the horse bends to maintain his place under you. It all *looks* easy.

He appears, says Barb, to be tucking up. By that she means he's losing some of that hay belly of his and starting to look more like an athletic horse.

August 20, 1999

My first solo training session with Dali goes well enough. No scoots, but then again, I ask little of him. My request that we trot into corners seems to rattle him, but he only braces a bit. Trying it first in a walk, then a trot seems to make it manageable.

At this stage in his training, he needs ample warning of my intentions. "Let him know the day before," Barb jokes from the sidelines. In the tight confines of the round pen, a simple serpentine will unravel if you fail to cue him of impending turns. Suddenly, you're at the wall, stopped dead. Dali likes to stop on little excuse in any case. But I also felt a level of trust in him that seems fresh and new.

What a wonderful summer it's been. I am a barn rat, trying to soak up the wisdom of Barb and Gilles. I sense my confidence growing: I now have no fear that Dali will kick when I clean his hooves. He, in turn, feels my confidence and thus no inclination to kick. It's embarrassing to report how much I enjoy stroking him.

Yesterday, Barb shampooed his mane and tail and I expected to see some class in my horse today when I went to his stall. But this morning it rained, he rolled in the mud, and he looked a complete ragamuffin. A brown crust covered his face and back and rump. I used a sponge to lift it off, and he took well to the mopping.

August 25, 1999

I am awash in the myriad details that go with saddling and tacking a horse. The world of bits and bridles and girths seems like one of those hedge mazes: The paths are all connected but it's easy to get lost.

I have decided to buy the used Passier, opting for old quality, trusting that Jochen Schleese or one of his helpers can adjust the tree and flocking. Meanwhile, I'm in that hedge, pondering the turns. Eggbutt snaffle or full cheek? Copper in the bit, or not? Bridle with a flash, or without? Leather girth or fabric? Kathi, as usual, has thoughts on all of this.

She tends towards the classic and time-honoured systems. A good quality overlay girth made of leather is her recommendation. Her choices seem the most costly, but not always. She urges against spending a fortune on a bridle, knowing how easy it is for a rider to lose focus long enough for the horse to step on a rein and snap the leather.

Kathi's thoughts on copper bits (the metal is said to aid in salivation) similarly reflect her conservative tastes. A simple snaffle made of stainless steel does the job, but she always runs her hands along the metal looking for burrs or imperfections that would nag at the horse's mouth.

And not for her fancy foam pads. "That's why you paid Jochen all that money," she says. "So the saddle fits well." A plain and simple saddle and standard stirrups (though Kathi does favour the Australian safety stirrup, with the sculpted outer edge that allows the foot to slide out more easily). I suspect that my outfitting, like my horsemanship, is not a static thing and that what passes muster now will not a year hence.

August 27, 1999

Yesterday, before Barb took Dali outside to ride, I checked the cinch, judged it loose and tightened it. That move, Barb said later, changed him. "He seemed funny. I thought he was going to buck me, but then he went wonderfully."

I suppose we were due for a day like this. Today, in the chase and join-up, I was watching Dali without really seeing him. I moved through the routine as if programmed. My feet, apparently, were the giveaway. "Are you in a hurry today?" Barb asked almost sarcastically. She was lunging Prime Time in the ring just outside the round pen and periodically looking in to monitor my progress (or lack thereof). My movements in the ring, she told me, were quick; my feet, especially, were those of a New York commuter.

Dali got rank and I failed to see just how miffed he was. At one point, Barb looks at me in the saddle and says, "Don't do anything. Just breathe." I was reminded of what Chris Irwin had talked about, how you can absorb the gentler philosophy, accept it as gospel, then step into the ring and start pushing buttons like the predators we truly are.

The lesson never recovers from its bad beginning. Dali does not buck or spook. He simply shuts down. His steering is heavy and recalcitrant; were he a car I would guess the power-steering fluid was low to empty. In the outdoor ring he feels aimless and sluggish. He is particularly loath to turn right and we have several battles at the south end of the ring, where it happens that a white plastic chair amid some farm equipment induces much fear in him. His trot is leaden and he folds into a walk every chance he gets. My exasperation grows by the minute.

Afterwards, we look for reasons. Was it the full moon? The heavy heat and humidity? The fact that Barb was also in the ring on Prime Time, Dali's turnout boss? Has Dali soured on the join-up routine?

We determined that next time we would lunge him a little, try to vary the routine.

Training a horse feels a little like building a house. A few years ago I spent the better part of a summer playing carpenter's apprentice to a skilled builder as we both worked on my square-timbered log cabin on our small acreage southwest of Kingston. "Larry's folly," Ulrike would dub it.

The excitement of seeing a dream unfolding never disappeared during construction, but the path was as pitted and winding as any I had ever travelled. The marriage of 170-year-old hand-hewn timbers with new building materials proved difficult. But wood and stone never failed me the way flesh did. That summer I acted as my own general contractor and I learned just how disappointing hired hands can be.

The work site some days fairly hummed with workers and the sound of hammers, drills and saws. By degrees, the cabin took shape. But sometimes work had to be redone. I hated that part: the forward steps followed by backward ones.

Like the training of Dark Fox Dali, the cabin was not built in a day. I cherish that cabin and I can now laugh at the anguish its reconstruction caused me. My affection for Dali grows too, and one day, perhaps, I will look back and be amused by the time, say, of his steerlessness.

August 31, 1999

I spent two days painting at the cabin Thursday and Friday and am anxious to know from Barb how Dali had schooled in my absence. Fair to middlin' might describe it. At one point he gave a little kick—"not a head-down buck," says Barb, but a clear sign of petulance. "He's been giving us signs that he's not yet ready to canter to the left," she continues. "He's a horse that worries easily. And what worries him is the rider on his back."

Barb's strategy is to move back to the trot and work on steering. Clearly this five-year-old has spent a long time grazing in pastures and living the life of an unemployed horse. Riding, at the moment, seems like work. But Barb is convinced that by building up his strength and confidence, he will become willing and disciplined. To force him or to do battle with him would be a mistake.

Even moving from the arena to the outdoor ring has become for him a small issue. Barb had to circle him a few times and she made a point of coming back into the arena before going out again and letting me on him. With her up he did state his clear preference to go right, and not left as Barb was asking, and there followed a bout of panic that saw him rush the fence. There were other moments of skittishness, too, but as I rode him in circles, always in a walk, he seemed to me more himself. He does fly off the handle, this horse, but he always comes back quickly. The education of Dark Fox Dali, and his rider, continues.

September 1, 1999

The cloying summer heat has returned, only somewhat diminished. I wear my heavy green chaps in the ring because I like their grip and they spare my jeans, but their weight only raises my body temperature. My body's thermostat is the Irish model, not made for equatorial heat. Yesterday in the ring I spent a mere five minutes on Dali, never exceeding a slow trot, and my pumpkin head (or so my son Kurt says I look in my Troxel riding helmet) already looked steamed.

Barb may have figured out why Dali balks at going left. A young horse at Blue Haven had suddenly developed a similar problem, even rushing towards the fence with Barb aboard. On a hunch, she called in her vet who discovered the source of the horse's aggravation: a wolf tooth, which he extracted. Barb showed it to me: a mere sliver compared to the hefty number that Mark had removed from Dali.

Significantly, Dali is a different horse going to the right. His trot extends, he seems lighter, less worried. Moving counter-clockwise requires on my part more muscle, more inside leg, and sometimes ends with the horse halted at the fence while I yank left. I insist on winning these little skirmishes, and I do, but they are tiresome. Is the problem as simple as a tooth?

Mark Rutherford dropped by within hours of my call. He found the gum sore on the left side of Dali's mouth where a wolf tooth is trying to break through. His strategy will be to punch a small hole there to let the tooth come through and then extract it at a later date.

If the problem is merely dental, we should have Dali going nicely to the left in a few days. If the problem is behaviourial, it may take longer.

Precisely one week ago Dali gave me the worst ride yet, aside from that first eventful one. Today he was almost wonderful. I tried as best I could to be considerate of that left side of his mouth, releasing pressure the second he looked to be into his turn. I praised him, rested him after particularly good moments and took some sustenance from this little bit of progress.

September 5, 1999

Mark makes two holes in Dali's mouth, one for the wolf tooth and another for a canine tooth. The former he then tries to extract but without success. Dali's bloodied mouth is swollen on that troublesome left side, and when Barb rode him Friday with only a halter, my horse was almost comically one-sided.

Pauline, who owns the land behind Blue Haven, had apparently stopped by briefly to watch Barb school Dali. Barb does a bending exercise in which she asks Dali, on a soft rein, to bring his head around towards the saddle, releasing him the second he goes soft. Barb has the good sense not to force the issue, and so she must have stayed there, her left hand wide on the rein, waiting and waiting for his head to come. Watching this must have been like watching paint dry. "Did you ever get that horse to turn his head?" Pauline asked the next day.

Turns out the answer was *yes*, but much time passed before the blessed event.

When I rode Dali it seemed I was the benefactor of Barb's patience and four days of healing. He looked ragged, having rolled in the mud that came with the morning rain. But he was agreeable to being lunged—a first for both of us. And though the day was appallingly hot and humid (I have never experienced a Labour Day weekend like it), he generously turned left on command. He felt light in my hands, his trot was smooth and agile.

Later, at Barb's suggestion, we rode in the grassland near the paddock and around the house. Dali was all ears and I felt a surge in his walk I had never experienced before. He was more horse than I had previously known, and his joy at this new environment ran up through his body and into my hands. Our small first hack was pure joy.

September 8, 1999

Today marks a revelation, a little epiphany that drives home Chris Irwin's point about horses expecting their riders to be just a little better horse than they are.

Monday, Dali had been superb. Light and quick when that was called for, supple in my hands. His tooth-induced crankiness seemed a distant memory. Tuesday he was still responsive but less so. Today he is stroppy from the get-go, and he lashes out a little with his left hind when I am cleaning the hoof. I dive back, loudly hitting a stall door and alarming him. I return to the foot and he settles down, but I take the message. He was turned out in the ring earlier, owing to rain, and he is feeling frisky. That old attitude of his has come back.

He continues, as he had Tuesday, to circle to evade my mounting him. The trick, said Gilles, who was offering advice, is to make him circle more. Make the wrong thing difficult.

I worry less about the mounting than his dullness under saddle. He feels heavy, almost lethargic. His trot is a resentful shuffle and he has reverted to his bad habit of cutting into the middle. I had to use a lot of leg to keep him to the outside and moving ahead in the trot. Leg yields (the horse is asked to move forward and laterally at the same time) come an inch at a time or not at all. A canter seems beyond us both.

Enter Gilles Dupuis. "Why are you sweating so much?" he asks me. My black T-shirt is already dank. I keep looking at my watch. All I want is some high note to end on.

Gilles could see that the horse was heavy on the forehand and leaning into the bit. I would have to get him working more from the hind end, he said. Ask gently for his head, he instructed, using your left rein until his head is almost at your knee (Gilles even had me scratching Dali's head with my free hand as a reward for giving me his head) and then apply your heel to his side. Then we worked on the other side. Ask for his head, hold, release as you apply the heel. Dali got to like it and to anticipate.

The hope was that with his hindquarters thus engaged, Dali would go forward more easily. But he was only marginally more responsive. Gilles next taught me to put some meaning into the clucking sound I make when I ask for more speed. He had me sit Dali and at the moment I clucked I was to give him a mild pump with both feet. When I did so I suddenly had a lot of horse under me, and the next time he slowed and I gave him a cluck he responded instantly.

Gilles was marching out orders now. Walk. Faster walk. Trot. Fast trot. Canter. Dali had no time to say, "I can't do this." We breezed through the transitions.

Gilles was full of praise afterwards. "I'm impressed," he said. "You guys," he said, meaning Barb and me, "did a nice job on this horse."

September 13, 1999
The heat has finally abated. Morning breezes have a cool edge now,

and days of rain have turned the scorched lawns an emerald green. The fall painting of the trees has also begun, and at Blue Haven there is serious talk of a trail ride.

I have Dali dreams, dark little fantasies my psyche spawns, no doubt to preserve my body. In one, a bridle breaks and Dali is hell-bent for the barn from some distant pasture. Or I get a foot caught in one stirrup and he drags me along like a rag doll, my head bouncing off the rocks. Or, while cleaning his hoof, he finally connects with one of those roundhouse swings.

These are cautionary tales, conjured, no doubt, to keep me alert.

"There is nothing, and I mean nothing, easy about owning a horse," my friend Sarah tells me. She rides a sometimes acerbic grey Thoroughbred mare at the novice eventer level, and while she is committed to both her horse and her sport, she does on occasion reflect on the cost.

"If I didn't have Maddy," Sarah says, "perhaps I would own a small house. I would have more time to spend with friends. Sometimes it's hard to convince your partner that the horse does not come first." Schooling a horse, she now knows, is like having a second job. Sarah drives from her office to a stable an hour north of Toronto three or four times a week. Some evenings, after schooling, bathing the horse, cleaning tack, it's 11 p.m. when she gets home.

Her mood after she finishes a schooling can vary from elation to misery. The horse is a gifted athlete who can also be aggressive when she senses that Sarah is unsure. Sarah has had to cope with her own fear and the mixed emotions that close contact with a horse can engender.

"The highs are intensely high," she told me. On some nights she wants to cry. On other days, when Maddy jumps cleanly and elegantly, when the connection between horse and rider is seamless and easy beyond words, my friend feels whole.

September 14, 1999

Today Dali takes the bit almost happily. Our task, and we work hard on this, is to make him supple, to get that thick frame of his bending nicely around my inside leg. Stops now include a bend, even after he comes down from a trot. I simply shorten my inside rein and draw it to my leg so his head comes around. And though he might circle for up to eight seconds, I leave the rein at my leg until Dali stops, and when he does I instantly release as reward. Dali soon gets the hang of it and his circling diminishes.

I approach mounting, another worry of Dali's, in a similar way. When he moves forward to avoid my boot in the stirrup, I ask him to circle, keeping his head bent and forcing his hindquarters around. Make the wrong thing difficult . . . Soon, I hope, mounting will see him standing stock-still.

There is a mighty scoot at the beginning of the lesson—a response to loud voices in the woods beyond the sand ring—but he quickly composes himself.

Still, his quickness astounds me. I think I'm set, then I'm left behind, one foot is out of the stirrup, I'm making silly whoa sounds and my heart is pounding. "Go with those scoots," Barb tells me. "Buck Brannaman says those panic attacks are typically brief, but if you try to stop the horse in the middle of one of those flights, you make it ten times worse."

"Go with him," Gilles used to say in the early days, when Dali was ducking the halter or the hose. The advice still applies.

September 15, 1999

Chase today too hot. I asked for too much canter, got him too excited, and the result was that instead of coming to me agreeably at the end, he did so slowly and hesitantly. He made faces, would not follow me when I walked ahead. Barb's suggestion: Ask for the canter, and insist on getting it the moment you ask, but ask for less of it.

Still, Dali is a forgiving horse, and there were times in the ride when he was fluid. Gilles urged me to trust him more, give him more rein. The second I did that he was a happier horse.

I'm trying, as best I can, to teach him collection, too. A collected horse holds his head up and close to his body, with his hind legs more under him. The collected horse, Margaret Cabell Self wrote in *Horsemastership*, is "alertly balanced," capable of quickly and easily increasing, decreasing or changing gaits.

I aim to teach Dali collection by riding him with a firm rein, and the second he tucks in his chin, I am to release and go soft. He does give me something but it's subtle, almost undetectable. I pray for softer hands, for cleaner, clearer signs. No doubt they will come. All in due time, horse time.

September 16, 1999

Awful day. No other words for it. Dali's latest evasion, a circling away when I go to mount him, is now a patterned response. And the feet, for months a non-issue, are threatening to become one again.

In the ring he is surly. Ears back, cantankerous. We take our horses out into the paddock this bracy, windy day, there to discover that they steer like rudderless sailing ships. Dali improves when we head for the barn, but moving in the other direction he turns his shoulder in and drifts radically left and right. I have an aimless horse with almost 1,200 pounds of attitude.

His steering and outlook improve, but I have trouble conjuring the light smooth horse of the day before.

"Green horses," Barb sympathizes.

"Tell me this will all be a distant memory come spring," I plead.

"And what year might that be?" she teases.

The end of the ride stirs a new resolve. I am going to have to swallow my pride and return to the mounting block, a grey recycling box. I thought we had fixed the problem of the slipping saddle, but when the girth is wet from Dali's sweat it's more inclined to slide.

After the ride, I decide to remount several times and so end on a high note. The first attempt flies; the second one fails utterly. Nothing works. He circles, the saddle slips, and we leave it at that.

I drive home reeking of resentment. On Monday we'll go back to the western saddle. My romantic notions are coming undone. I imagined that my horse would love me, certainly respect me. But Dali remains standoffish and some days he fights me. I flip through my "Buying a Horse" file, feeling like a dumped boyfriend and wondering if I have made the wrong choice. Maybe I should have bought one of the pricier, fully trained horses on offer? Does there exist such a thing as a fully trained horse?

There is the truth as the breed extollers would have it. Canadian horses are people-friendly, docile, smart, versatile. And my hunch is that one day I will be able to list all those virtues and hang them like a plaque on Dali's stall. But he is, at the moment, mercurial, occasionally combative, delicate and inclined to worry, and he tests me all the time. I suppose that even these traits could one day make him a fine competitive endurance horse.

September 20, 1999

Throughout this journey, Kathi has been my touchstone. She always finds light when I feel engulfed in the worst sort of equine darkness.

This morning when I explain how discouraged I am by recent events with Dali, she offers what should have struck me as obvious: We are working him far too hard and he's telling us as best he can to slow down. Two hours of riding, says Kathi, is far more than is necessary. She and Dick ride their horses six days a week, but no more than an hour at a time.

"You're right to go back to the western saddle," she says. "But I'd cut way back on his workload. Ride him 20 minutes a time for the next few days, then take him out to a field and hand-graze him. Let him know you're his buddy and not his taskmaster."

She also strongly advises using a mounting block, since it dramatically reduces stress on the horse's withers. Dick uses one, and a horse chiropractor who once examined their horses knew without being told that was the case, for he could tell from the healthy state of the withers. I'll try to think of that and not male pride as I henceforth use the mounting block.

It may well be, as Kathi suggests, that factors combined to sour my horse. New tack. Longer hours. He may be sore, his brains may be fried from all that classwork. Small wonder that lately he's seen me coming and silently groaned. Thus the ears back, the bite threats, the way he's suddenly slow to let me pick up his feet.

"You're doing the best you can. You're really trying to get into the mind of that horse," Kathi says. "So don't worry. This too will later be seen as a blip." And not the nuclear explosion it seemed on Thursday.

She tells me of times in past years when Dick would come in from the barn shaking his head in despair. Things could not be better for them now. Dick has won the last three eventing competitions he has entered, and that's without precedent.

Kathi's diagnosis may well have been on the money. Three days off may help explain the Dali I ride today. But another truth offers itself. A truth exquisitely simple: The horse must respect his rider, and by moving off as I attempt to mount him, Dali is showing no respect. Gilles, off to the side, chuckles at this sideshow.

"All right," Barb tells him. "You try."

Gilles approaches Dali, lets the reins hang over his neck and mounts the horse before dismounting. When, on a second try, Dali drifts off to the right, Gilles goes to the horse's right side and moves him back. Shuts off the escape route. It took only that bit of firmness to arrest the Dali shuffle.

My own mounting—and Gilles has me do it four or five times—was clean and effortless. I am instructed to push against the saddle, to encourage him to brace. That done, I am to spring up off that right foot and into the saddle. No hesitation. It works at the beginning of the schooling, and at the end. A potentially major issue has been defused in a matter of minutes.

"He's a smart horse," says Gilles. "If he wasn't smart, it would have taken a lot longer to deal with that evasion."

The ride itself in the sand ring is smooth enough, far less fractious than the one before. Gilles oversees the lesson while Barb works with her little Arab mare in the shade of a tree. Gilles observes that I work too hard in the saddle, grip too much with my knees. I try to emulate his loose leg, using my heel more than my leg. Gilles's tactic is to give the horse every opportunity to perform a maneuver with as little guidance as possible—to go, to stop, to turn. But if he won't stop when asked, for example, that's when you apply the emergency brakes. The hard left pull to the inside.

"If you rein back hard every time you ask your horse to stop, you harden his mouth," says Gilles. "And eventually you'll have no stop at all. You'll ask for a halt and he'll be gone," and he makes a motion, with the palm of his right hand skimming overtop the palm of the left before his whole arm shoots out. The international symbol for *vamoose*.

All in all, it feels lighter up there. Dali is happier. And so am I.

# CHAPTER II

# SHOW TIME

---

ROSS FARM MUSEUM, NOVA SCOTIA, FALL 1999

*I was to enter the forest with Barry Ward on a plain farmer's wagon. The pair he had chosen were a three-year-old stallion—"a hellion" with a week in harness to call upon—and a seven-year-old mare disinclined to suffer youthful exuberance. Both handsome black Canadian horses, neither ever paired with the other.*
*"Hope your insurance is all paid up," Ward laughed as we set out.*

SAVING WHAT'S LEFT OF OUR HISTORY—heritage horses, heritage seeds, heritage architecture—falls to the fearless few who embrace lost causes. Such people, because so rare and so passionate, are often seen as curiously eccentric or hopelessly reactionary. The battle to con-serve and preserve wears on them, and the louder they protest the

Above: Barry Ward, Dolly and Frannie near New Ross, Nova Scotia.

---

more the mainstream ceases to hear them.

I vividly remember two decades ago entering one of the grand old bank buildings of my city—Limestone City, for it is distinguished and defined by its old stone architecture—and hearing a teller complain that renovations on the place had stalled, owing to objections from what she called the Kingston Hysterical Society.

My days as an editor at *Harrowsmith* magazine had also given me a glimpse of those who persevere in collecting and sharing the same vegetable seeds the pioneers would have used. Operating out of places like West Elizabeth, Pennsylvania, and Decorah, Idaho, and calling themselves the Seed Savers Exchange or Heirloom Seeds, these tiny businesses seemed worlds apart from the giant seed companies. The big money was in hybrid and genetically altered seeds. Glossy catalogues heralded the new, the improved, leaving hippies, skeptics and purists clinging to the wreckage of the old ways, the old seeds. I rather like the idea of these folks paddling against a mighty current. If they are kooks, as alleged, they are my kind of kooks.

In the late 1970s, the fate of the Canadian horse seemed as grim as an heirloom pumpkin or a century farm in the path of a developer's bulldozer. A few hundred purebreds remained, but only in Quebec, and all previous government attempts to ensure a future for the breed had ended in apparent failure.

Alec Hayward, keen on Canadian heritage and a friend of the breed, found himself allied with a horsewoman named Ginny Dailley. Hayward, the formidable retired heavy-machinery dealer, and Dailley, the sprightly daughter of a military man, became convinced that one way to spread the news of the little known Canadian horse was to get his image on a stamp. They got petitions circulating, they lobbied, they made nuisances of themselves.

In 1991, Alec and Ginny, their lawyer in tow, marched into the Ottawa office where mandarins choose art for postage stamps. When they entered and Ginny uttered her name, a woman at the desk knew immediately who she was. "Oh yes," she said. "I'll go get the *big* file. . ."

Posted letters in this country have yet to be graced by the Canadian horse (though Big Ben, the show jumper, and Northern Dancer, the racehorse, were among four individual horses who made the grade in the summer of 1999), but should it happen, and should the breed endure as now seems likely, the accomplishment will owe something to Ginny Dailley. Though she failed to put Canadian horses on a stamp, she did give them another place—on stage.

What struck me about Ginny Sealy (her married name) is how ageless and youthful this mother of five seemed. In the fall of 1999 she talked to me on the phone about needing to retire from performing with horses. For many years, she had put the Canadian horse in the limelight at African Lion Safari in southwestern Ontario, but that long string of performances was about to break. I expected to hear some fatigue in her voice when I met her. Some evidence that all those years pounding the drums for a beleaguered line of horses had sapped her a little.

What I found instead was an almost coltish woman I took to be in her mid-forties. There was also about her, and I may be wrong about this, a charming naiveté. I had seen Ginny and her Canadians on video, and it seemed to me that what she did in the ring with four spirited horses running "at liberty" was extraordinary. I told her she had a gift. She shrugged it off as a fairly simple matter: Figure out the individual horse and train him. Then work them as pairs, and finally as a foursome. The astonishing thing is that Ginny did it all in several months.

I went to her place in the rolling countryside west of Toronto one early fall day when the leaves had turned but not yet dropped. The horses in the barn were lined up in standing stalls, and to coax each one out to be suited up in surcingle and leather halter Ginny just spoke warmly and tugged a little on his tail. Even the horses thought she was charming.

Her house is a 19th century square-timbered log house recently covered in white stucco after years of its owner wrestling with chinking, leaks and flies. Owner of a pioneer's cabin myself, I know all about that. Someone, though, should tell the folks down at African Lion Safari entrance about the stucco. Staff there directed me to "the log house at the top of the hill."

The inside, though drywalled, still has the occasional square-timbered beam from the old structure. The view from the windows is of fields and fence lines, though I imagine on summer nights, when the windows to Ginny's house are open she can hear on the wind the call of the elephants and camels and the other exotic creatures that roam those grounds. Maybe the horses hear it too, and answer in their own way.

As she had promised she would, Ginny demonstrated the liberty show in a small round pen near the house. Wearing a white and red jacket that advertised for her husband Kevin's karate school, she moved around those horses like a girl acting out a play she'd devised with her cousins. Some sort of common energy, or common blood, seemed to course through them all. In each hand she held a long dressage whip, waving each like a conductor, but never actually touching the horses, while issuing soft verbal commands.

Beautel, 13, Ariss, 13, Zephyr, 16, and Farro, 16— "the boys," as she calls them—performed for an audience of one. They queued up and trotted around the perimeter, they paired up, criss-crossed, reversed and waltzed. It was a bit like the Mounties' musical ride, but there were no riders in red tunics; just this woman conducting an exquisite little ballet. At the end, one horse reared on command, then stretched out his right front leg, tucked the left under and bowed like a courtesan. Finally, he raised his left leg in a farewell wave just before he and another horse reared up together.

"Where did you learn to train horses?" I asked her after the horses had been put away.

"I don't know," she replied, a hearty laugh rippling through her answer. "People ask me that. The liberty was just common sense— common sense to me."

Ginny's father was a military attaché posted in the former Yugoslavia, where she took riding lessons as a young girl. "I remember the horse was chestnut and very, very large," she recalled, again laughing at the memory of her first horse. "And my instructor would make us ride without hands or stirrups . . . that's where it started." Later, back in Canada, she joined the Pony Club.

But there was no one mentor, no abiding influence. At some point early on in her life with horses, Ginny must have come to her own conclusions about how to communicate with them. Every horse in her circle would have picked up immediately on her confidence, her inner calm and sublime skill. She seems to know when to press, when to prod, when to praise. The horses perhaps sense in her a strength of purpose, a sunny disposition, even a joy in the work.

"I could be in a foul mood because everything else is going wrong," she told me, "and you get in the ring and do liberty and it just makes me happy. They're funny, those horses. They make me laugh."

Ginny's mother was a ballet teacher who taught her dance between the ages of 9 and 16. "Ballet," Ginny says, "is precise, and you do the same thing over and over. I got used to that kind of training, and knowing that hoped-for results were sometimes far down the road."

Ginny trains each horse separately to voice command. Each horse assigned to the liberty performance, then, has to know *out*, meaning to hug the rail of the ring, and their names, of course. Eventually they'll have to know *walk*, *easy* [go slow], *relax* [everything's cool], *trot*, *move up* [closer to the one ahead], *double up*, *waltz*, *counter-clockwise*, *four up*, and *come here* [when they gather before her at the end].

"Everything starts out slowly at a walk," Ginny explains. "You say their names, then you pause, then you ask for the command. The pause gives them time to think. If the horse doesn't do it, you keep on correcting. Nothing rough. Maybe you jingle the lunge line. You *always* praise when they do the right thing. Each horse would get 15 minutes of schooling, in the morning and then in the afternoon. It seemed like they were in their stalls thinking, because in the afternoon they were much better.

"As a trainer," she says, "you're kind of good guy and bad guy at the same time. You can't let them get away with anything, otherwise they'll run right over top of you. But as a woman, I can't bully, I don't have the strength; I have to use the brain. There's a lot of horse there. They can get mad. So, you back off a little; try something different. Every time there would be something a little bit wrong; especially with Zephyr. Every day something to fix. But I had a purpose and I felt very strong."

Once she had a handle on an individual horse's mind, she felt confident in knowing how to proceed. "If I know they know what I want, I'm inclined to say, 'Smarten up.' It doesn't take much to scare a horse. Just flip the lead shank and smack him on the chest, it makes a noise and they go . . ." She makes a wide-eyed face of fright to illustrate the horse's reaction.

And if push wasn't right, pull was. She tells of trying to teach Farro dressage and him getting impatient, stomping his foot in anger. "He was one you worked the other way," said Ginny. "I'd say, 'Oh, come on, Farro, you're a good boy . . . ,'" and she said *good boy* in that tone some of us use on dogs we love, dropping the *d*. "And Farro thinks, 'She's wonderful, and so maybe I'll try one more time.' He was doing piaffes, the difficult trot in place, and you just couldn't push him. Farro's very quiet and sensitive. He does not like to be yelled at. He's a very sensitive fellow. But very clever. He's got a lot of heart, though, and he wants to please, but you have to know how to work him."

One time she put her husband, Kevin—his father is Joe Sealy, a musician well known on the Toronto jazz circuit—on Farro. "Kevin doesn't ride that much, but he has good balance and a quiet demeanour. And Kevin asks me, 'What do I do if he whinnies at the mares?' I said, 'Tap him with the crop and say, 'Don't do that.' Well,

Farro does whinny and Kevin taps him on the neck, not realizing that this was a cue for Farro to waltz. So around they went . . ."

Farro is of the Fox line, as Dali is, and I wish I had a dollar for every time I heard that line decried, and then, in the next breath, celebrated. "A lot of people don't like that line," said Ginny, "but Farro is wonderful. It's a clever line . . ."

Ginny concedes that she may be more "no nonsense" than she thinks she is. But it says a lot that her secret weapon is an orange vegetable. The day I saw her in the ring, Ginny carried with her a goodly number of carrots. "Men at the Royal Winter Fair," she recalls, "used to laugh at me because I was always giving my horses carrots. But the horses don't do what I ask them to because of the carrots. They do it because they *have* to do it, because I ask them to do it. They're not being paid. They would rather get hooked up to a carriage and go down the road; that's a horsey thing. Not the liberty, show after show. So I was always rewarding them. It's just recognition."

Her Canadian horses do, though, clearly prize the carrots. Ginny tells the story of training little Zephyr and how one day it was going badly. She was determined not to give him a carrot. It so happened that Zephyr, previously, had been taught to fall for a role he had in a film. All of a sudden, amid this disastrous day of schooling, he fell flat on the ground. "I thought I'd killed him," said Ginny, warming to her story, her eyes large. "I thought he'd had a heart attack. But his mouth was open. What Zephyr was saying was: 'You won't give me a carrot for the liberty, so how about *this* trick?'"

Ginny calls Zephyr "the tinker of the crowd. You have to watch him. Sometimes, during a liberty show, my mind is always thinking Zephyr, and when he gets out of my sight I'll just call his name, so he thinks I'm watching him." At the Royal Agricultural Winter Fair (where Ginny took the liberty demonstration for many years), "there was a post in the middle of the ring, two and a half feet by two and a half feet and all the way to the roof. The little tinker knew I could not see him, and he'd muck up. So one show I peeked around the post and he saw me and he just about jumped out of his skin and went right back into place. He just makes you laugh. You're mad at him but you have to respect him."

Ginny had long worked with Thoroughbreds and found the Canadians far more forgiving. They learned quicker and retained what they learned: Little tricks she taught them one year and then forgot would suddenly reappear the following year, the way spring shoots in a garden issue pleasant reminders of last fall's harvest. She also found the horses wanted to be with her, which sometimes was a problem. Ginny would be fixing fences, for example, and the horses would have their noses in the way and Zephyr would run off with the hammer.

The 13-year-long affiliation between the Canadian horse and African Lion Safari began in 1985 when Ginny announced to her father that she wanted horses to be part of the Safari experience. She was vague on the details and then knew nothing of heritage horses. It should not have surprised her that her father was open to horse-powered theatrics.

Born in Winnipeg, Gordon Dailley was attending university there, but he was, as Ginny puts it, "misbehaving," and his British-born parents sent him to England in hopes of straightening him out. Later he would captain the hockey team that won England Olympic gold in 1936. "Dirty Dog" Dailley, as he was called, set up the winning goal in a 2–1 game that handed the Canadian team a stunning defeat. At the games and earlier, Gordon Dailley almost created international incidents when he first refused to accept Adolf Hitler's autograph and then turned his back on the Nazi leader.

Ginny remembers him as a funny and unpretentious man who loved to wear old clothes. "He was a well-educated man who loved the arts," she says. "He was also an entrepreneur who was open to ideas that were *out there*." African Lion Safari brochures paint him as a man ahead of his time. "Long before conservation and eco-tourism became fashionable," it says, "Col. G. D. Dailley, Founder of African Lion Safari, had a vision: *To provide an environment for self-sustaining*

*populations of declining wildlife species.*" He realized this vision by creating displays where visitors were 'caged' in their vehicles and the
animals were allowed to roam freely."

Well, not exactly freely. The game reserves are ample all right,
spread over 750 acres, but double fencing does tend to define the
animals' freedom. And as for the colonel's vision, Ginny remembers
it differently. During a visit to England in 1967, he discovered the
lions of Longleat. A man named Jimmy Chipperfield had launched an
unusual zoo in which patrons drove through a reserve to see roam-
ing lions.

After retiring from the military in his mid-fifties, Colonel
Dailley took that novel idea and, by 1969, had established a much
grander version in Canada. His partner in the beginning, until he was
later bought out: one Jimmy Chipperfield.

But how did Canadian horses get tossed into the mix of elephants and giraffes? The aforementioned brochure features a collage
of animal attractions at the park, including tigers and lions and birds
of prey. Down in the right-hand corner is one called Animals and
Man Performance. It depicts a handler in period costume driving a
Canadian horse pulling a sled and what looks to be a 19th century–
vintage barrel.

In 1985, says Ginny, "We bought three old liberty horses from
an American circus. They were maybe 28 years old. It just happened.
The Safari elephant guys and I were trying to put a show together
and we thought, we'll try these old horses." Shortly after that, Anne
Hinrich, a friend of Ginny's working at the Milton Agricultural
Museum, heard about Canadian horses through Terry Veevers, who
continues to train them and use them on his farm nearby at Puslinch.

The world of Canadian horses is tiny, but I was amused to learn
that the sources of Ginny's horses in 1985 were pretty much my
source too. She bought Beautel and another called Velour from
Jérôme Aumond and Ferme Saroma, where Dali was born. Beautel
and Ariss were by Alec Hayward's stallion, Viger Duc.

LITTLE HORSE OF IRON

For 14 years, "the boys" were featured in a small way at African Lion Safari. As Ginny came to know and admire the breed she had not known existed, it appalled her that no one else knew about them either. It became her mission to spread the word.

"I really believe in the breed," Ginny says. "These little guys have worked their little hearts out—ploughing, taking kids to school, they've gone to wars and they've never complained (I guess because they can't). I think they've really helped. But no one was putting them in beautiful barns the way the Lipizzaners were. We stick them out in paddocks. This is our national breed. Other countries treat their national horses with such honour, and we have not done that. I wanted to give them a pat on the back. Our country is extremely young; it has so little history. We have to hang on to every little bit."

An entire generation of pupils in southern Ontario now knows about Canadian horses, thanks in no small part to Ginny. School kids would come in buses: up to 40 buses a day, with 50 pupils in each. Some years there were costume dramas that vividly depicted the role of the Canadian horse in early history; and always there were the liberty shows: three a day, seven days a week for seven months straight over 14 years.

Adults, too, were mesmerized by these horses. Ginny would be walking up the hill to her house after a show and look behind to see people following her. "They were amazed they had never heard of the Canadian," Ginny recalls. "They would always say 'the Canadian what? Trotter? Quarter horse?'" "No," Ginny would reply. "Just the Canadian." They had questions about the horses' history and personality, about how many existed and where. Some wanted to buy one. Ginny would direct them to breeding farms in Quebec. And in the years Ginny took the Canadians to the Royal Agricultural Winter Fair in Toronto, the telephones at those breeding farms, she later learned, similarly lit up. Until Ginny brought hers, Canadian horses had not been featured at the Royal Agricultural Winter Fair in 50 years.

"I considered it," says Ginny, "one of my jobs, besides education, to make people aware. If Canadians are not aware of this wonderful horse, they are not going to buy them or breed them. It's marketing is what it is." But marketing did not inform her endeavours. Nationalism did. The irony is that marketing brought those endeavours to a halt.

We had traded phone calls as I planned a trip to see her and her Canadians. On September 7, 1999, she called, a little breathless: a few weeks previously, African Lion Safari had told her that the show of Canadians would no longer be a part of the park. Though she is a Safari co-owner, along with her brother and another partner, others decide what creatures will hold centre stage there. "It took my breath away," she told me. She sounded in shock.

Later, in person, she was somewhat more sanguine about the whole affair. "I was going to retire in two years anyway. I had had enough. I want some peace in my life. The other shareholders think it would be more of a pain to work with another trainer and they don't want to be bothered. It's a real shame. I understand that with all tourism places you have to have something new all the time, but to me the liberty is something very special and the history is something very, very special. I would have liked to pass on the torch . . ."

Ginny quietly let it be known that her Canadians were for sale, and within days several were snapped up. It must have been unbearably sad to see the foursome split up and the horses she had acquired as two-year-olds going down the driveway in trailers. Ariss and Beautel were sold to Americans who plan to use them for light hacking; Farro went to a semi-retired trainer who does work with filmmakers; Zephyr went to a colonial museum in Virginia where he pulls antique carriages three days a week. He was the hardest to part with. "I cried and cried when I sold him," Ginny told me. "My young son said to me, 'Mom, he's just a horse.' Well, he was so small he was barely a horse, but he was *such* a character."

Yet, in watching them go off to good homes, Ginny was at least spared something she had begun to dread. "I always wondered what would happen to these guys when they're 21 years old. I didn't want to see that. They need to be worked, they're too young to retire. It's nice to have someone buy one as a hobby horse, go out on weekends. They've worked hard enough; they need some fun time. The breed is on the upswing, so I don't feel too bad. Maybe that job is done."

African Lion Safari offered a literal stage for the Canadian horse. Show time there meant performance, kids and tourists in bleachers, backdrops and microphones. In Nova Scotia, the Canadian horse works a different kind of stage: a small working farm-cum-museum meant to re-create life in that region circa 1870.

The first French horses to arrive on the shores of what is now Canada arrived in Acadia in 1610. Their stay would be brief: An American raider named Samuel Argall made off with them in 1616. But the horses that ultimately became the Canadian would find their way over time and by circuitous routes to Boston, to New France and even to Sable Island.

Barbara Christie, an intrepid researcher and the author of *The Horses of Sable Island*, published in 1995, is, by her own admission, an elderly lady. But if you call her at her home in Halifax and ask her a question, any question, involving horses and history and Nova Scotia, she will excuse herself, you will hear a great rustle of papers and she will invariably return with the answer or the promise of one. For 20 years, she has been poring over equine history. Though her other passion is flower gardening, I had the sense that her home is awash in paper. I imagined documents set out in boxes, arranged alphabetically, atop tables and counters. There would be a typewriter somewhere. Christie is old school. She owns neither a computer nor a car. She is, though, a great fan of the Canadian horse.

"I love them," she told me. "You can't deny them. They're a super, lasting, all-purpose horse."

It seemed natural, owing to the Canadian horse's four-century-long association with Nova Scotia, to go there. I wanted to know from the people who worked closely with Canadian horses what their experience had been. What conclusions about the breed had they reached? I knew as I asked the question all over Nova Scotia—in New Ross, Elmsdale, Louisbourg—how flawed a question it was. Surely I knew by now that every horse is different and that to paint an entire breed in a certain light—"they're all like *this*"—was simplistic. My encounters with Canadian horses on the coast told me that some of them were true to the literature. The thing is, the literature on the breed is mixed. There are references to *docile,* but mentions too of *nervous.* Which word is closer to the truth?

Barry Ward's four years of working almost daily with Canadian stallions and mares and geldings at Ross Farm Museum northwest of Halifax have taught him to reconsider that word, *docile.* On this 60-acre working farm, some nine Canadian horses, along with other heritage animals—Berkshire pigs, Jersey cows and Cotswold sheep—help re-create a sense of life on a Nova Scotia farm in the latter part of the 19th century. The horses plough fields, haul lumber from the woods for the shake mill, take visitors on wagon rides and sleigh rides past the lake. No mere decoration, the horses work. And so it is that Barry Ward, Ross Farm's teamster and a harness-maker in his other life, has a keen sense of the Canadian horse's character. He has indeed come to certain conclusions.

"I would read about the history of the Canadian horse," Ward says, "and I kept seeing that word, *docile.* And I thought it meant sleepy, laid-back, lazy, stupid. The Canadians are not that. They're alert and very ambitious: They want something to do. They love to work and prefer a day in the woods to a day in the barn. I've had lots of Clydesdales and Percherons, and these Canadians would outwork them; they're more sure-footed. They're very quick, very smart and careful, and not always quiet. I'm not one to take a stick to a horse, but it wouldn't work anyway with these horses. You have to work with them. They're a damn good little horse."

Ward carries with him the physical memory of these horses. Frannie and Dolly and April and the rest. Sit next to him, close your eyes and you can conjure leather, horse, shavings and hay. It's a grounded, ancient scent, one my own grandfather and Ward's grandfather would have worn proudly. My son tells me I wear the same scent after my Dali-ances.

Ward is not an imposing man, and while he speaks obliquely of illness in his past, neither could you call him frail. Wiry, maybe. His hands, critical to communication with his team of horses, are large and strong. On the chill October morning I followed him to the horse barn, he was wearing fisherman's rubber overalls hung on his small frame by suspenders, a wool jacket and cap, all varying shades of grey. Only his rubber boots (a mossy green) and a flash of yellow on his suspenders (where they crossed on his back) lent him any colour at all. The many photographs I took that morning depict a man older than I remember and seeming to swim in his clothes. Everything, even his moustache, seemed two sizes too big. The man in the photos looked ungainly. The photos lie.

Watching Barry Ward tacking up the team told me much about the horses and their handler. For all the bulk of Ward's clothing, he moved among the horses with ease and grace, and they, too, fell into place with astonishing dexterity.

Ward has had a varied life, farmed a little, sold tractor parts, run a co-op farm supply store. But always in his life there were horses. He guesses some 117 horses have passed through his farm in the past 14 years. They were horses with character flaws, conformation flaws, horses nobody wanted or could handle. Ward's task was to set them right and then to part with most of them for more than he paid.

I had been most anxious to meet this wrangler, who had earned a certain reputation as a gifted and sensitive horse trainer. "If he asked those horses to go through a knot hole," one of his colleagues at the museum told me, "they would try for him."

The first thing that struck me about him was his confidence. He wanted to take me deep into the woods to bring back some firewood, and I had already been warned by the museum's director, Allan Hiltz, that the road was rough. Implicit was the notion that only the most sure-footed and rugged horses would dare tackle it.

Further, I was to ride with Ward on a sturdy but plain farmer's wagon built by the Mennonites in Elmira, Ontario. Over a steel frame and between a pair of small tires, the builders had placed heavy wooden planks. Our seat would be a bale of hay. Safety brakes there were none, and the pair of horses Ward had chosen were a three-year-old stallion he called Frannie—with a grand total of a week in harness to call upon and a reputation as "a hellion"—and a seven-year-old mare named Dolly disinclined to suffer youthful exuberance. Both handsome black horses. Neither had ever been paired with the other.

"Hope your insurance is all paid up," Ward laughed as we set out.

I will admit to a little trepidation, but only a little. I knew, the horses knew, we were in good hands. With the horses, Ward's contact, verbal and physical, was constant. He would touch this one's tail as he passed by to put on a bridle, would call another by name, and he never stopped reading them. As needed, he chided, he praised, he admired, as a father would a child.

"My wife kids me," he said. "She says I speak nicer to the horses than I do to her. Sometimes I wonder if the Canadian isn't more of a woman's horse. That's how important it is to show them affection. They give," he concludes, "what they get."

The stallion, smaller than the mare, showed his respect by sidling up warily as both were tacked up. Despite the circumstances, Ward's trust in them (and his own judgment) was almost unassailable. When the mare ventured forward before the stallion was in place, she got an admonishment. "Dolly, you know better than that."

Teamsters often like help when they tack up two horses. Not Ward. There were many times, during tacking up, moments in the woods and upon our return, when the reins were left on the wagon or a horse would be trusted to stand alone, unhitched, while another was attended to. And one of the two horses, remember, is a three-year-old. A stallion at that.

By a series of verbal commands (*gee* for right, *haw* for left), he parked those horses where he wanted them. Later he would back up and park the wagon using the same and other verbal commands. Ward even has one voice command that sounds like *whup*. "People laugh at that word," he told me as I pitched on that hay bale over the ever more hostile path, "and they want to know what it means. It's a cross between *whoa* and *up you go* and I use it when I want the horse to lift his feet over an object on the ground."

What ground there was was fast giving way to rock gardens, black slime and mud up to the horse's knees, and all manner of natural obstacles. Once we came across a sizable fir tree that covered most of the road and I offered to disembark and swing it off to the side. Ward pressed on without pausing. "Don't worry about that," he said as the horses responded to his *whup*, delicately lifting their feet over the tree and the tires rolled up and over the limbs and branches. I was on a two-horsepower all-terrain vehicle.

Sometimes the wagon would drop from a boulder and land with a thunk on the dirt road or splash into water-filled trenches in low, soft ground. I struggled to keep my balance, flexing my thigh muscles and trying to achieve a grip somewhere on those planks. I was only a few feet from two horses but riding was never like this. I longed for stirrups, saddle, reins.

How, I wondered, did Ward maintain his balance and keep just the right contact? "It's all in how you handle the mouth," he had said earlier in the morning. If my perch was precarious, surely so was his. His grandfather had apparently taught him a lesson about the value of a steady hand.

"He was not a rough man," says Ward, "but he could be very stern with horses." And, it seems, with grandsons. On one occasion, when the young Barry was driving a team with his grandfather seated beside him, the boy either forgot his delicate touch on the reins or let it slide with the rolling of the wagon. For suddenly there was his grandfather's elbow in his mouth followed by a warning never to be so careless again.

Ward has learned that the slow way with horses is the quicker way. Presented with a horse terrified of entering a trailer, Ward once spent an entire summer overcoming that phobia by putting the horse's hay at the trailer's entranceway and moving it farther inside each day, an inch at a time; one day he tried for three inches and the horse would have none of it. Finally, the horse went all the way inside, and Ward had the good sense not to close the door behind him but rather to send him outside immediately. Next time, Ward led him in as if it were all old hat, which, by now, it was.

On we went into the forest, still shrouded by the same dense fog that had greeted the dawn. The narrow, primitive path circled and dipped. Now it crossed a brook, a flat expanse of boards serving as makeshift bridge. As if the fog had stilled even the birds, a heavy silence hung all around, broken only by the tinkling of bells on the horse's collars, water falling in brooks and the sound of the horses as they plunged on and up the slick trail. These days the bells were there to lend a romantic touch to wagon rides, but in the days of horse transport they served a practical function: to warn teamsters at dangerous bends of approaching horses and to keep to the side.

We stopped once en route to a clearing where the wood lay piled, not to rest the horses, who showed no sign at all of fatigue or breathlessness, but so Barry could have a cigarette. The horses waited patiently, the steam rising from their backs.

Allan Hiltz tells a story of going to Quebec more than a decade ago to buy Canadian horses after deciding to make heritage animals a part of Ross Farm Museum. Gilles Racette was going to put Allan and a colleague up for the night at his home near Trottier Mills, and that evening Gilles's kids made a plea for a wagon ride. A 14-hand,

900-pound Canadian horse was hitched up and four kids and several adults piled on. At one point Gilles handed Allan the reins, and as they were going up what Allan called "this ungodly mountain," he stopped. "I'm used to stopping horses," Allan explained as he told the story. "Give 'em a breather."

One of the children said something in French to Gilles, who then translated it. "What's wrong?" the child had said. "Doesn't Monsieur Hiltz understand Canadian horses?"

Those who sell the breed prefer to sing the horse's praises; those who watch the horses being worked every day see them for what they are: good horses, but not horses without quirks. Barry Hiltz, farm and maintenance manager at Ross Farm Museum (he's no apparent relation to Allan Hiltz, though I joked that everyone at the museum is named either Barry or Hiltz), has a good sense of the Canadian horse's temperament.

"We've been on the verge of selling some of these horses," he told me. "They were sour and spoiled. They were doing little things but unacceptable things. One mare would bolt through doors, for example. Others were quite aggressive. Well, we still have all those horses. We didn't switch horses, we switched handlers."

They brought in Barry Ward. The Canadian horse intent on bolting through doors, it was eventually learned, had become hung up one day while going through. For an entire summer, museum staff had to back her through that door.

Hiltz now knows about the character of Canadians. "You can't get aggressive with them," he says. "You can't force them. If they don't want to walk past a wagon, and you try to make them, they'll only take so much and then they'll bolt. You can work them into it without forcing them. On the other hand, you can't let them push you around either."

Barry Hiltz's abiding impression is of the Canadian horse's intelligence. "Too smart," Ward sometimes remarks.

Foals get used to 50 kids charging off a school bus towards a paddock fence. The museum is visited by 6,000 to 10,000 school-children a year. One precaution taken is to remove yearlings from public view, lest they become nippers. Young children, especially those not comfortable around horses, will often present grass to a young horse but lack courage when they see the horse's mouth open. They pull back, the horse is quicker, fingers get nipped.

Back in the woods behind New Ross, Frannie and Dolly are engag-ing in a little equine testing of the waters. The stallion shows his youth by sometimes lifting his head, then dropping it like a stone. Ward would sometimes touch him with the tip of the whip, to get him to move up parallel to Dolly. Frannie had yet to learn Dolly's steady pace, and as a consequence she was often ahead and thus pulling a greater share of the load, a fact not lost on the mare.

Sometimes she would lean over towards him, for a second, then pull back. She was goading him, and he would fall for the bait, act up and find himself in trouble with teamster Ward. They were like kids in a classroom: A teacher turns back to the class from his black-board to catch a spitball thrower, who, though clearly guilty, was merely responding to someone else's missile.

Later in the morning, after we unloaded the wood, the sun emerged and Barry took me for a little spin by Lawson Lake. This time we used the wagon that carries visitors and it seemed the height of luxury—seats, footrests, brakes. The road passed the cooper's shed, the schoolhouse and the barn. Some of the buildings, with wood-shingle roofs and siding, still sat on their original foundations. Perhaps because the road traverses the farm itself, and we had no traffic to contend with, Barry felt free to hand me the reins.

This marked the first time I had ever driven horse and buggy, and I learned quickly what happens with too loose a rein. Within sec-onds, Frannie and Dolly picked up a rolling canter and I had to restrain them. After lunch, we took out a 16-hand, seven-year-old chestnut mare named April, and again I found myself admiring this high-stepping powerful Canadian mare and not paying enough attention to driving. In seconds she was off the road and onto the grass, and as we approached a hill she, too, struck up a lively canter before I brought her back.

Ross Farm occupies the site of an actual family farm that was worked from 1816 to 1869. In 1970, the province established a living museum of agriculture on the site. The aim was to portray an uplands farm; one, that is, more forest-based than the small coastal farms or the larger fruit farms of the rich Annapolis Valley. The uplands farm would have relied more on horse and oxen to haul timber, and both animals work on Ross Farm today.

The farm sits atop one of the many ridges that define this part of Nova Scotia. Some of the fields are tipped towards the valley below, and the road past the carriage barn and duck pond offers a steep incline where the horses always want to run.

In the cooper's shed, men in period costume make variously sized barrels of fir wood, but not nearly fast enough. Filmmakers buy them for period movies, such as the Canadian made-for-television movies *Road to Avonlea* and *Pit Pony*. Grocery stores buy them to lend period flavour to their produce displays. Farm-gate operations in the Annapolis Valley want them for their apples. People buy the waterproof models as rain barrels. The wood for those barrels, along with the pine and spruce used in the shingles for farm siding and roofs, are all hauled by the horses.

When Allan Hiltz procured Canadian horses for the museum, there was only one other purebred Canadian horse in the province. Now there are some 25. So impressed with the breed is Hiltz, who runs a farm in his off hours, that this year he bought a Canadian for himself.

The museum has become known as a place where the Canadian horse is promoted and celebrated. When Hiltz and a colleague travelled around Quebec in the late 1980s eyeing horses, they met breeders reluctant to let their horses leave the province. Alec Hayward and Donnie Prosperine had encountered similar reluctance when they horse-hunted in Quebec a decade beforehand.

The attitude of Quebec breeders, certainly to Ross Farm, has changed. Hiltz credits the good work of the farm in featuring the breed and economic factors—the Canadian horse is now fetching a lot more than a decade ago.

Hiltz tells the story of their mare, La Gorgendière Fox Miria. Like Dali's sire, she was a horse raised at the Deschambault farm in Quebec. "Some don't care for the Fox line," says Hiltz, cupping his hands atop his head and leaning back in his tiny office at Ross Farm Museum. "We have great respect for the Fox line."

Miria was a handful in the beginning. Unused to the harness, she would throw herself out of the traces. Now anyone, says Hiltz, can drive her. She's a regular in the annual Annapolis Valley parade celebrating apple blossom time. Some 100,000 people, a thousand floats and bands warming up: None of this rattles her now.

I caught sight of Allan's chestnut Canadian as we rounded his long driveway later in the day. This being Nova Scotia, I had myself a dinner invitation, as did Barry Ward. "Don't expect anything fancy," Allan warned. His wife, Bernice, had prepared a fine and ample supper, drawn mostly from her own garden. The meal consisted of mashed potatoes, corn, carrots, meatloaf, apple pie crowned with cheddar, tea, and the best well water I have ever tasted. I stopped at three glasses.

You could say I fell *for* Dali the moment I fell *off* Dali. The sight of him dashing across that field was somehow imprinted on my brain, and by degrees I warmed to him. But Ginger, Ginger was one of those horses I fell for at first sight. Even in her stall she had bearing. Here, I would have told Barry Ward, had he been in that barn, here is *docile*.

She's a two-year-old filly bred at New Ross and now residing at the splendid Woodhaven Stables northeast of Halifax. Ginger is a liver chestnut, 15.1 hands and likely 1,100 pounds. I liked everything about her. Kind eye. Sweet disposition. Elegant conformation and smaller feet but still in that sturdy Canadian mould. Curious. Quiet. Playful.

The stable manager, a woman named Susan, put a halter on her and brought her out into the barn aisle so I could get a better look. Ginger, she said, is turned out with a Thoroughbred right off the track and always beats her when they race towards the water. As we spoke, the filly would nuzzle my jacket or mouth a paper bag hung outside a nearby stall.

"I hear the breed is making a comeback," Susan said, "and I'm really glad to hear that. I remember seeing a Canadian horse in Prince Edward Island who was so calm and trusting that there really was no breaking-in. When the time was right, they simply bridled her and saddled her and off they went."

Ginger might not be quite such a snap as that, but my hunch is she will be very agreeable. Her co-owner, Gordon Russell, of Halifax, told me he bought the horse for his wife, Joan. "We had watched the Canadians at Ross Farm," he said, "and I liked the way they worked, their disposition. I bought Ginger for my wife who has been around horses a long time but was nevertheless leery. She's no longer afraid of horses. Ginger has changed all that."

Russell did, however, note the spark in Ginger. "She can get hot. She can be stubborn." Turns out she and Dali are distant relatives. She has Fox blood in her: Her great-grand-sire is La Gorgendière Fox Kosmos, a full brother to Dali's grand-sire, La Gorgendière Fox Larry. "The Fox line," Russell had heard, "can be crazy, sparky. With this line you better have a bit of experience. So we decided to get professional help." With a trainer, they are slowly bringing Ginger along. In the weeks before I saw her, they had introduced her to the bit and begun to long-line her.

"Everybody who owns a horse," says Russell, "has something to say about their horse's breed, something that distinguishes that horse.

'My horse is a second cousin to Big Ben,' or something similar. What Joan can say about Ginger is that 'My horse is a heritage horse.'"

Some 500 kilometres away at the Fortress of Louisbourg, Greg Joyce offers an unequivocal assessment of the Canadian horse.

"There's no horse like them," he says. "We have a two-and-a-half-year-old gelding. He'll dig in and pull, he'll go anywhere, inside houses, inside tunnels. He's unflappable; it's incredible."

Among his other duties, Joyce oversees the animal program at the reconstructed 18th century fortified town at the northeastern tip of Nova Scotia. The fort has three Canadian horses, with another on the way: One of their mares was bred to Frannie of Ross Farm.

Joyce has owned horses and will own them again. And when he does buy another horse, he will buy a Canadian. He tells the story of the gelding at five months jumping a fence to go to another pasture. But when it came time to jump back in, he was jumping from lower ground and got hung up on the fence line, cutting himself badly in the chest. "I held him," says Joyce, "without a halter while the vet patched him. The vet could put his arm right inside the wound to clean it. The vet was astonished. That's the temperament we're dealing with."

The gelding, named Guillaume, comes from the Henryville line of Canadian horses, known for its docility. And the horse would have need of it at Louisbourg. The fort, a replica faithful to the architecture of the 1700s, features lots of low-hung, narrow tunnels six feet high. His first time in, Guillaume simply followed his handler.

The other gelding at the fort was so calm he could have been left a stallion. They chose not to breed him, but the gelding process made him no calmer. He was mellow before, mellow after losing his jewels.

The mare, concedes Joyce, was more of a handful. "Obviously, she had had some trauma in her life." Now 20, she came to Louisbourg when she was 9. "She was quite difficult for a while. She was never nasty but she had an awkward gait and did not want to pull heavy loads. We got around it through trust and loyalty."

Like Ross Farm, the Fortress of Louisbourg will sell the occasional Canadian horse raised there. And the interest, apparently, is high. Small wonder when Greg Joyce is there to sing their praises. "I couldn't ask those horses to be any better than they are," he says.

The Canadian horse is featured at other pioneer villages scattered across the country. King's Landing Historic Settlement, for example, re-creates a 19th century New Brunswick village, and thus uses some of the horses that would have been used at the time. They have two Canadians, both mares, named Zeta and Gail, 12 and 13 years old respectively. Zeta came from Gilles Racette in Trottier Mills, Quebec; Alec Hayward provided Gail.

Similarly, Heritage Park Historical Village in Calgary features Canadian horses, as did Black Creek Pioneer Village in Toronto until quite recently. Upper Canada Village near Morrisburg, Ontario, on the St. Lawrence River, re-creates life in 1860s Ontario in part by putting some 20 Canadian horses to work on the site pulling wagons and stagecoaches through the village, cutting hay, towing scows on a canal and operating an old treadmill.

"The Canadian horse is quite alert," says Dave Dobbie, Upper Canada Village's supervisor of farms and domestic interpretation. "They're very trainable, with a good disposition. Here they have to be. We've had kids run under the barrel of a horse."

Dobbie says people are amazed when you tell them that the horse is a Canadian, for it's news to them that such a breed even exists. But every now and again an elderly man will come along and there will be this shock of recognition. "We had horses just like that," he'll say, "when I was a boy on the farm. But that was a long time ago."

# CHAPTER 12

# "HE'S *SO* QUIET . . ."

LAKEHEAD STABLES, OCTOBER, 1999

*A bruise the size of my hand and the colour of a ripe plum has formed above my buttocks.*
*A companion bruise, bigger but fainter, has formed on my right buttock. It's all quite*
*arresting, and I find myself at bedtime nude and twisted around before my dresser mirror to*
*monitor the strange, almost autumnal progression of the colours.*

September 21, 1999

IT IS STILL EARLY DAYS with Dark Fox Dali, and no shortage of issues to be resolved. The business of the feet loomed large for a time, as did mounting. It seems, in retrospect, that Kathi and Gilles were both right. There were matters of respect and trust to be resolved.

Today, as I twice readjust his girth, he curls around to see what

Above: Dali on his last day at Blue Haven.

I am up to. I gently but firmly use my hand to suggest he best look to the front. I also, as Gilles suggested, lower the left stirrup by three notches. This proves a great help in mounting, for I am a stiff old bird trying to get up without using a mounting block. Since I no longer strain to get that left foot up into the stirrup, my right foot has spring as I launch into the saddle. Once up, I readjust the stirrup.

I also heeded Kathi's advice. Yesterday I shortened the lesson and afterwards hand-grazed Dali for about five minutes. Alongside the outdoor ring is a right-of-way where the grass grows thick. Dali tore into it like a child surprised with ice cream on a hot summer day.

Today, perhaps, pays a few dividends from such gestures. I give Dali more rein, and he responds in kind. This late September day, the canter comes, despite complaints, ears back. But at lesson's end I have a relaxed, contented horse, one perhaps anticipating a walk in the grass.

September 22, 1999

The phrases "killing with kindness" and "We are the authors of our own destruction" come to mind. Today, I tighten the girth only to the fifth hole. It seems secure, though I had it at six yesterday. This is my first mistake. I also forget to secure the throat latch on Dali's bridle. And while I do shortly notice the latter, dismount and attend to it, the girth almost comes back to haunt me.

I noticed the saddle loose and sliding left early in the lesson, but out of laziness and a worry that a third mounting would disinter that troublesome business, I let it go. I simply shifted my weight to centre the saddle. Barb was issuing orders in the middle of the ring— "Come down the centre in a trot, turn right, then canter all the way around"—when the saddle began to lurch dangerously to the left. I was leaning over Dali's neck, saying "whoa" in a pleading, mewling sort of way.

Early in the lesson, he had scooted several times in one corner, almost unseating me. Pride bade me act as though it were nothing.

But when Dali began to scoot as the saddle slipped, I thought we were in trouble.

"Are you all right?" Barb said when we finally came to a halt.

"This damn saddle," I replied as I dismounted, reset the saddle and went to notch six.

By now, the third mount, Dali had grown weary of the up and down. He moved ahead as I went to put my foot in the stirrup. I went to his right side and backed him up; that and a stern word did the trick. On the bright side, he did let me on and he did stop when the saddle began to slip.

In *Horsemastership*, that classic book published in 1952, the author warned against matching green riders and green horses. I am not so much green as mentally lazy. Forgetting the throat latch? Casual about the girth? This comes of riding lessons at stables where details are left to others and the horses are safe and reliable. Today I almost took a tumble because I let details slide.

Still, the day was not without one small pleasure. When Barb, on Rocky, led Dali and me outside the ring and into a little park near their house, Dali came alive on that little bit of trail. That felt good.

I continue to hand-graze him after every ride. He tears at the grass and loads it in his mouth as if there might not be another opportunity. As if winter snow was imminent. The low afternoon sun caught the highlights on his coat, the flecks of yellow and gold, and as I held the black shank in my hands and leaned on my horse, I felt a rare sense of privilege.

September 27, 1999

*Less is better* emerged as the theme of today's lesson. Dali lunged agreeably, though my request that he lope sparked a minor explosion. Lunging is supposed to take the pepper out of the horse, but there is an art to it. I still wrestle with it and with small details, such as forgetting to switch the lunge line from one side of the halter to the next when I change directions.

Dali appears to forgive me my transgressions. When I ask him to stop in anticipation of my turning him the other way on the lunge line, he invariably comes into me. I read in a horse magazine of a trainer who never lunges more than 10 minutes and always ceases the minute the horse comes into the centre. Perhaps I don't need to lunge Dali?

Still, he tests me. Bridling him sometimes requires perseverance. He never runs off, just ducks and swerves like a boxer. As I mounted him today, he did his little sideways dance, but I had only to back him up from the right side and he obliged.

During schooling he got light fast. In the canter, though, he turned into the centre of our counter-clockwise circle. Barb quickly diagnosed the problem: I was oversteering. The trick is to use my inside leg to push him out and use the outside rein judiciously. Little corrections.

Later, Gilles, on Prime Time, and Barb, on Rocky, we all of us went for a trail ride. Dali was a happy horse, wanting to dip into the alfalfa but stepping out strongly.

"He looks good out here on the trail," said Barb. "Which is a good thing," she added. "Because that's his job."

October 2, 1999

Rode Dali at Blue Haven for the last time a few days ago. Rain forced us into the round pen, where he seemed agreeable, but towards the end his ears came back frequently. Something was bothering him.

"Every time you went down in your post," Gilles said later, "the ears went back. I think you're banging his back." A little test in the stall—Gilles pressing down where my seat would typically land—caused Dali to pin his ears and swing his hind end around.

I left wondering: Am I behind in my posting action? Are my stirrups too short and my feet forward of the girth? If my horse has a sore back, will it improve if I simply ride him better?

The move from Blue Haven to Lakehead Stables, which had been my plan from the beginning, came at a good time. It offered

Dali a four-day rest—time to adjust to his new surroundings, for that back to recover, for me to think about form. Longer leg. Softer hands. Follow the motion of the horse.

I will miss Blue Haven. I'll miss the ritual of going there, greeting fat old hound dog Daisy, and Tara, the little white terrier, stealer of carrots. In a way, Blue Haven will keep in touch. I have asked Gilles and/or Barb if they could watch me ride for the next few weeks, correcting my mistakes, suggesting a course of action in the schooling ring. Dali, I know, will keep testing me.

We trailered him Friday morning, one of those bracing fall days when the light lends new clarity. The wind chilled bare skin, but in sheltered areas the sun warmed. Dali came off the trailer, head high, eyeing everything nervously. I thought back to the last few times he walked off a trailer, to Blue Haven and at the vet clinic in Kemptville. There was no comparison: This version of Dali was a little imperious, but more calm than not. I took him into the paddock that had been cleared for him, showed him several piles of hay and a trough of water, then released the shank and let him go.

In a cool-as-a-cucumber trot, he inspected the borders of his paddock, introduced himself to his neighbors, and quickly settled into a meal of hay. Within minutes, he was rolling on the ground. "I love to see that so soon," said Lil Grooms, his new keeper. I had thought she might keep him in his stall for a day or so to get him adjusted, but this seemed a kinder arrangement. Dali, for today, had the middle paddock to himself, allowing him to see his new herd while affording him early protection and security. Barb was sure he would settle in nicely.

Earlier that morning at Blue Haven, Barb had let him out in the sand ring, convinced he would be stall-bound for a day or so in his new digs. Camera in hand, I walked out to him. It warmed me to see him stride purposefully my way. I scratched his throat and he lowered his head in contentment. When I bent low to take his photograph almost from ground level, he lowered his head even farther, curious about my camera.

For the last time here, I put him in the cross-ties, cleaned his hooves and groomed him. I ran the rubber curry comb over him as a massage then brushed him with the body brush. His coat, just starting to thicken for winter, shone in the sun when I took him out to the long grass for one final graze. I thought him devilishly handsome.

October 4, 1999

A night of rain and a bitter morning wind derailed my plan to take Dali for his first ride in the sand ring at Lakehead. I did, though, stop in to see him. He had his back to the stall door but immediately swung around at the sound of my voice. He was happy to have his neck scratched and even to have his muzzle stroked. Then he sighed, as Dusty, our dog, does when she settles in for a snooze.

"He's *so* quiet," said Carol Peterson, a fellow boarder who had just bought an unruly four-year-old Oldenburg named Rocky. Her horse pushed with his head and butted; my horse was content to be caressed. What a change from four months ago when he would not be touched and certainly not around the mouth.

October 6, 1999

"Don't expect much from your first ride at the new stable," Barb had warned. New surroundings and all that.

Lakehead Stables is a modest outfit, home to 10 or so horses. I like the fact that you may have to skirt frisky newborn calves on your way to the ring, or perhaps a chicken, escaped from the henhouse. I like the quiet professionalism of the two barn cats hired on as mousers, the way they sleep together on a saddle pad in the tack room, curled around each other like snakes in the sun. The place lacks all pretension, but with about 200 acres of back fields and forests for hacking, it sprawls deceptively.

Lil and Gerry Grooms—both "retired," a label at odds with

their rigorous labour—run it most days. Daughter Kellie owns it, son Chris helps maintain the old barn, and daughter Kathie and her husband, Francis Groenewegen, run the fancier counterpart down the road. The elder Grooms coddle the horses, worry that they've had enough to eat, find excuses to praise them. If a horse could be said to have grandparents to spoil them, Lil and Gerry would fit the bill.

I always go in the stable's side door, where Swiss bells hanging on a wrought-iron horse tell the horses in their stalls that someone approaches. In this little anteroom is stored the grain. What greets your nose, then, before every ride, is fuel for that ride: oats, sweet feed, molasses, all in plastic garbage pails with horses' names on the cover—Rocky, Ras, Bogi, Danny, Scooter, Misty, Jasper, Bayly, Sadie, Dali.

The tiny tack room is lined with trunks, mine plastic and plainest of all. Saddles hang on sturdy wooden trees, folded blankets have a metal tree of their own, while bridles hang on horseshoe-shaped holders carved from wood, some with the names of horses overtop. The room has the feel of an equine museum, eerily quiet and full of untold stories.

Some stables have tall metal grates that prohibit each horse from putting his head out and into the corridor. Not so at Lakehead. Were the horses keen, I could walk down the length of the barn and high-five every one. This was Dali's new home, and he seemed to like it fine.

But perhaps he was still getting his bearings. Even lunging that day was an adventure. Occasionally rearing in imitation of Trigger and yanking powerfully on the line, he finally backed into the two strands of hot electric fence at the gate, snapped off one plastic handle and broke the line, got loose and almost bolted. He stopped outside the ring, panting and snorting and looking like a frightened colt. It could have been far worse. He might have tangled a foot in that wire or run into the woods beyond the paddocks.

What had gone so wrong? An entire week off, to store up energy, could not have helped. He has also bonded with an older horse in his paddock and he whinnied to him several times as I tacked him up. In the cross-ties he was restless, stamped his left front foot after I cleaned the hoof, and generally acted the renegade.

"He's *so* quiet," Carol had said. She should have seen him today. She wonders if, in buying her Oldenburg, she has bitten off more than she can chew. The same thought now, and not for the first time, crossed my mind.

I stopped at Blue Haven on the way home and huddled with Gilles, who was astonished to hear of Dali's shenanigans, especially the rearing. His analysis: too much grass and grain, not enough work.

I am sporting a swollen finger on my right hand, plus various cuts and rope burns courtesy of Dali tugging hard on the thin nylon lunge line. Next time I will use a thicker, cotton line and work him far from the gate, down in the corner. Who knows? Maybe I'll actually get on him.

October 7, 1999

Tomorrow was another day. The high winds had abated, and the sun was warm enough. With both Barb and Gilles looking on, Dali was more his old self. Gilles lunged him at first, and they fought a little, especially when Gilles asked him to go the other direction from the one he had been going.

"I don't want to be fighting him all the time," I told Gilles. "I want all this to be soft." Then Barb thought she'd give it a try.

Barb deployed the same ground work she had used on Dali all summer long. She would ask him to go round one way, using her hand rather than the whip to keep him going. Then she would stop him with a *whoa*, let him come in, change the lunge to the other side then back him using her fingers. And away he went the other way. Nice and easy.

Many elements conspired to make yesterday woeful. High winds made him hot. (Chris Irwin says wind can leave the horse worried that his senses can't be trusted: Wind distorts the horse's sense of smell and hearing and puts branches in motion, offering cover for predators. The horse, feeling vulnerable and thus high-strung, believes his best defence is to stay in flight.) Factor in, too, new ring, separation from his paddock mate, increased grass and grain rations, and finally, and perhaps most important, my own inexperience. What was I doing holding a whip in my hand when Dali was so hot that he cantered from the get-go? I should have dropped the thing. Got him into a walk. Taken my time. Gone slow.

"If a horse is acting up when you bring him in from the paddock, make him work," advised Gilles. Get him circling, stopping and starting, walking over poles. Don't just haul him to the cross-ties and hope for the best.

Riding in the ring, I was conscious of Gilles's eyes on me as I posted, softly now, my stirrups lower, my hands over the horse's mane. Gilles saw a world of difference and Dali was clearly grateful.

"What I'm coming to realize," I told Barb and Gilles later, "is that training a horse is like baking a cake. Except the cake is never done." It is what has taken me most by surprise about working with a young horse. How things can get worse before they get better, how issues you thought resolved crop up again like weeds in a garden, how the horse burns a hole in your soul. It seems I will need to emulate Barb's softness, Gilles's firmness. Dali occasionally needs to have his chains rattled, and yet there is no sense in coming at him. He needs assurance and a kindly manner, but he must also respect me. Every day I will have to ask for that. Otherwise, he'll run me over. That's just the way Dali is.

Got a call this evening from Wendy McCullough, a family doctor who rides Ras at Lakehead. A call of welcome and encouragement. Tiny had told me about this woman, who only took up riding a year and a half ago and was now flying over jumps and immersing herself in the world of horses. Ras is a purebred Arabian and a lovable rascal. Together, Wendy and Ras took the top novice trophy on the Ontario competitive trail riding circuit in 1999.

Wendy knew that as a novice trainer I might need to hear of her own perilous journey, the moments of grave second-guessing. Days when she wanted to sell Ras. Days when she feared her ineptitude would ruin him. Times when fear consumed her and she wondered what had ever possessed her to take up horses.

Her assessment of Dali? A handsome horse with a lot of spirit and a great sense of fun. Released into his new paddock a few days ago, he tore around, so much so that Wendy grew alarmed. But later she became convinced he was just glad to be out there, with his grass and his buddy Ras. Wendy went out and spoke to Dali, who got all soft, and when she turned away he followed her around the paddock like a lovestruck puppy.

"Don't get discouraged," she told me. "He's worth it." Someone who hangs out at the stable for hours, she has haltered Dali often in the paddock and come to admire his manners and gentle nature.

Maybe I should keep him after all. . . .

October 8, 1999

I awoke and was not pleased to see a stiff wind tugging at the leaves on the trees outside. I aim to ride Dali, wind or no.

This was a marvellous day in Dali-land, but I do go on learning valuable lessons the hard way. After Wednesday's fiasco, for example, I have learned not to lunge him by the in-gate and to read his mood more carefully. I have learned to insist on respect, so that today as I took him towards the ring and he looked longingly back at the 16-year-old gelding (with whom he has fallen hopelessly in love), I snapped him a little with the shank. Pay attention, I said. Focus on me, not your boyfriend.

Bridling, mounting (using the handy block in the ring) was a dream. The ride, too, had a pleasing feel. Until, that is, I grew cocky at the end and thought I would ride without stirrups, to improve my seat. (My actual seat would not thank me.) As we posted a little quicker, Dali scooted. In a stride he was in a bold canter heading for the gate and I lacked the sense or reflexes to turn him and apply the emergency brake, as I had been practising for weeks; in seconds I bailed out, rolling left off his back as he made a hard right. I landed rudely and squarely where my butt meets my back.

Dali, bless his soul, did not bolt for the barn. He turned into the ring and stopped, then looked back at me. I dusted myself off, touched my back (which felt numb, as if someone had taken a sledge hammer to it), brought him to the mounting block and rode him twice around the ring in a trot. Call it making a point.

Though my back was searing my heart was glad. Dali did not abandon me, did not flee or panic. I may lack brains, but more and more am I convinced I have a good horse.

Some of the women riders in the barn—I am the lone male— have nicknamed him The Kitten. They love how sweet he is, how agreeably he comes to be haltered and led, how calm in the stall.

"I'm not sure I like that nickname," I told Kathi. To which she replied, "Would you rather his nickname was Crazy Horse?"

October 11, 1999

Too sore to ride, I went to the barn just to see my horse. I walked him, brushed him and hand-grazed him in the grass by the barn. He seemed mellow, and perhaps I imagined this, but when I winced after picking up a hoof, I thought I caught a look of alarm in his face. He lifted that front left foot even before I asked for it.

"Thanks, Dali," I told him. "This old guy needs looking after."

My lower back feels like a thick hard Jell-O has formed beneath the skin. A bruise the size of my hand and the colour of a ripe plum has formed above my buttocks. A white V flares at the crease, as if someone had branded the letter in white, now stark against the deep purple. V for what? Victory? More like Vacuous or Vapid. A companion bruise, bigger but fainter, has formed on my right buttock.

It's all quite arresting, and I find myself at bedtime nude and twisted around before my dresser mirror to monitor the strange, almost autumnal progression of the colours.

Four days later my bottom was as sore as the day it happened. I can fake it on the flat, but mounting stairs gives my trouble away. Putting weight on the right foot to ascend a step provokes little stabs of pain in my back. The Jell-O stretches a little, then snaps cruelly back. This rider needs a walker. At home I lean on the banister at a 45-degree angle and lurch up the stairs, longing for the stairway elevator that Katharine Hepburn deployed in the film *Suddenly, Last Summer*.

As I limped around the cabin amid family all Thanksgiving weekend, declining the golf tournament and walking like a codger, I tell all who ask that I did something in my sleep.

There is some truth in that. I was literally asleep at the switch when I decided to ride Dali without lifting up the stirrups and crossing them, and without taking a firmer hand. I have a hunch one of the stirrups, which are large and heavy, hit him hard and he took it as a cue to canter. Looking on the bright side, I wonder if he took the correct lead. At least he was listening.

It has been a week of hard lessons. The third finger on my right hand is still sore, still hot and red, blue and swollen. The cuts on that hand look infected, requiring antiseptic ointment and Band-Aids. Wounded I am, and walking, though barely.

October 13, 1999

The mellow Dali continues to be the one to greet me in the paddock. True, he's looking for the apple I bring him, but he is also content to be scratched under the chin. There is a softness in his eyes, a trust and calm that feel new.

Still too sore to ride him, I did feel up to lunging, which has become routine. I bring the whip but never use it. My voice and clucks are enough to move him. Now and again he shakes his head, but it's a slim version of what he used to give me. I spoke French to him the entire time today, as much out of gratitude as anything.

Today offered one more reminder of Gail Mosher's dictum about the nose horses have for trouble. I was hand-grazing Dali by the barn when he stepped on the shank with his left foot. I tried to ease him back but he raised the foot, caught the tip of his hoof on the halter and in an instant stripped it off. There he stood, startled and uneasy at his freedom, a busy county road not 40 feet away.

Talking to keep him—and me—calm, I slipped the shank over his neck as he bent down once more to his grass, knotted the rope, reset the halter and slipped it on. In a few minutes, my heart stopped pounding and the headlines in my brain ceased to form: "Runaway Horse Killed on Highway . . ."

I was lucky. The Kitten stayed calm.

October 15, 1999
A pattern is revealing itself. Fail to work this horse for a week and you have a lot of horse on your hands. Owing to my sore back, I didn't ride him, though all that time I did lunge him three or four times.

Barb was to ride him today and she was looking on as I lunged him. He seemed dutiful as he circled, but all of a sudden he was up on his hind legs, then scooting around to my right, and I was on the ground spinning like a fisherman's lure behind a powerboat. I was dragged briefly, and from ground level watched the lunge line trailing off across the ring. Dali ran to the paddock gate and parked there, hoping he had ducked some work. Muddied, my finger bloodied (the same one from last week's episode), I retrieved him and went back to lunging.

The ribs on my left side felt sore; the apple I had tucked into my left pocket was crushed. The Kitten had exploded once more. These episodes trouble me less and less, but must there be so many?

After today's antics, Barb taught me how to brace, drawing the lunge line across my body and securing it at the hip. The key is to anticipate these runs of his. She also warned me always to shut the barn door behind me: She drew a mental picture of Dali racing into the barn and catching reins and stirrups on doors and latches.

Barb had picked up on Dali's mood right away. She saw him shaking his head, and her response was quick and instinctive: Control him. "Make him move faster the second he shows sauciness," she told me. "Make him see you noticed, and brace if he runs." We lunged him long, maybe 15 minutes or more, and Barb had me changing pace often, bringing him in then sending him the other way. "No mercy," she said. "Let's keep him busy thinking. He can trot that easy trot all day. It's changing pace that tires him out."

But even after all that, Barb still saw friskiness. "I'm just going to sack him a little," she said, and tossed her jacket against his chest, over the saddle and against his flank. He jumped a little. He jumped again when Barb moved suddenly, bouncing an inch high off the ground, and she stayed on her invisible pogo stick until he more or less stopped reacting. The sacking was an old lesson. The standing jumps were new.

"We can't be pussyfooting around this horse," she told me. "Act like he's a real quiet horse and he will be quiet. But if you tiptoe around him all the time . . ."

Gerry Grooms had remarked on the phone that morning how Dali had startled when some hay was dumped in his stall. Gerry felt the need to talk to him, calm him.

Later, when Barb was up in the saddle, I asked her, "How is he?"

"He's thinking," she replied. "But so am I."

There was mischief written all over him. Barb worked on turning his head, keeping it bent till he went soft, releasing the reins as reward.

"When you turn him like that," she told me, "you're reminding him that you have control. And he knows it."

She had to work hard to keep him to the outside, fighting his tendency to cut into the middle by using her leg. Then she would bring him to a circle stop and send him out again.

"This is a horse you want to respond to you," Barb said as she was leaving. "You don't want him reacting to things around him, you want him responding to his rider."

Back or no back, I intend to ride him each day for the next five days. Take some of the cat out of The Kitten.


October 16, 1999

I feel sluggish and flu-ridden and my back aches. I actually dreaded going to the stable. Did that sick feeling in the pit of my stomach perhaps owe something to a fever I once contracted in North Africa and occasionally must battle? Or was it the prospect of battling a bay named Dark Fox Dali?

As Barb had suggested, I kept Dali guessing on the lunge line. I hung the line on the buckle just under his chin so I could easily change directions. I altered pace and direction, especially if I sensed him getting hot. After 15 minutes, he seemed focused and soft.

The ride went well and it offered a true test for several reasons. A stiff wind replicated conditions of the other day; and some people were training sheepdogs on their flocks in the adjacent field, which lent some adrenalin to the day. Dali eyed those sheep and the darting border collies, and seemed not keen to hug the south side of the ring.

We worked it out. He earned his apple. Even my back was grateful.


October 18, 1999

With the ring too wet, I opted to take Dali to the hay field, where three cows showed little interest in us and Dali reciprocated with ambivalence of his own.

He lunged passably, but he still shakes his head by times and ambles into his trot. Next time I might bring the whip and just hold it to see if he respects it. It's all about reading him; I want no repeat of him bolting off the lunge line and me taking what Gilles called "flying lessons." But neither am I happy with his petulance, the little acts of rearing a foot off the ground.

He rode well but he felt heavy near the end, and I wondered if the footing was tiring him out. I quit then, determined to make his first foray into the field a pleasant one.

And it was pleasant. A fall day, the sun casting shadows from the few oaks at the edge of the field, the sodden earth absorbing Dali's footfall, the space so quiet you could hear the dry reeds rustling. This was more like what I dreamed of when I dreamed of owning a horse. Coasting across a big field, cows for company, riding towards a warm setting sun. A man and his horse.

October 20, 1999

With my horse so much in my thinking, a good day has become, by definition, a good day with Dali. And this was another one.

"You guys are making progress," Barb said from the centre of the ring. It was yet another windy day and himself had been prancy in the cross-ties, worrying about banging doors and the whine of power tools as Gerry worked on the barn. But Dali calmed. That right hind foot went into rest mode. Even the rain that suddenly blew in just as suddenly left, and we had the sun again.

He was mellow on the lunge line, sometimes too mellow. One time he jumped into action and I heard Barb yell at me to brace, but when I looked over she was laughing. She had induced the spook by jumping on her pogo stick as Dali passed.

"You be sure and do that when I'm in the saddle," I rebuked her.

In the schooling, Dali was soft. He stops wonderfully. Even the canter work wasn't bad. All in all, a fine day. Now I'm off to the Maritimes for three days to meet some other Canadian horses and their handlers, so I may have my hands full Sunday afternoon. I'm praying it won't rain.

October 27, 1999

Today was yet another of those days I had hoped for when I determined to buy a horse. One of those near-perfect fall days when the leaves are almost gone but so are the horse-, house-, and deer flies that make you and perhaps your horse actually long for winter. The crisp little edge that came with this morning's wind has been banished by the noon sun. You're moving through forests and open fields on horseback, feeling blissfully apart from, yet at one with, the world.

Wendy had called me mid-morning. After near burnout, she now practises medicine about two-thirds of the time, having decided that riding and Ras merit at least some of the other third. Would I like to deke out for a trail ride?

I had no idea how all this was going to go. Would Dali spook at the three cows he had snorted at earlier as they lounged outside the ring? Would he balk at crossing streams? And just how friendly were he and Ras anyway?

Later in the ride Wendy told me that three other horses—like Dali, new horses on their first trip past the back field—had been so nervous they had to turn back. I hoped for better: little wind, Dali calm, his paddock mate for company. Conditions for that first trail ride seemed right.

There was real spring in his step. His ears were forward, and he was animated. Ras, notoriously hydrophobic, balked at crossing the first stream. Dali expressed no initial desire to cross it either, and I had worried that his habit of dancing around mud pies in the sand ring would make water on the trail a headache. But then he crossed almost without hesitation.

The trail, and this augurs well for future rides, is fabulous. Plenty of clean, long two-track paths to trot and canter, lovely little trails snaking through pine or maple forest, and in one clearing a derelict limestone house and its ornament—a blue '69 Merc easing earthward, bushes pouring out the side windows like green filigreed smoke.

So calm was Dali on this trail he had never seen before that he took to snacking, often timing his moves. Once I leaned over to stroke his neck and he chose that moment to bite a leaf. Even white cedar and white pine seemed delectable to him.

After despairing of him, I could have kissed him. The crowning touch was how sensible he was when we came the back way into Kathie Groenewegen's sprawling horse farm. There was much for Dali to be wary of: huge circular bales of hay wrapped in white plastic and glistening in the sun, all manner of farm machinery, horses prancing in paddocks. Dali snorted and checked everything out, but never lost his cool.

In the outdoor ring, Wendy offered me a choice: take the back way through the fields to Lakehead, a 10-minute ride, or walk five minutes along Sydenham Road, a busy county road. This gave me pause, but then, we had been riding for two hours and Dali had remained steadfast and calm. So I walked him in the deep ditch along the road, coming up to the gravel for the last 50 metres. The sheep by the fence gave him pause, but only a little. Traffic, even the big water truck that roared past, bothered him not at all.

Wendy was terribly impressed by Dali's composure. As was I.

October 28, 1999

"He seems to save his antics for when somebody's around," Barb observed today, with her usual raucous laugh.

She was looking on as I lunged him, then decided to step in when she observed him "gawking" at the sheep and other horses, or perhaps not moving with anything like the alacrity she wanted. She got him going all right. His head came up, he got prancy, but Barb read him perfectly. He wasn't in a bolting mood, just a full-of-himself mood.

In mid-lesson, me up, Dali spooked at something down in the corner. I got a little left and a right and a do-si-do. Once more, the wind had sparked fire in him. But like Wendy, I'm starting to find these shenanigans amusing. They come like storms in the desert; the rain barely lands before the clouds disappear.

Barb put Dali's current state rather well. "There's nothing on the trail he's scared of. He's still more worried about you up in the saddle. And that means you have to be his number one. If he's looking off at sheep and not paying attention to you and he spooks and finds himself in a jam, he'll hold you responsible for that. He needs you to look after him." My task is clear. Save Dali from Dali.

November 1, 1999

Rode on the trail again on Saturday, with Wendy and Ras. Dali was more up this time, at least in the beginning. I tacked him up at the south end of the stable, not his usual place at the north end, and there was much to-ing and fro-ing around him. Gerry and Lil and their helper, Barbara, were cleaning stalls and moving newborn calves. Dali snorted his displeasure.

But on the trail he was once again superb. He lets me know of wildlife in the bush, and he gave great pause when we chanced across a young cat. We even got a canter in at the end, cutting across a hayfield.

I conveyed all this today to cousin Kathi and she was overjoyed to hear it. "Don't be too quick to take him out on the trail by yourself," was her only advice. As usual, good advice, and I was well in step this time.

Lil's daughter, Kathie Groenewegen, a fine horsewoman in her own right, calls my cousin Poke—as in Pocahontas, a nickname that remembers her pigtails as a girl and that all her friends know her by. Kathie G. says my cousin is unlike anyone she knows in terms of her instincts for horses, her ability to size them up and know them. "It's almost scary," said Kathie G. as she showed me the indoor ring where I will ride Dali this winter.

I remember two things my cousin said when she first saw Dali: the remark about his sturdiness, the other about his inner calm, how she thought she could ride him down Princess (Kingston's main street) without any problem.

An overstatement, but I'll say it again: I am pleased he takes to the trail so keenly. "He's very brave," said Wendy on Saturday, who has watched a parade of horses come undone at new wrinkles, new trails, new riders.

November 9, 1999

Another day of high wind at Lakehead, yet mild. So mild the flies had returned, and what I took to be impatience on Dali's part as he stood in the cross-ties and stomped his front foot was actually the little blighters. Dali seemed happy to see the green bottle of fly spray coming his way.

I find myself talking to him now like I talk to Dusty. He's more trusting, lets me fuss with his head when there's mud there, lets me clean around his eyes. He has even stopped whinnying to his buddy Ras when I tack him up. The new Dali?

November 17, 1999

This new Dali is not keen—or not yet anyway—on roads and traffic. If, as the phrase has it, "seven falls makes a rider," I am well on my way.

Dali seemed laid-back during lunging in the ring, but as soon as we departed from schooling routine and joined Ras and Wendy heading out the front door of the stable and into the grassy ditch that runs beside Sydenham Road, I could see him grow agitated. Flurries were forecast and a stiff breeze blew. Dali had not been ridden in five days, weather and the farrier intervening. He was up.

Our destination was the Keppler side road, a hundred metres north past the stable, so we'd have a minute's walk along Sydenham Road, a veritable highway where cars and trucks travel at up to 100 kilometres an hour.

Dali's walking pace quickened. Having to brave traffic is simply part of his and my education, but I do wish these were all quiet back roads. The position of my stable in relation to the indoor ring a kilo-metre away means we'll have two options this winter: walk 5 min-utes along Sydenham Road or 15 minutes through back fields. My nightmare is Dali loose on Sydenham Road with a truck bearing down on him.

Today he was perilously loose near that road—twice.

Dali was afraid: the cars too close, the stretch of black pave-ment too unfamiliar, he too fresh from his layoff, the sound of his own new metal shoes on the tarmac unnerving him. And so he reverted to an old evasion: He scooted as I mounted him. In hind-sight, I should have walked him farther on.

There were a lot of *should-haves*: On mounting, I should have grabbed some mane (just in case), for he did give me warning. The first time I tried to get on him he moved sideways, which he hadn't done in months. He was clearly telling me something was not right, and I failed to heed the sign. I should have backed him up, restored calm, walked him down the road and away from the sound of traf-fic. Finally, I should have ridden him beforehand in the ring.

In any case, he dashed forward the moment I mounted him and he headed for Sydenham Road. For that was the direction I had him pointed; one more pilot error.

I tried to bend forward and grab the left rein, make that one-rein circle stop. At least I was remembering the right thing to do. But his propulsion kept me behind the motion, back in the saddle and, in seconds, off the saddle. I remember a real estate signpost looming just ahead of us, Dali veering hard to the right, me coming out of the saddle and turning in the air so my back now aimed for that post. I waited for the sound of a crack, from my spine or that square cedar pole.

Somehow I missed the post and there was no crack, but now I was on the ground, on my back, and looking up into the loins of my horse. Dali must have circled, come back. It was like being prone on the tarmac as a 747 swept noiselessly over you. I wondered if he

would scuff my brow with his hooves as he passed, or worse. He did
not. I felt instant gratitude. And my landing on thick grass was almost
pleasant. I now had other falls to compare this one with, and it
seemed I had drifted down.

But Dali had sped on a few metres and I wanted desperately
for him to stay where he was. I got to my feet and called out his
name. He stayed put, though his eyes were far too wide and white
and the sound of road traffic seemed to get louder as I slowly walked
towards him. Would he scoot for the safety of his stable? Or just
panic and run?

I never took my eyes off him. I was afraid of what might come
barrelling around that curve, though I imagined the worst: a septic
tanker late for a pumping appointment, an 18-wheeler with a
foghorn, a Winnebago festooned with flags, a Harley with the muf-
fler off. I feared this was a turning point, some terrible moment in
the play where I had been cast as a central character. My own tragi-
comic *Equus of the North*.

Years ago while visiting my sister in British Columbia at her
riverfront home, it became suddenly apparent to her and to me,
before I had even had my morning coffee, that her older boy, then
seven, had broken a cardinal rule of those who live by rivers: He had
left his five-year-old brother down there. Like the sound of the traffic off Sydenham Road, the roar of the spring-swollen river could be
heard even inside the house. My sister went pale and silent. She may
have simply mouthed my name in whispered horror, beseeching me
in some nameless way, though of this I cannot be sure. Theresa's husband, Ken, a commercial fisherman, was up the coast and so it would
fall to me to go down to the river.

I remember my descent down that steep riverbank, shirtless and
barefoot, sliding feet first through the tangle of brush and plopping
into waist-deep water. There, only feet away, was my nephew, looking into a whirlpool as if into a mirror. "Trevor, don't you move!"
I shrieked at him, which had the desired effect. Then I slowly walked

towards him through the water and plucked him from the rock.

Dali loose by the highway had the same prosaic ending as nephew alone by the river. Dali stood sideways to me and let me come to him. I remember grabbing a stirrup (not the wisest of grips) because it was closest to me, then the reins. This is one of the good things about the Canadian horse I often call "mon vieux" in imitation of Gilles Dupuis: He dumps me, then stands stock-still with a shocked look on his face. "How did you get down there, you crazy Anglo?" I led him on a little farther and got on him.

Later, as I described the day's events to cousin Kathi, she described a phenomenon of delayed stress called "payback": Your horse on a cross-country course vaults the tough jump but balks at the easy one that follows. "It could be that his first shoeing was more traumatic than he let on," she said. "He was saying, 'Something's not right here.'"

We talked more about the marriage I have embarked on: green rider on green horse and how that's usually a recipe for disaster. "But you're such a student of the game. You think about it day and night. You'll be all right. Just ease up a bit the next few days."

"Sometimes I wish I'd bought an old plug," I told Kathi. "This horse is way more horse than I'm used to." "Yeah," she countered, "but who'd want to read about that? Too boring." Then she made some joke about me borrowing her husband's body protector, a flak jacket meant to soften hard landings.

For the rest of the trail ride that day, Dali had lots of go and not much whoa. In the ring I can stop him with my seat alone, even from a trot; adding a *whoa* brings him to a shuddering and not terribly elegant halt. It's not so much a smooth transition—trot to walk to stop—as it is a collapse into an invisible glass wall. It's so sudden I invariably pitch forward a little as he splays out those front feet, like a horse in a cartoon.

But this day he wanted no part of that and I turned him on one rein about a dozen times trying to restore a disciplined pause in his forward motion. It worked only occasionally. His mind was elsewhere.

Like him, I did not much enjoy having to travel so long on pavement. The passage of a tractor pulling a load of hay unnerved him somewhat and we deked into a driveway; a hundred metres on, we again encountered the tractor, idling now alongside two border collies who monitored our passage. Nice doggies. This was not the trail I longed for. Eventually we came to rights-of-way, a 50-acre field and the gem on this route: an old railway bed as straight as a nail but soft underfoot and stretching off through marshland to either horizon. You could put your horse into long canters or gallops and be dead sure of the ground.

At the end of the ride, I dismounted at the same place I got tossed. Another mistake, for Dali visibly remembered his last time here. He had no interest in stopping, but when he did, I dismounted, perhaps too quickly, and slipped on the pavement in those western boots of mine, falling backward until I was flat on my back. The reins got long as Dali—who wore a look of incredulity that said "Now what?!"—pulled back until finally I could hold no longer. He was loose yet again. I cursed my ineptitude. This time he simply joined Ras; Wendy grabbed his reins. It's acutely embarrassing having to chronicle all this. Lawrence of Arabia riding his first camel surely had less trouble.

By now, owing to the three-hour ride and the stress of my tumbles and the traffic, Dali was extremely wet beneath his girth. I put his sheet on for the first time and walked him for half an hour trying to cool him out; he was still wet. I towelled him another 10 minutes and we decided to park him in his stall. Wendy brought in Bogi, the old grey in the stall next door, to keep him company.

Just when I think I am reading this horse well, he holds up a big sign that says "I'm afraid" and I don blinkers. The third finger on my right hand, the one that bears the stress of the reins, has yet to recover from the lunging incident. Now it's a swollen red curl clamouring for ice. Later I would discover a welt and a small cut on the lower left side of my back; it seems I made contact with that post after all.

Still, I ducked several bullets today. My body hurts like the devil, and my spirits are low, but the angel assigned to me continues to watch over me and my horse.

# CHAPTER 13

# THE CANADIAN HORSE AS SPORT HORSE

*"The American trotting horse is an American creation. The material has been taken from various sources, but more largely from the short, quick-stepping French-Canadians than from any other source."*
—National Live Stock Journal, 1881

THE WORLD SINGLES DRIVING CHAMPIONSHIPS were slated for Gladstone, New Jersey, on October 18, 2000, with some 60 entries from 22 countries anticipated. Plans had been under way for two years. The chosen site was Hamilton Farm, a splendid 5,000-acre complex with a rich tradition of carriage competition. I had my own reasons for wanting to go: the lead Canadian entry was a gifted Canadian horse. Here, I thought, was an international showcase for an

Above: Navigator Ken Mott, driver Sue Mott and Caesar at Ste-Justine de Newton.

almost forgotten breed. A win would boost its prospects and perhaps lend a storybook flourish to *Little Horse of Iron*.

Alas, at the eleventh hour, a mosquito brought everything to a resounding halt. Some carriages were already en route from Europe on September 19 when organizers took the agonizing decision to cancel the event. Outbreaks of West Nile virus in the United States and France meant that no one could guarantee the safety of competing horses.

After a rigorous, two-year-long selection process, Canada had planned to send a team comprising three entries, including the lead driver Sue Mott, who lives just north of Toronto. Her horse? Du Coteau Lalou Caesar, a purebred Canadian horse. Mott and Caesar had already beaten the American entries on several occasions, and while she was cagey about their prospects against European competition, I was privately pulling for a grand victory: individual honours for Mott and Caesar, team honours for the three Canadian entries.

And as Sue Mott described what an odyssey it's been training this challenging horse, I took sustenance. My horse and hers sounded like brothers, but Caesar, at the age of seven, had blossomed and seemed poised for a real shot at a world championship.

Consider his record. In the two years leading up to the world championship, Caesar and Mott entered 14 advanced competitions, earning 10 top-three finishes in dressage. In 2000, the tandem won both Gladstone, the most prestigious event on the continent's combined driving circuit, and the Laurels, site of the North American single horse championship. Those two victories helped earn Mott the Jaguar Triple Crown and a handsome prize—an all-expense-paid trip to the Royal Windsor Horse Show in England in May 2001 and the use of a new Jaguar while there. (Regrettably, the show was cancelled owing to the outbreak in Britain of hoof and mouth disease.)

Caesar's future is bright. He would have been among the youngest, if not the youngest, horse competing at the world championship. And the spare horse in that competition was to have been another Canadian horse, Zenith, a mare owned by Bill Graham.

"I've thought of you often in the past year," I told Mott on the phone when the news broke of the cancellation. We had talked about a year and a half earlier when she was selling two Canadian horses, but her price was too steep for me. "I've spent so much on trainers for my green horse," I told her, "that I might have been better off buying one of your fully trained models."

Mott described Caesar as a 16.1-hand, black gelding with heaps of attitude. "He's quite domineering, with a strong personality, but he's kind and easy to work around." That was not the case when she got him at the age of three.

Jean-Paul Gauthier, a friend who had competed with Canadian horses at the world championship level, had heard she was looking for horses. One on the farm of Germain Laberge at Thurso, Quebec, caught his eye. She describes the scene:

"Germain has an interesting farm, with more than two hundred horses. After foals are weaned, he halter trains them and then lets them run free until the age of about two and a half to three and then he hitches them up to a sleigh to break them. Caesar had pulled a sleigh but he was wary of men. Even to touch his legs and pick up his feet was impossible. There were wolves in the area and he was very handy with his back feet.

"When I first saw him it was 30 below, the snow was up to his knees, and he had all this hair. But Jean-Paul saw something that I could not and I simply trusted his judgment." Mott had lots of experience with ponies and warmbloods but this was her first Canadian. She bought Caesar and two others that day.

At home she got Udo Hochgeschurz to begin the task of training him to drive. This coach, with all his experience, said Caesar was unlike any horse he had ever worked with.

"Caesar was so bull headed," said Mott. "He had a watchful eye and it was months before we could even pick up his feet. There were times we thought it wasn't worth going on. We'd take a few steps forward and then a couple back." But by moving slowly, with lots of ground work, walking and lunging, they did make progress and in 1999 everything began to click. Caesar's extensions got better from all the work they did with cavalletti poles raised up to 18 inches off the ground. "He got lighter on his feet," says Mott. "He used to sound like 10 horses coming down the road."

Caesar's inner calm and great mind have become his great strengths. While the warmbloods have the natural gaits, they are prone to fretting. "He has opened a lot of people's eyes," says Mott. "The Americans love him. One wants to buy him but I've told him the horse is not for sale. He's so elegant but still so big and powerful."

Living in an age of specialization, we lose sight of what true versatility means.

A versatile horse, for example, is one we can all admire, but our first instinct is to lower our expectations of that horse. For surely the price of great range must be paid in performance. A decent carriage horse might also serve as a child's saddle horse, but surely it would be asking too much to have him haul logs during the week and then race him against elite trotters and pacers on the weekend. The historical record of the Canadian horse bids us think again.

If, as now seems likely, the Canadian has rebounded from obscurity, the breed's versatility deserves some of the credit. Canadians today are used to pull show carriages, to plough fields, as trail and distance horses, even in show jumping and dressage. In 1999, the winning show jumper at the Jeux du Québec (the Quebec Games) was a Canadian stallion who weighs more than 1,200 pounds and who works all winter in the bush hauling firewood for his rider.

The Canadian breed's range was evident almost from the very beginning. The Canuck, as the Americans called him, came from France as a warhorse; farm duties called on his power, but soon enough his speed was recognized. *Habitants* earned a reputation as fast and reckless drivers and, whether deserved or not, modern Quebecers are still tarred, 300 years later, with that same brush.

The racing of horses in Canada goes back almost to the day that Louis XIV sent horses across the Atlantic. The first races, in defiance of laws against it, occurred between horse-drawn *carrioles* after Mass or on Montreal streets.

Riders in New France were just as enamoured of speed. Pedestrians were forever being run down, until finally an ordinance was passed that fined a rider 10 *livres* (pounds) plus costs for every person he knocked down. Racing even occurred at night, so much so that laws were passed forbidding it out of concern for horse stock. These laws, too, were ignored.

By 1739, New France had almost 10,000 horses for a population that still only numbered 44,000. The French governor became concerned that all these horses were more about sport than farm work. And no doubt he had a point. Inevitably, the friendly racing took on an edge. Someone would brag that his horse was faster than another, and out of nowhere, like a seed on the wind, a bookie would materialize to take wagers. Army officers took to racing horse-drawn sleighs and by 1760 horse racing was well established in Quebec society.

Historian David Street describes how devoted, and daring, the *habitants* were in racing on ice.

> At every possible opportunity from small gatherings of friends to more formal festive occasions, the French horses would gallop at full speed across the ice, racing cariole [sic] against cariole [sic] on the treacherous surfaces of river and lake. It was a common, and sad, sight to see horses with broken legs. Those who escaped the ice races unharmed were expected to stand steaming in the freezing winds, without blankets or covers, waiting patiently to pull the farmer and his family back to the homestead at full pace.

Even when visiting neighbours, Street wrote, farmers drove recklessly.

After France's defeat on the Plains of Abraham, the English took up racing with similar relish: the Quebec Turf Club would establish its track in 1789 right on the battleground. The English, too, had tried banning racing in the streets several decades earlier and had had about as much luck as their French predecessors.

The British had known horse racing since the 17th century, and by 1764 Quebec City had a "raceground." The *Quebec Gazette* published the first recorded racing results on July 9, 1767. A mare named Mondesty, owned by a Captain Prescott, took home the $40 prize. By 1808, races in Quebec City drew up to 4,000 spectators, or one-quarter of the city's inhabitants.

The Canadian horse was already known for his uncommon strength and endurance, his resilience and vigour. He lacked the pure speed of the American trotter but it became clear that crossbreeding the two types created a superior horse.

The Americans, especially as their road network developed in the 19th century, had need of good roadsters. The Canadian fit that bill perfectly, and it proved a small step from there to the track.

After the War of 1812, the trade in French-Canadian horses took off, and by 1830 most of the trotters in the northern United States were of French-Canadian origin. Smart breeders came to realize that crossing Canadians with even ordinary stock produced superior horses. The stagecoach drivers of Boston clamoured for them, and Canadian crosses there fell into legend.

Meanwhile, the Canadian pacer, a blend of the Narragansett Pacer from Rhode Island and the old strains of the French-Canadian horse, contributed mightily to that doyen of the racetrack: the famous American standardbred.

Here is the *National Live Stock Journal* of 1881:

> The American trotting horse is an American creation.
> The material has been taken from various sources,

but more largely from the short, quick-stepping French-Canadians than from any other source. We run against the Canuck blood almost everywhere in our trotting pedigrees. . . . The Kentucky trotting pedigrees are full of it. . . . New York trotting pedigrees are full of it. . . . The New England pedigrees are full of it . . . and in Mr. Thompson's excellent work on Maine-bred Horses, you encounter this Canuck blood on almost every page.

The celebrated sons of Rysdyk's Hambletonian, Bruno and the Brother of Bruno, and their full sister, Brunette, were all out of a Canadian mare. Bruno, especially, was astonishingly fast for his time. Gift, a chestnut gelding by Mambrino Pilot, was out of a small pacing Canuck. His owner issued a challenge through *Spirit of the Times*, a track publication, to run against him for a $1,000 purse. There were no takers. The bay stallion St. Lawrence was another notably fast trotter. Other Canadians who achieved fame in their day included Copperbottom, Daniel Boone, Drennon, Corbeau, St. Clair, Smuggler, Clearbit and Blue Bull.

Perhaps the most famous Canadian was Pilot, whom legend has crossing the border into the United States pulling a pedlar's cart. One historian, Charles Plumb, says Pilot was foaled in 1828 in Quebec; he died in 1853 on the farm of Robert Bell, near Henderson, Kentucky. "He bred," writes Plumb, "both pacers and trotters and rendered valuable service to the American racing horse interests."

Pilot was a black horse, 14 hands high, with a heavy mane and tail and a somewhat nasty disposition. Several of his owners were afraid of him. Observers of the day also commented on his remarkable power, far in excess of his size. "The little black ram," he was often called.

What set Pilot apart, in a state renowned for the wealth of its stud farms, was his prepotency. Mares of all breeds were brought to him and he passed on to his sons and daughters his own great stamina and vigour. Historians of trotting may know these names: Tecumseh, Roanaki, Nigger Baby, Native, Pilot Jr., Tom Crowder, Old Tecumseh, Ole Bull, Young's Pilot and Chew's Pilot. All could trace their bloodlines back to Pilot and all produced many fine trotters and pacers.

Plumb also refers to a horse bred in Canada called Kittrel's Tom Hal: "It is said that he was much abused in his time and was ridden nearly to death over rocky roads by a drunken wretch in an elm-crotch saddle." He was the sire of various Hals and the famous Little Brown Jug. Another of his offpsring, Brown Hal, sired Star Pointer, a legend in the pacer family.

From dashes home after Mass, to Kentucky racetracks, from farm horse to sport horse. It seems an unlikely trajectory. Today, the Canadian still competes with the best, but now the sport is combined driving.

They call it combined driving because the carriage sport combines three events: dressage, navigating around cones and other obstacles, and a cross-country marathon that may go as long as 20 kilometres. In dressage, judges consider these and other matters: the horse's obedience, the correctness of his gaits and transitions, his harmony, suppleness and freedom of movement. In the obstacle course, the challenge appears simple: keep cones and balls up. Finally, the marathon tests the ability of horse and driver to travel at an even speed, although quickness is essential when travelling through obstacle zones since each second spent there counts as a fault.

In advanced-level competitions, a navigator on board may keep three stop-watches: one running forward (to compare the team's time at each kilometre marker with the ideal); one running backward (starting at the maximum time allowed, so the team knows how much time is left); and a third stopwatch at the ready (to record any time delays caused by other competitors). One can imagine the discussions that occur between driver and navigator on a tension-filled course. Late in May 1999, I spent a day at Ste-Justine de Newton, just inside the Quebec border at southeastern Ontario. My aim was to learn more about the sport and the Canadian horse's role in it.

The competition—at Windedge Farm, an elegant equestrian complex just outside the village—marked the first time that an FEI (Fédération Equestre Internationale) sanctioned event in combined driving had taken place in Canada. Combined driving looks like such a genteel sport: the women in natty little hats with feathers, men and women in driving aprons, leather gloves, bowler hats and ribbon ties. The elegant carriages are always polished and gleaming.

But the day before, during the cross-country event, two carriages, including one driven by Bill Graham, who uses Canadian horses, flipped. No one was badly hurt, and Graham's horse, Zenith, did not panic or bolt, but stopped after about five paces. The carriage was righted and Graham and his navigator finished the course, but the mishaps serve to counter the notion that the sport lacks risk.

I remember Maxine Kumin, the Pulitzer Prize-winning American poet, once telling me that her family worried about her competing in driving events in her seventies. Every show, it seemed, somebody's cart went over. But even their worst fears could not have conjured what happened in the summer of 1998. A loose horse at a competition triggered a traumatic memory for her horse, Deuter, who bolted. Kumin's moving book, *Inside the Halo and Beyond*, describes her brush with death and the terrible ordeal of her recovery. The "halo" of the title refers to the contraption of metal cage, screws and bolts that housed her skull for months.

Kumin's book ends with her finally being able to mount and sit Deuter, whom she utterly forgave for his bolt. She had thought the moment of rising onto his back would feel like an epiphany. "Instead," she writes, "I feel merely at home. I am back in my peaceful kingdom."

In his immaculate grey fedora and matching moustache, Graham looked at the Ste-Justine competition like an actor about to walk onto the set of a Victorian-era film. He only came to the sport six years ago and here he is: president of the Canadian Driving Society and enamoured of the Canadian horse.

Graham came to horses very late (even later than I did) and now, at the age of 64, he competes in combined driving at the world-class level. He had just returned from two months of competition in the U.S. "There's a love affair building down there between Americans and the Canadian horse," he told me on the phone a few days before the competition. He also sang the praises of his mare, Zenith, who was content to stand stock-still for the better part of an hour while passersby patted her and she patiently waited her turn. But when it came, "she was a piece of dynamite."

Graham loves the temperament of the Canadian horse. And he is astonished that despite their low numbers, the breed has an out-standing record in international competition. He cited the case of Morris Kerr recently winning with a Canadian horse in Gladstone, that mecca for combined drivers. Graham and I chatted only briefly, for his duties at the show weighed heavily on him, but we agreed to connect later.

It struck me, as I wandered the grounds at Ste-Justine de Newton, that there is something a little incongruous about the sport of combined driving. For one thing, the carriages being pulled by one or two or four or more horses are taken over carefully groomed ground. This means that the natural partner to all these 19th century images of horses and carriages—the clip-clop of hooves on cobblestone—is missing. And in one competition, called "the cones," these horse-drawn carriages, throwbacks to another time, are asked to go through pairs of very modern, very bright icons: the fluourescent-orange markers favoured by construction and utility crews all over North America. Little balls half filled with water are set atop the cones and any carriage wheel that comes too close to the cone causes the ball, or the cone itself, to fall. Each such incident costs the driver five faults.

What looks easy is not. Let the horses out too much and the speed has ramifications on the sometimes serpentine course. The carriage begins to snake a little, skid sideways, maybe casting up earth or creating a minor seismographic tremor at the base of the cone: Balls come tumbling down.

I was struck by something Chris Irwin, the horse gentler, said about combined driving when he gave a clinic near Ottawa in the summer of 1999. It hit me like a revelation, for I had always looked down upon the carriage sport as the quaint preserve of wealthy eccentrics. Those costly rigs, those top hats, all that harness and the sound of those bells. It was about showmanship, not horsemanship. Wasn't it?

"You want to see world-class equitation?" Irwin asked his audience. "Go see world-class combined driving. See if *you* can keep a horse in a buggy going in a 20-metre circle. And if you can't, *bow*."

The sport, a throwback to a time when a farmer had to know how to hitch a team and the horse was the real engine of the farm, has its own arcane language. On a six-horse team, for example, the pairs are called leaders, swingers and wheelers, depending on their position. The working of the drivers' hands, merely to execute a turn, seems profoundly complicated. Those hands must be delicate, connected as they are to all this: tons of horseflesh (the big Belgians can go 19 hands and weigh 2,600 pounds), up to 900 pounds of leather harness and 230 feet of line. Guiding young Dali across a field, an adventure itself in the early days, pales in comparison.

In pleasure driving, the range of carts is dizzying: gig carts, spider phaetons, buckboards, doctor's buggies, park drags, stagecoaches. From Terry Veevers's video on competitive driving, *The Box Seat*, I learned that Harry Witteveen, a Dutch-born driver from St. George, Ontario, trains in a little cart derived from an old Fiat car.

There were lots of Canadian horses at Ste-Justine de Newton. Carole Dailley, sister-in-law of Ginny Dailley, was here with a black Canadian mare called Doris. I counted seven altogether, some with wonderful names: Morris Kerr drove Jimmy Peach; Sue Mott took a fifth place with Caesar; Gérard Lambert drove Africa and Chivas (what, no Regal?).

Peter Taws, a member of the show committee at Ste-Justine, told me the sport of combined driving had almost disappeared a few years ago. Now it's come roaring back. I wonder why. Is it aging boomers looking for an elegant horse sport that forgives soft bellies and weak backs? It seems a sport neither for the young or the impecunious. These carriages can cost $20,000 and $30,000, and the horses did not look cheap either. Then there's the cost of a trailer big enough to accommodate horses and carriages, plus the cost in fuel.

Competitors came to Ste-Justine de Newton from as far away as Pennsylvania, Massachusetts, South Carolina, Indiana, Florida, Manitoba and Alberta. Taws told me that 20 years ago Prince Philip broke his arm in a polo accident and took up this sport while he recuperated. Blame the royals then?

Kirsten Brunner, Patricia Cooper's instructor, did well today: a clean performance and third overall in the advanced single horse competition. Kirsten's mother, Erica Brunner, was once quoted thus in a magazine piece about driving: "You develop a very special relationship with your horse—in this sport, trust is everything. In riding, you can use your body, you have the horse between your legs. In driving, it's all in the reins, in the hands."

For hours I sat in a lawn chair with Terry and Walter Hellyer and Greg Mackenzie and heard them discuss the merits of light versus heavy carriages, how to navigate through those cones (it's not so different from lining up the left bumper of your car with the white line), which pairs they liked and what the head carriage of the horses told them.

This is a sport about obsession. Imagine the days of preparation, the hours on the road, the early rise—all this for two minutes in the ring. And for all its laid-back atmosphere, there was pressure here. Many of these drivers are trying to earn spots on their national driving teams. The focus in their eyes as they competed was plain.

Despite relatively small numbers in the sport, the Canadian horse has an enviable record in world and continental competition. Two Canadian horses, Nip and Tuck, driven by Gerald McCallum and owned by Alec Hayward and Donnie Prosperine, won the 1987 North American Pleasure Driving Pairs Championship. And in 1997, two Canadian horses won the presentation class at the World Combined Driving Pairs Championship in Germany before 60,000 spectators, beating out entries from 20 other countries.

In that win, Jean-Paul Gauthier of Guelph, with Jane Lyndon as passenger, drove Canadian horses named Asmon and Vélo to victory. Vélo and Asmon are 16 hands plus and weigh 1,400 pounds each. They were selected by Jean-Paul Gauthier, who aimed to show the world that Canadian horses could compete with the best. Judges were assessing the quality of the horses' gait, the conduct of driver, groom and passenger; the physical condition of the horses, their elegance; the condition, style and setup of the harness, the style of carriage and much else.

A month after Ste-Justine de Newton I'm at an auction in the Ottawa Valley. Auctions are typically seen as places where bargains can be had, where neighbours lament the weather and poor crops over chuckwagon coffee, and the auctioneer tries to bully and cajole the gathered into ever higher bids. But seen from the seller's viewpoint, an auction can be a sad event. Possessions amassed over a lifetime are carted off by strangers, sometimes for unconscionably low prices. The "what-am-I-bid, what-am-I-bid" sometimes nets a yawn and forces the rubber-tongued auctioneer to toss another item onto the pile to make it go.

The auction at Frank Prosperine's mother's farm was such a one. The gentle, burly man, who showed every evidence of the Italian blood in his veins, was selling off some 30 carriages, all collected by his father, Donnie, during a lifelong obsession with horses, including Canadians. Donnie's old partner, Alec Hayward, looked on with dismay of his own. Many of those buggies had fond memories attached.

"There's no reserve bid on any of these carriages, save one," he said. "They've all got to go. Whatever the final bid is, that's the price."

Frank had been putting off this day for 10 years, since the day his father died. The will called for the estate to be divided, and not all Frank's siblings shared Donnie and Frank's passion for horses and buggies. The auction had been in the works for weeks and Frank looked exhausted from the effort. He leaned on a cedar-rail fence and gazed off into a north field. "I'll be glad," he said, "when this day is over."

A hundred or so people, standing in small circles under the shade tents or sitting in the buggies themselves, looked on as the auction circle followed the auctioneer from a hay wagon to old ploughs set on the ground and towards the tack-laden tables.

Most of the stuff went for a song. All a preamble to the gems of the sale. There was a black surrey built around 1890, a cutter, a mountain wagon, a trap, a pony wagon and a vis-à-vis—all from the same era. There was a sleek green "rockaway" once used in the filming of a movie and pulled by Maggie, one of Donnie's black Canadian mares. There was a dump cart, a Concord buggy, a swan-neck cutter, a doctor's buggy, several governess's carts, a carriole, a farm sleigh, an express sleigh that was the farm pickup truck of its day. Some had been placed under the shade tents, others were parked in the hot sun, where a merciless wind assailed them. One of the surrey's black tops was showing its age, and where time had cut fist-sized holes in the canopy the hanging bits flapped forlornly.

But before the carriages went on the auction block, bearskin rugs, carriage lamps, saddles and tack and all manner of horse-and-buggy gear were sold. I did not stick around for the carriage sale, but I did walk in the barn where Judy Prosperine, Frank's wife, was showing someone around. The barn is home to some 20 Canadian horses, all black and all pretty friendly once the stranger had been gone over with a soft muzzle.

Late in April of 1999, I took a ride in my friend Patricia Cooper's buggy—a Withybrooke, named after the place in England where they were originally made. I wish I could say her buggy offered a smoother ride than it did. I even took my notepad up into the carriage, thinking I could take notes as we went along. I took notes all right, but were you to see them you would guess them penned by my off hand as I emerged from a general anaesthetic.

As carriages go, this is a plain one. The four-foot-high wheels are painted a bright sun-yellow, and Maple Lane Rebel Tom—now 14—cuts quite a striking figure with Patricia at the reins in competition. I've seen the photos: a short, fair-skinned woman in black driving apron, white blouse buttoned to the collar, her fedora set off by a jaunty red feather.

The whole effect is to transport the onlooker back in time. It looks so elegant, so 19th century. It even looks smooth. Tom's trot is even, and hints at power under wraps. But the image that came to me as I rode in that Withybrooke that sunny cool day in April was of those jiggling machines from the 1950s: Imagine a girthlike device attached to a motor, with the user wrapped loosely behind at the hips and back. It was thought that the jiggling would help lose weight.

By way of warmup, we rode round and round Patricia's half-acre paddock. The fencing, on two sides, borders on a pine forest, so that the trees themselves act as vertical supports for the horizontal boards.

"It was pretty strange at first," Patricia says of her early days in the carriage. "When you ride in the saddle you get used to that immediate contact. Your aids are your legs, your hands in contact with the mouth through the reins, your seat. It's all very direct. But in driving, it's your voice, the whip, and your hands—but the horse's mouth is eight or nine feet away from your hands."

She's convinced that driving is actually safer than riding. The remoteness of the control, though, seemed quite alarming at first. The first time in the cart, Patricia described a snake pattern with Tom, not because Tom wasn't paying attention but because he *was* paying attention. The hands have to be kept even; Tom was doing exactly what Patricia's hands were telling him to do—one S after the other.

Patricia, a novice driver, typically drives at Tralee, an astonishing facility north of Toronto owned and operated by a vet named Dr. Ray Cormack. Local lore has it that his family once owned a big farm in what is now Mississauga, a vast community and industrial heartland west of Toronto. It seems the doctor has a penchant for antique carriages. That day, Patricia, her son Alex and I were taken on a tour of the several board-and-batten barns that house the collection. The farm manager who took us around lamented the low ceilings that he said failed to lend the distinction these carriages deserved. There was a turn-of-the-century hearse, an Irish jaunting car in which the driver sits off to one side and leans into the centre on his elbows. A German spider phaeton. Some 40 carriages in all, many of them restored by a carriage maker in Bromont, Quebec, named Alain Benoit.

There was even a Russian carriage (whose tin fenders and shoddy craftsmanship the farm manager scoffed at) that required the two outside horses in the four-horse team to turn their heads absurdly to the outside. A photo on the wall showed the carriage moving at what looked to be great speed, the dust swirling magnificently, and being pulled by four white horses. It had the feel of a scene from *Ben-Hur*.

In May of 2000, I had a longer talk with Bill Graham and learned of his own connection to Tralee and Dr. Ray Cormack.

"About eight years ago," he told me, "I read an article in *Canadian Geographic* magazine about the Canadian horse. I had bought two riding horses the year before, but I was quite green about horses. On the other hand, I have one way of doing things and that's full speed ahead."

He made inquiries, and over the phone bought (subject to vet check) a stallion and a gelding from a North Bay horseman. Graham's farm is at Lions Head on the Bruce Peninsula, about 200 kilometres northwest of Toronto. The horses arrived in an old cattle trailer, along with an even older carriage and some older yet harness.

At about the same time, Graham went to a horse show at Tralee, liked what he saw, introduced himself to Dr. Cormack and said he wanted to learn to drive. And it was arranged that Jack Braithwaite, a fine driver who worked for Dr. Cormack, would take him on as a student. "One thing," said Graham, "led to the next."

It seems that Graham is as talented as he is impulsive. He calls himself "an old jock" but he has impressive credentials. In 1959 he played centre for the Belleville McFarlands, world hockey champions. He also played pro football, lining up at halfback for the Hamilton Tiger Cats in the 1950s and playing in four Grey Cups, his team winning two of them.

What drew him to the Canadian horse? "I'm a diehard Canadian," he said. "I like the country, but it seems we are always hiding our light under the bushel basket."

Graham has 11 Canadian horses, all from the Fox and Henryville lines. "I like the Canadian. I find they have good action, good temperament. I never bother with cross-ties in the stable, for example. And wherever I go, people just fall all over them. People are looking for quality horses, easy keepers, smart people-oriented horses. That's the Canadian."

But Graham agrees with Terry Veevers that the Canadian horse has a strong disposition. In the winter of 1999, Graham was in North Carolina, where he hired a prominent American trainer to cure one of his Canadians of her habit of being overly strong on the right rein. "He's a good trainer this guy, but he's also pretty firm. And the harder he pulled, the harder she did. I changed to a softer trainer, and used apples. It's working. Our approach has always been soft. For me there is no choice between stick and carrot. It's always the carrot."

Meanwhile, Graham's adopted sport of combined driving has become what he calls the fastest-growing equestrian sport in North America. The Windedge Farm show that drew 34 competitors in 1999 drew 76 in 2000, and they came from all over North America.

Sue Mott and Caesar, meanwhile, will continue to train for whatever competition lies ahead. That storybook chapter in the long saga of the Canadian horse may yet be written.

CHAPTER 14

# SEVEN FALLS MAKES A RIDER

LAKEHEAD STABLES, DECEMBER 1999

*Dali is very much under my skin. His scent settles on me, and no matter how hard I wash my hands it lingers there. The other night I was watching a performance in my son's school auditorium, my chin in my hand, and Dali's essence was wafting all around me, taking me back to horse and barn and leather and that day's ride. Maybe, I thought, someone who smells like a horseman will eventually become one.*

EVER SINCE COMING OFF Dali two days back, on November 17, I've felt uneasy. Driving my car, watching a movie, awake in the small hours, I keep rehashing the moments that led to the fall, and I dread a recurrence. I continue to wonder at the breadth of my foolishness—a rider of modest experience buys as his first horse a raw, sparky five-year-old.

Above: The author in a pensive mood.

Today, curiosity bade me return to the scene of my unseating and I was appalled to see how distorted my mental map of the scene had been. I had the real estate sign 20 metres in from the road. It's actually about five. And when Dali made a beeline for that sign, he was on a collision course with Sydenham Road, just where it curves.

That trajectory would have had him facing traffic as the vehicles rounded past, a little like that stark Colville painting where the galloping horse is on a collision course with a train. Had we continued in that line, him picking up speed and me bouncing in the saddle struggling for a grip on the reins and out of my stirrups, we would have gone onto the highway.

Dali, I now see, curled hard to the right just before the real estate sign, as if to carefully deposit me on one of the few patches of grass in that whole area. Then he must have curled left again, away from the highway, and stopped.

I was more terrified today, seeing the true layout, than I was on the day the fall occurred. Had I landed on the pavement of Keppler Road or cracked that post, or, worse, been deposited on the highway . . . It will be a long time indeed before I mount Dali near that road. The rail bed, tempting as it is, can wait till spring.

A few days later, I followed Kathi's advice and put liability insurance on Dali: Imagine the consequences—physical, legal, emotional—if someone in a vehicle was hurt while trying to avoid a loose horse on the road.

A young horse up the road bolted off a lunge line the other day, the line trailing wildly behind him as he scooted over Sydenham Road. This is a valuable and much-loved horse, and I can imagine her owner's terror as she watched him roar down that long lane. He had some luck, for he avoided traffic and even got help. A woman in a passing car, someone familiar with horses, stopped, got out and held him while the grateful owner caught up to him. Insurance, says Kathi, is wise in any case. If your horse kicked someone in the stable or damaged property, you're covered.

I described my adventure to Barb and Gilles, and the more I talked, the more I came to conclusions and solutions. *Always* ride this young horse in the ring before a trail ride. "*Good* idea," said Barb, "just to make sure all the connections are there." *Always* consider his tail, his head, his eyes, looking for fear or worry when you mount him. Go through your checklist, like a pilot before takeoff. *Always* ensure he's focused on you, and not on sheep or cars or another horse. *Always*, after a long layoff, take the measure of him. Almost all the "incidents" have occurred after five-day layoffs. This is a horse best kept busy. "This is a horse," Kathi told me, "in need of a program." Maybe this is a stock expression, because Maxine Kumin would say the same thing when I told her of our adventures: "He needs a program," she told me.

I found in my notes in the "Buying a Horse" file something that Ray Lalonde, a Canadian horse breeder in Ottawa, had told me. He was describing his horse, Albert, a Fox-line horse, like Dali. "He's got a good temperament as long as he knows who's the boss," said Ray. "He will take advantage and he would be a challenge. A lot of people think that line is hard to handle . . ."

Dali requires just the right blend of confident handling and softness. Too much bold stuff and he gets wide-eyed. Too much soft handling and he frets, worries that I cannot or will not make the right decision. I have tilted in both directions in the past, but my natural tendency is to get close to him. Like a boy to a teddy bear. Dali enjoys some of that, but when I layer it on I suspect he construes it as weakness.

Today I was determined to be more demanding. When I saddled him he put back his ears, likely remembering the ugly episode just past, but I rebuked him for that. On the lunge line, I asked for quicker trots, moved his hindquarters and never let him crowd me. But it was all preamble to the moment of mounting, and I would have been so forlorn had he scooted. He did not, though I was not pleased to see that he walked on a step or two. Near the end of the lesson, I got off and remounted. That time he was fine. And he improved as the lesson progressed. We worked on transitions. I wanted him responding to my seat, stopping for that invisible glass wall he brakes for, and it came.

I left pleased, but drained, too. Chris, who owns the Morgan gelding named Prime Time, Dali's former paddock boss at Blue Haven, confided in Barb the other day that if people knew what was involved in training a horse—"in actually trying to do something and not just park him in the paddock" is how Barb put it—fewer people would own horses.

I sometimes find the intensity too consuming. This, too, shall pass. It always does. Like a Dali explosion, like a snow squall that darkens the winter sky then gives way to the sun.

Someday I'd like to spend a few hours just out in the paddock, keeping Dali and Ras company. I've never had an eye for individual horses; even horses I've ridden often seem unfamiliar once unsaddled and loosed in a herd.

But Dali, Dali I could pluck easily. There's a quiet dignity about him, even when he ambles over to me after I call him. He shuffles, like a left fielder heading out to play his position. Ball players trot almost reluctantly, as if parsing out energy one step at a time. But you know that the second the ball is hit they can explode into motion.

Sometimes Dali will spot me crossing the farmyard, maybe to pull back the electrified fences leading into the ring prior to a lesson. His head will come up, and stay up. His focus is arresting and quite singular. When I enter the paddock, halter and lead line in hand, he'll go back to grazing. As if to make a point: I saw you, but I have this grass to attend to. . . .

Then I'll call him, walk towards him and stop. My gesture says, I'm meeting you halfway. I've tried staying at the gate and calling him; doesn't work. His reward for coming is an apple. I am *always* glad to see him. I like the way he closes his eyes in pleasure as he crunches that apple and accepts the halter. I may stroke his neck, fuss over him, complain about the mud from his rolling.

I like his rugged athleticism, his playfulness. I keep hearing, from Wendy and Lil and Gerry, how he and Ras tear around that paddock with a vigour that sometimes alarms them. Lil calls him "a high-energy" horse. One time I went to see him at dark, when there was a Chris Irwin clinic at Kathie Groenewegen's barn, and I dropped in to give him an apple. I flicked on the lights and woke all the horses from their slumber. Dali blinked repeatedly, trying to see me, like a child rubbing his eyes at dawn. He looked so vulnerable.

November 22, 1999

I am trying to put behind me that tumble of the other day. It's the kind of memory I want to roll into a ball and bury in the nether regions of my tack box. I must not forget, I cannot forget. I just want to park the thought and move on.

Dali was fresh today; he still hates it when I ask him to move his hindquarters around on the ground, and he wants to crowd me as I do it. I back him off with my upraised hand, and one time when I did that he raised his front feet a little.

There was a time that action would have alarmed me. Now I push back. When he has moved his hindquarters to my satisfaction, he comes in and lowers his head: I used to think he was wanting a hug, now I'm inclined to think he's pouting.

He's more disciplined on the lunge line these days, not so many twists of the head or sour looks.

Mounting was good. Once up, I made a point of doing nothing but praise him when he stood stock still. He was soft to handle, yielded well, turned nicely both ways with his hindquarters. Backing up is almost a private joke: "*Recule*," I tell him, using Gilles's Franco-Ontarian slang for "Back up," and assuring him I have all day. Which is about how long he takes to back up.

Still, he was good. Good and wet. Have to buy, and soon, some winter blankets for him. That thick coat of his gets drenched under the girth with less than an hour of work, especially today with the temperatures around 12 or 13 degrees. At home, with Christmas only a month away, I watched as Queen's students on Rollerblades skated past in their shorts.

November 24, 1999

It turns out that the expression is "Seven falls makes a rider." Here I thought it was 10. At the rate I'm going, I'm a cinch to hit double figures. I admit it. I'm sore, discouraged, and my confidence has been severely shaken.

"Green on green," cousin Kathi consoled me, "is a hard combination. You're taking your lumps." I hope my green horse is feeling better than his green rider.

Today, with Barb there to give me a lesson, we worked on backing him up and getting those hindquarters over. And though he tuned out at the beginning and flatly refused to back up, he came around later on. But on this gusty, blowy day, Barb had to shout her instructions and I still couldn't hear her.

The explosion came as I asked Dali to canter at the lower end of the ring, site of past spooks. But those were quick little tempests. This one had legs. Once again I found myself behind his motion and struggling to regain control.

We've done almost no canter work lately, for I've lacked the fortitude, and maybe Dali sensed that now as we picked up speed. Maybe it was the wind. Maybe all that backing up and hindquarter work soured him. But when I asked for that canter, giving him more rein to enable it, he found himself in the boogey corner and racing into the wind. He spooked. We rounded the corner at a gallop and near the one remaining standard in the ring I came off his left side, hard onto my shoulder blade where it meets my neck. I could hear and feel the cold sand rattling in my helmet and cascading down my back. I had spun in the air, just as I had last time, and accordioned headfirst into the sand.

I remember rising up, brushing off the dirt and saying to Barb, "I'm gettin' *real* fed up with comin' off this horse." There came waves of anger and disappointment and shock. I felt small, even silly, like an overmatched boxer, a bantamweight tossed into the ring with a heavyweight. Dali's saddle had slipped to the left, and I regretted not being more careful about checking the girth. Kathi had been in the stable earlier, helping fit my fresh young prince for a turnout blanket, and she had been on the off side and must have linked girth and saddle leathers one or two notches looser than I normally do. But the blame was all mine. I was judging tightness by notches, and not by actual tightness. A loose saddle did not help me ride my bronc, but the saddle was not the problem either. I must learn to ride these scoots—and fast.

I got back on him, suggesting to Barb that we do something simple before calling it a day. Dali moved sideways as I went to mount him at the block, and I simply said, "Don't even think about it." When he turned his head back to look at me, I firmly pushed it back. Eyes forward.

Within a minute, he had spooked again. Same spot, same direction. This time I had a firmer hold, and something approaching anger strengthened me. I turned his head in a one-rein stop, but he was so wired that he continued circling for about 40 seconds. In their paddock, two other horses—Danny and Bogi—had sensed the hot adrenalin coursing in the ring and started to buck and kick and tear. By now I just wanted off this horse. My horse. His tension was electric; I could feel it through the saddle.

I breathed a sigh of relief as my feet touched the ground. What the hell had I gotten myself into?

Wendy chanced along minutes later and offered her sympathy. She told me she once fell off Ras three times in one week. On the telephone later, Kathi told me how Dick, an experienced rider and successful eventer who does *not* come off easily, fell off a young horse three times in one hour. I've had no luck shocking the horse-smart people in my circle with my tale of woe: Sarah later told me she's fallen off Maddy at least seven times. All assure me that I will become a better rider out of this, and spooks that unseat me now won't next year.

Maybe I'll even see them coming. Wendy, for example, had ridden Ras earlier in the day but called it quits when the high winds brought down a big branch from a tree on the edge of the ring. Woodcutters call them widowmakers. Wendy had read the signs. I did not.

I now have an even longer list of *should haves*:

I should have considered heeding my instinct *not* to ride on such a windy day, knowing how wind spooks Monsieur Dali.

I should have lunged him longer, and even demanded some canter work from him on that circle. Got the lunge whip back out.

I should have gotten the trot and canter work from him early in the lesson, saving the backups, yields and hindquarter work for later when he was warm and, hopefully, mellow. And maybe have asked for less of them at a time.

I should haved watched keenly for the signs of a bolt: His head comes up, his ears go cockeyed. And even if my hunch about a spook was wrong, it does no harm to bring him around to a one-reined stop. Remind him continually that I have brakes.

And when he spooked like that, I should have had the courage and good sense to put him right back to work. Send him, as Barb used to say. The first spook was just that; the second, I'll wager, was a test. And my only consolation from this whole sorry episode is that I passed it. There are, I am sure, more tests to come.

"This horse should be moving forward," said Kathi. "He's just doing what all five-year-olds do. The trick, when he spooks like that, is to anticipate it, keep your seat, and when he scoots, ask him to scoot faster. You'd be surprised how tired he'll get of scooting."

The surprise, I am afraid, is ever mine. I am continually taken aback by the reflexes of my burly horse. Suddenly everything accelerates and I'm bent back like a sapling in the wind. How *do* I keep my seat when he scoots, darting right and left, especially right? That's his favourite deke, and I wish my body would remember it.

Should I take him back to Blue Haven for some more work? Should I ride him in a western saddle for a while, just so I have a pommel grip when he scoots? Should I—and my heart aches at the thought—embrace caution and trade him for an older, milder horse?

Gilles called this evening, concerned about my battered body, and wondered if I should ride another horse for a while, to regain my confidence. He voiced thoughts I have never articulated but that exist in some deeper part of my mind: Maybe Dali is too much horse. Next time I might crack my head in one of those accordion landings, or worse. Maybe it's too much to ask of a young horse who worries most about his rider, and an older rider starting to question seriously the suitability of his horse.

Gilles had that day ridden a young green Arab in his barn, but the second he got on her he knew something was not right. He worked her some more on the lunge line, got back on, and she was fine. Someday, maybe, I'll possess such an instinct, that ability to sniff the wind and know when an ill one is blowing.

Later I talked to Barb, who said that coming up to Lakehead for the occasional lesson put her in the awkward position of coming in cold. At Blue Haven, she saw Dali each day, had a good handle on his moods, saw for herself how schooling was going. In her delicate way, Barb was ending our loose arrangement. She's right, of course, but in losing her I've lost an anchor.

Kathi says Dali and I are going through what horse people call "a bad patch." What a delightful phrase for such a horrid feeling. My neck aches, but worse is that feeling in the pit of my stomach I thought I had shaken.

The plan is to take a few days off. Go to the cabin, cut wood, try not to think about my Dali-nquent horse.

On Monday, I'll lunge him and hope Dick has time to come out and ride him. "Now, why do you want Dick to ride him?" asked Kathi, wanting me to articulate my reasons, even though she herself had offered the idea. "I just want Dick to take the measure of this horse, maybe take the kinks out of him. . ."

"You want the full eight seconds," she replied, referring to the rodeo rider's hoped-for time on a bronc.

Kathi tries to see the world from the horse's point of view, but she is never blind to what she calls "naughtiness." She warned me to be on the alert for more naughtiness from young Dali, but she also assured me: "You will get over this. You have come a long way with this horse. You must not beat yourself up or think you're somehow raising a rogue horse. He's the equivalent of a 13-year-old boy."

Yes, and headed for reform school . . . .


November 30, 1999

Saw Dali yesterday, hoping to lunge him in the ring. Too sodden. Groomed him instead.

The air is still gone out of my sails. Dick's timetable wouldn't allow him to come up and sort out my now quite worried horse, though he would do it if I pleaded. I've contracted with Samara Warren, a capable young rider and trainer at Lakehead who uses old Bogi to teach her students, to ride Dali a few times. The plan today is that I tack him up, walk him over to the arena at Limestone Stables, lunge him and let Samara have her go at the full eight seconds. I do dread the trip over. If he gets panicky, we may have to turn back.

Still curious about Dali's bloodline, I called someone familiar with Dali's sire, Hobbyhorse Larry's Dark Fox. Elaine Ayre, in Linden, Alberta, remembers this horse competing at Calgary's Spruce Meadows. "Somebody had seen a picture of him jumping," she said, "and thought he would be good for the Battle of the Breeds competition. He loved to perform and he loved to jump," she said. That was the good news.

What about his temperament? "Well, he was kinda hot," she recalled. When Dali's dad stayed in the Spruce Meadows barn, and he was in cross-ties, they used to tie red ribbons around his mane and tail as a warning to those not informed that he wasn't a horse for patting and cooing over. He was cool and professional. "He wasn't friendly at all," said Ayre.

I'm sure I was more nervous about walking Dali the half kilometre up Sydenham Road than he was. On the other occasions he had Ras for company. Dali did snort much of the way, and on the way back, a school bus startled him and he pulled back some, but on the whole I was pleasantly surprised.

In the arena, though, he was wide-eyed. I walked him around several times so he could check it out. At one point I stopped and asked for his head—asked, in other words, that he arc his nose back towards the saddle, a bending exercise we had done hundreds of times, and he did so reluctantly then snapped his head back with a show of petulance. When two other riders came into the ring, I felt initial annoyance but shouldn't have. These quiet horses offered Dali moral support.

Samara watched as I lunged him, asked questions, tried to get a sense of him. When she went to get on him, he spun in a circle— here was a new twist on an old theme—but Samara wasn't bothered a bit. She went back to the mounting block, got on, then repeated the whole thing just to ensure mounting wasn't an issue.

But before even getting on him, she adjusted his bridle. She thought the noseband wanted to be tighter, and the bit, she believed, was too low in his mouth. Both adjustments, she said, would not hurt him and would help him behave. And though Dali fussed, and went back to having his mouth agape, he soon ceased.

Samara also remarked after a few minutes in my saddle that it was too low at the back end, and that a riser pad would help angle my body forward and into that athletic stance, better preparing me for any sudden flight from Dali. She said that when the saddle is low at the back end, it's easy for the rider's feet to come forward—she noticed it happening with her when Dali accelerated—and then a rider like me, whose riding posture could always use work, is vulnerable to a darting horse. The rider is leaning back at 45 degrees, and Dali takes both the loose rein and the pressure on his back as a green light. In Samara's words, meant to capture Dali's glee, "He says, 'Aw*right!*' and takes off."

Samara is a smooth, effortless rider. She's a dressage rider as well as an eventer who is training her own three-and-a-half-year-old warmblood, a gorgeous black horse named Nate—Chris Irwin's star assistant in this same ring a month back. Nate's sire, I later learned, competed for the Belgian Olympic team in dressage at the Sydney Olympics. Nate's pedigree is sterling but he is terrified, absolutely terrified, of cows, ever since a streaking calf caused him to panic and buck Samara off. Dali, next to young Nate, may seem calm by comparison.

Samara has soft hands but rides with more contact than I employed at Blue Haven. And Dali, who actually likes to know that the rider on his back is in charge, soon got mellow and did as he was asked.

Samara admired his trot, his solid feel and his willingness. And having come off tall Nate, she liked the fact that Dali's comparatively short stature put her a little closer to the ground, just in case. Her theory on scooting is that you essentially ignore it. Make the horse understand that while he, the horse, may occasionally succumb to fear, she, the rider, is not so easily spooked. I kept thinking of Kathi's explanation for Dali dumping me on that first ride in the Gatineau Valley: I was not a "worthy leader. . ."

*Practical Horseman*, I noticed not long afterwards, had some words of advice on how to handle a horse who panics in the cross-ties. The vets writing the column noted that "Fear has a herd dynamic. If your voice and movements tell your spooking horse that *you're* scared, he figures things must REALLY be bad." A chatty, conversational voice has a powerful, calming effect on a worried horse.

A light went on in my brain about Dali's little panic attacks: Sometimes no response is the best response.

An ounce of prevention would also spare me a pound of cure. Samara would try to nip Dali's scoots in the bud by asking for transitions to keep him focused and balanced. The aim is to have him go into the canter from a rhythmic trot, not the fast strung-out kind. The former transition is harder for a young horse to accomplish with a rider on, in the beginning anyway; the latter is more likely to trigger the explosions that have so unsettled me, and him. This latter method, Kathi later told me, is called "chasing," and while it's permissible with young horses, it's a method best not pursued.

Dali did scoot with Samara up, but they were tiny ones, and Samara ignored them. He seemed grateful.

She kept stressing how young he was, how hard it is for a young horse to canter in circles with a rider on. This comes with experience. The great risk, she said, is in asking too much too soon, so that he sours on both his rider and the ring. Even backing up, she says, requires tremendous mental agility on a young horse's part. I liked her sympathy for him, the way she kept telling him he was a good boy ("What a good *mannnnnnnn*," she kept saying), patting and stroking him. I thought of my own maternal grandmother, who liked to refer to any grandson in her presence as "my little man."

I was sitting on poles piled in one corner of the ring, and as Samara rode past me I described how foolish I had been to take this horse out onto Keppler Road. Two fairly green riders on two more or less green horses. "I saw you guys going out that day," said Samara, "and I was hoping you'd be all right. And yes, it's true that a young horse and a novice rider don't always make the best match, but you're doing this right. You're analyzing, you're getting help."

After the lesson, we put a cooler on Dali and walked him. I told Samara about the white marks on his mouth when I first got him. "He wasn't interested, at first, in me getting on him," said Samara, "so at some point he's been ridden by someone who was hard on him. He's still not sure he can trust us humans. But that will come."

Samara liked him, liked the fact that he worked through his worry about this new rider and made no attempt to ditch her. He looked like a trustworthy school horse as Samara did figure eights, walked him in circles, asked for trots and lengthened strides. She did some canter work from a slower trot, and when he couldn't manage it initially, that was fine. She simply asked again from a trot and eventually it came. The troublesome clockwise canter would have to wait another day, for by the time an hour was up, he was wet from his exertions, and perhaps from working in this new environment down that worrisome road.

Samara's advice: Three workouts a week is fine, and not more than 45 minutes each. Keep him interested, keep him happy. Mix up schooling and ground work and trail rides.

Samara said, in a way, what Kathi had said: You've come a long way. Don't give up now.

December 1, 1999

Kathi tells me that a British eventing magazine titled a recent piece "Where Have All the Horsemen Gone?" The article takes a critical look at the new "fixers" and "gentlers" and wonders what ever happened to the passing on of horse wisdom, the sharing of knowledge within a family farm or stable.

I know now that fixes are like plugs for holes in dykes. New leaks invariably appear. As for gentlers, they can point the way, but the shaping and schooling of a horse, like that of a rider, only ends when breathing does. Like music or poetry or any body of knowledge, riding has simple beginnings but no end of complexity.

I too easily forget this, and come to my ride with an agenda, a shopping list, things I want to cross off. Little did I know that my pen issued bold strokes one day, invisible ink the next.

Dali has already been the benefactor of some fine horse people: Barb and Gilles and Samara, cousin Kathi from a distance. But he has also had to bear the brunt of my growing up in a Scarborough bungalow, my riding limited to occasional walks on some sad-sack rental mounts at Hilltop Stables.

I wish my grandfather were alive. Leonard Flynn was strict with his horses but he loved them. He would, no doubt, have had thoughts on Dali.

December 7, 1999

They say getting there is half the fun. With Dali, it was that and more. Took Dali the back way today, the long way, from Lakehead to Limestone Stables. The road seemed too risky; but the other way had its own delights.

During the 20-minute walk, as we got farther and farther from his buddies in the barn, Dali grew more and more alarmed. Call it separation anxiety. "Where the heck," he seemed to be saying, "are you taking me?" He would dance and tug, get all tense, whinny repeatedly to the herd back home. Several times he lifted those feet off the ground and pawed the air—"a pretty aggressive thing," conceded Samara when I told her.

I wasn't going to risk a confrontation out there, for I worried he'd bolt. But neither could I accept such defiance. I snapped his shank, moved him back, let him know with my voice I didn't like it. He kept stiffening, staring into the bush as if it were teeming with bears. I sang, I praised him when he grew calm and lowered his head. I hoped I wouldn't slip in the mud.

When I told all this to Kathi, she likened it to going to war with a rubber knife in my hand. The halter gave me no leverage. Better would have been a halter over his bridle, with both in my hands. If he pulled back, the bridle would put pressure on his poll. Of course, if he bolted, he might step into those reins . . . Oh dear.

Kathi's advice: Buy a long lead rope with a chain on the end of it, and have Samara show you how to fit it over his nose, then school him with it in the ring so he gets to feel it and, better, respect it.

"These are called hard miles," said Kathi, "and we all go through it with young horses. Dick doesn't even go down to the mailbox leading a young horse without a chain on. Dali has never been back in those fields without a buddy. He's been kept in his stall for a few days because of the rain. With just a halter on him, it's no contest. I'm surprised you were even able to hold him. I know that underneath all this he's a sensible horse. He's not a 17-hand lunatic Thoroughbred, but he's young and he has to learn to be properly led, and to trust you."

Kathi also advised using a Tellington-Jones method: The rider walks the horse forward with the butt of a dressage whip in his left hand, and when the horse barges forward, or whinnies to his pals, the handler flicks his wrist and lightly bops the horse on the nose. In time, the horse should stop when you do to avoid that discipline. And there's always food reward when he does it right.

"He won't be like this when he's seven," Kathi assured. I'm sure Dali will see seven, but will I see 51?

Down the long lane we went, through two gates, up a little hill to another gate, crossed a field then zigzagged on some untilled ground serving as pathway between fields towards the Limestone barns. Dali seemed relieved to see them, and though he scooted a little outside the arena when the grey in the closest paddock decided to show off and canter past, we did make it. But how I dread these trips. The thought of them keeps me awake at night.

Once in the ring, I released the shank and let him go. He'd circle me, in a trot and sometimes in a canter, as if on the end of an invisible lunge line. There was the usual shaking of his head, but I thought I caught some glee, too. With all the mud in the paddocks, said Samara, he hasn't had a chance to go for a good run. We also borrowed another rider's saddle pad, with a riser pad built in at the back. It made a difference.

Dali was far less tense with Samara up than last time. She gave him a long warm-up in a walk, eased him into trots, worked on upward and downward transitions. He fell into a nice groove, and though he scooted once or twice, they were the old scoots, like little flares that come off an oil well on the prairies.

Samara is convinced that the scoots arise out of some old instinctual fear. He darts, typically when Samara puts extra leg on him, to ask, say, for a canter. And it must trigger some memory, maybe of another rider. The scoot builds on itself, like a snowball rolling down a hill, because now he's convinced that he's in deep trouble with his rider. Samara wondered if a previous rider punished him for his scoots. She likened it to him saying progressively louder, "Oh my God!" "OH-MY-GOD!" "OH-MY-GAWWDDD!!!"

Her tactic of ignoring the scoots worked well. I will endeavour to do likewise, but I'll need her inner calm, her balance, her seat. Pity these things cannot be packaged, drunk like a potion.

Not long before this moment in Dali time, I was in Wolfville, Nova Scotia, en route to see some Canadian horses, and I was drawn to a used bookstore, where I chanced across a bibliography of British horse books published after 1851. In 19th century Scotland, I learned, there existed secret horsemen's societies whose members believed fervently in potions to cure equine ailments and in charms that gave the trainer power over horses, even fractious ones.

In East Anglia, one took the bone of a frog or toad, ritually prepared it, buried it in an anthill and baked it in an oven. The ritual, not the bone itself, bestowed absolute confidence. A century later, the bone business seems silly; the matter of confidence still has the ring of truth.

My young horse, meanwhile, without ever intending it, is teaching me to be a better rider. And one day, perhaps, a truly confident one.

December 8, 1999

Dali continues to surprise me. Today, perhaps showing some fatigue from yesterday's workout or simply knowing now where I was taking him, he was a prince as we walked down that muddy lane. He never whinnied once to his pals, who were all out in their paddocks and watching him leave. His head stayed low the whole way. Several times I stopped and gave him a chunk of apple and thanked my stars.

I've changed my thinking on this back way. "It does give you a chance to just hang out with him," said Samara, and she's right. Walking with him, especially across the field to that break in the hedgerow that leads to the other side, I felt his calm become mine. One day my calm will become his.

What a difference from walking along Sydenham Road, trying to be small, hoping that gravel trucks choose another time to scream past. The back way is at least 10 minutes longer, but it's good horse time, and until snow and weather make it impassable I'll take it when I can.

As I walked I thought of yesterday's antics. Was this about him being kept in his stall for days and no work for a week? Was it sweet feed hotting him up, or some lunar phase? I had gone to the stable expecting the same, or worse, as yesterday. On Kathi's advice, I had bought a lead shank with a chain on it. No more knives versus guns.

I had seen such a device used on unruly horses (Carol's horse Rocky was so equipped routinely). You can simply attach the shank to the bridle, and sometimes the sound of that metal snapping will call a horse to attention. Another, sterner, option is to run the chain through the halter. When you pull down on that arrangement, it puts pressure on the horse's nose. It's a loud call to attention, and one I will use the next time Dali's actions endanger us both.

But today Mr. Mellow could have been led by a string. Who *was* that horse yesterday?

"Would you call him a nervous horse?" I asked Samara as she rode him.

"No, he has his moments," she replied, "but in general he's very quiet, very sensible." Samara has seen too many hot horses who stay hot. She admires how Dali stands to be bridled and haltered (though he still, as a game, turns away once or twice before signing on the dotted line); she likes his name, says it suits him. That he managed our somewhat eventful three-hour trail ride she called a feat.

I owe a great debt to Blue Haven: They civilized Dali, got him started. Samara's job is to undo some of the worries I poured in his head, and to refine my own seat and balance.

The other day Dali gave her a few mini-scoots and, later on, a sidestep when some outside noise startled him. She kept her athletic stance, went with him and about her business, and she assures me, as Wendy did, that what unseats me now won't a year hence. What a pleasant thought: riding without hitting the ground.

I finally asked Samara her age today. I wouldn't have guessed she's 24; some days she appears much older and more mature. She has the perfect skin and clear brown eyes of a young girl; the reserve and discretion of a genteel young woman. She always wears black jodphurs and black sweater, black helmet and delicate black leather gloves. She gets on Dali as if she were whispering to a friend in a cinema: one foot up, pause a second to check his response, up and oh so lightly over. In the dismount, she comes out of the stirrups, leans onto the pommel as a gymnast would and swings over, careful not to touch his back with her feet. And though she informs me that much suppling work has to be done with my horse, the truth is that at times she makes him look as if he's gliding on air.

I like her keen sense of detail and order. I left a cooler, lunge line and my fluourescent workmen's vest (bought when braving Sydenham Road was an option) piled on jumping poles in one corner of the arena, intending to pick them up after parking Dali in his paddock. When I returned, the items were gone. They were in the tack room: the cooler neatly folded, the lunge line tied securely in no-knot figure eights, the vest on top. My pile looked like a decorated cake. The only thing missing was a sign: Samara was here. Later, I learned that someone else in the barn, perhaps Shannon Knox, the barn manager, or the owner, Kathie Groenewegen, had created the pile. But the gesture was entirely in keeping with Samara's character.

She already possesses a degree in psychology from Queen's and has embarked on a six-year course in osteopathy, an alternative form of medicine that uses palpation and manipulation. On graduation, for example, Samara would treat arthritis, back pain, headache and an array of other debilitating problems not always handled well by mainstream medicine. "There'll be lots of work for you," I assured her. "My generation is falling apart." And I told her how gatherings of my male friends have become seminars on tennis elbow, lower back pain and other, more sinister, ailments of the aging body.

The mind, too, is suspect.

"Working on another book?" a woman in the tack shop had asked me. I had told her why I was buying a shank with a chain on the end.

"Yeah," I said, "it's about a foolish man my age who buys a young horse. It's a tragedy. No, it's a comedy." And she laughed heartily, assuring me that a great many horse owners who know something of humiliation like stories about the humbling of others.

December 9, 1999

Another *very* pleasant trip through the lanes and fields over to the arena. Finally, a bright day and warm—a sweater day. We marched through mud. Dali has begun to look for the bits of apple he gets along the way, and so I stop to deliver them at the same place: a clump of birches at a spot where we begin to lose sight of the other horses in their paddocks.

He seemed almost lethargic in his walk. The combination of reduced grain rations and three straight days of work have taken the pepper out of him. I am so grateful, so glad, when he's mellow and happy.

But Dali has also taught me the strength and power of a horse, and how even sleepy puddinheads, as he sometimes is, can so quickly come alive. As we rounded the silo at Limestone Barns, Dali jumped sideways about four feet and I had no clue as to the cause. "I should have warned you," said Francis Groenewegen, up on the roof doing repairs. Dali has this spatial map of that area, and suddenly his radar spotted a moving, living creature, up high, where none had been before.

With Samara as tutor, I rode him. Not without some edge; no doubt he felt the same, remembering the last time his "dad," as Samara would say, was on board. We kept it simple: walks, trots, transitions. "Keep him busy," she advised, "just in case he's scheming."

Samara is revamping my seat, my legs, my hands. She wants me to ride with a deeper seat; ultimately, she says, a safer seat. "Think about riding on your pockets," is how she puts it. She's also prescribing greater rein contact, which, ironically, is what Dali first experienced. I remember how Jérôme rode him, how firm and straight those reins were.

But I also remember how worried Dali was about his mouth and, later, how getting him to accept the bit was such an ordeal. Fate has interceded kindly on my horse's behalf: Barb and Gilles had us riding on a loose rein, and Dali learned not to fret about his mouth. And now, having come full circle, Samara has me riding a little like Jérôme did. Except now Dali knows more. He actually seems to like the contact.

"It's like you're holding his hand as you make that circle," Samara said while we arced past her in the ring.

Samara has me back thinking about classical English riding. She wants me bending Dali around my leg, not the heel in the western way, but the calf. Toes forward. Squeeze that outside rein on the circle. She's rebuilding me as a rider, repairing the terrible blow to my confidence, equipping my seat and balance and hands for that scoot that lies in waiting.

Later, as I hot-walked him, Samara sat on the poles piled in the corner and wrote out a receipt. As she handed it to me, I passed her the money, and Dali took a sniff of the notes and considered eating them.

"No, Dali, you can't eat the money," I told him.

"Well, in a way, he does eat money, doesn't he?" said Samara. Indeed he does. She has suggested Woof boots for his hind legs; we need a riser pad as a temporary fix to the saddle, metal clips for that rug I bought so we can secure it at his neck. There is no end, it seems, to the tack.

But he was so sweet in the arena, so agreeable on the way home. Bless him, he walked behind me, did not barge, refrained from snacking after I asked him not to. I am astonished at his capacity to forgive, even when I know he will never forget.

December 15, 1999

Trudged through six inches of snow to get to the arena. Dali not so mellow—the wet snow had recast the land and it all felt new to him. But he well knows the way, and was not so alarmed that he did not know to ask for apple bits at the birch clump or to try for weed snacks en route.

In the ring, under Samara's tutelage, we worked more on me than on Dali. My sloppy form, a loose blend of western from my days at Blue Haven and whatever my body recalled from English riding at Wilmarny, has made me vulnerable to Dali's scoots. Samara wants my feet back under my hips so that when I look down I can't see those western boots of mine. I am to sit deep in the saddle and, as I ask for a canter, lean back. My hands should be over Dali's mane.

I like the combination of aids. The seat is indeed deeper, and with that rein contact I feel more engaged with Dali—and Dali's brakes. Leaning back as I ask for a canter makes sense too. If and when he ever scooted, his acceleration wouldn't drive me back as it used to, when I would lazily lean into my canter requests. Back? I'm already back.

He was a sweet horse under me. Went over poles on the ground (though not without first refusing), trotted fine, even gave me some little canters. He'd been off for almost a week and I wondered if he'd be a powder keg. I never bother with the lunge anymore, just use the whole arena as my 50-foot round pen. He issued lots of bucks and the odd flash of the front feet as he ambled around, but the slog over in the deep snow had already taken something out of him.

On the way back, a rug gathered at his neck like a child's scarf, he can seem so vulnerable, so much in my care. I would bleed for him then. Maybe I'm just grateful he didn't put me on the ground. Maybe it's a feeling you acquire, that elusive something between human and horse.

The literature talks a lot about how careful the Canadian breed is, and Dali is that. "Nervous and docile," the literature says. And I always thought they were contradictory, but now I see how my horse offers both. He has a wonderful, smooth trot and he's become a real pussycat in the paddock. He comes when I call him; in the cross-ties he's agreeable and quiet. He's smart, with plenty of spirit. He has taught me so much. About the power of a horse. About how nimble and quick a big horse can be. And how with horses there is no such thing as a quick fix. Nice and easy does it. The slow way saves time in the end.

For all the bruises Dali has laid on me, for all the days when I've come home discouraged or angry or fearful, I've never stopped feeling for him. He's very much under my skin. His scent settles on me, and no matter how hard I wash my hands it lingers there.

The other night I was watching a performance in my son's school auditorium, my chin in my hand, and Dali's essence was wafting all around me, taking me back to horse and barn and leather and that day's ride.

Maybe, I thought, someone who smells like a horseman will eventually become one.

# THE LONELINESS OF THE LONG-DISTANCE RIDER

DUFFERIN FOREST, APRIL 1999

*"It takes two years to know whether you've got a good horse or not."*

—Nancy Beacon, endurance rider

ONE KIND OF STORY RECURS OFTEN IN THE LITERATURE on the Canadian horse, and while some narratives seem stretched into legend, there is at least a spirit of truth in them. The stories are too many and too widespread to ignore. The stories all say that the Canadian can go all day with a heart and willingness unmatched in any other breed.

I had thought that a horse able to trot so long and so effortlessly would be a natural as a distance-riding horse. The recorded history of the Canadian has certain specimens trotting, for example, from

Above: Stan Alkemade, right, checks a horse during competition.

Quebec City to Montreal, from Montreal to Cornwall, and from Montreal to Plattsburg, Vermont, the distances ranging from 125 miles to 185 miles. In each case, the horse only stopped trotting when his driver paused for ablutions.

I had thought that might make the Canadian a natural distance horse. But that was before I actually went to the competitions and saw Arab after Arab coming in to the vet checks, and heard the vets themselves talking about the astonishing cardiac recovery of Arabs and how too much muscle is a bad thing, for that muscle mass has to be cooled down. Still, I thought, the little horse of iron would do well in these events. Dali and I would not embarrass ourselves.

I had thought, naively, that after buying Dali in the summer of 1999 he and I might try a competitive trail ride late that fall or sometime during 2000, and that this venture, too, might be part of the book. I was wrong, almost comically so. Distance riding, I would learn, is for mature riders and mature horses. But the more I learned about the sport, the more I became convinced that it was the one horse sport I wanted to try for myself.

I remember Deb Ottier, a reproduction researcher with the Equine Research Centre at the University of Guelph, once saying in a lecture to Canadian horse owners that the sodium content in horse sweat is 10 times that of humans. Small wonder that horses get dehydrated when ridden hard on hot days.

That came back to me late in April 1999 as I watched horses coming through vet checks at the first competitive trail ride/endurance ride of the season put on by the Ontario Competitive Trail Riding Association (OCTRA). It was a windy day under a bright though not overly warm sun; still, a day later, my face and neck are a hot red from the wind and sun. And a lot of horses are home in their paddocks sore and tired.

There were 29 riders entered in the 50-mile ride; 57 in the 25-mile event. Some were from Quebec and the United States, most from across Ontario. I saw a lot of Arab horses and Arab crossbreeds, many of them wide-eyed, wary of having their mouths looked at, their rectal temps taken. One Arab chestnut stallion put on a show of twisting, neighing his supremacy and sending people scurrying. "A crazy sport for crazy horses," is how one vet put it.

All in all, a useful and rewarding day.

Near Rosemount, north of Toronto, Dufferin Forest is tall pine, with an ample parking lot for the many trucks and trailers and mini-corrals of temporary electric fencing set up alongside. Horses were everywhere, being exercised, hand-walked, grazing in their enclosures. A horse-centred village had sprouted on the edge of the forest.

Di Lindblad struck quite a sight. This 60-something woman in green sweatsuit and old straw hat sat in a field in a wingback chair with floral pattern that seemed to match the dry leaves swirling in the wind. I liked her immensely. The chair had been an unsold yard sale item that remained in her truck and made its way out on the field as a place for her to sit during downtimes in the vetting sched-ule. There was a stripe of masking tape high on the chair declaring that one might have the chair for $10; I played the role of would-be buyer, asked Di to step out of it, expressed deep satisfaction as I sank into the chair and then wondered aloud if Di had another for herself since this one suited me fine. "Getttt out," she said, and I knew bet-ter than to cross her.

Her instructions to riders blended the firm and the friendly, and were always delivered with mild authority. "When you're trotting your horse," she told one as he led his mount down to the cones and back, "pay attention to your horse. Give him his head."

Di's not a vet, but one who has been riding long distance for some time, and who was, in fact, instrumental in forming the Ontario Competitive Trail Riding Association in 1968. The name does no jus-tice to a sport that amounts to a true test of horsemanship.

What struck me at the end of the day was the camaraderie: the vets with their kindly advice and encouragement, the laughter, what care was lavished on the horses by riders and crews. I had the feeling I had entered a close-knit community. The event is run almost entirely by volunteers, maybe 20 this day; even the vets are paid only a nominal fee. People help each other: Last year in Penetanguishene a rider fell from his horse, who ran off, and the entire entourage of riders and volunteers searched until they found him.

I began to understand a new language. Capillary refill time. Mucous membrane check. Dehydration pinch test. Gut sounds. Thumps. P&R. The chine line.

Capillary refill refers to the time it takes for the small capillaries in the gums to return to normal after pressure is applied by the hand; a similar test is done on the jugular vein. In both cases, less than two seconds is good. More than that means penalty points.

Mucous membrane is a check of the gums, which should be pink, not pale or muddy.

The chine line runs horizontally along the lower side of the horse. The word *chine* has several meanings, one of which is "a deep and narrow ravine cut in soft rock by water." In a dehydrated horse, the gut muscles all clench and you can see quite clearly a demarcation as the stomach heaves.

In the pinch test, the judge gathers the horse's skin between thumb and forefinger: It should flatten in a second. More than that means penalty points or, in severe cases of dehydration, elimination.

Thumps refers to an electrolyte imbalance that leads to the diaphragm heaving at the same rate as the heart is beating. It's quite visible on the horse's body. The world authority on electrolytes in horses is a Canadian: Gayle Ecker.

One of the critical tests in distance riding is P&R: pulse and respiration. The idea is to stress the horse just before the P&R test, say, by trotting in at a brisk pace to the vet check area, and then 30 minutes later see how pulse and respiration have come down. These two parameters offer telltale clues to stress or injury, including problems not easily seen by even the most learned observer.

Arab horses—because their blood is so close to the skin, because of their large trachea and because their desert genealogy gives them other advantages in long rides—have a fantastic ability to recover their normal pulse and respiration after stress. All horses can be conditioned for distance riding, but Arabs start with an advantage on the trail, where markers show the way: Red means turn right, blue means turn left; red and white warns of any pending turn; and white means straight on.

What I like about the sport is the way it blends elite riders, who may enter hard fast races stretched over three days and 300 miles, with Sunday riders content to mosey towards the finish line after 15 or 25 miles. Distance riders have three choices: easy, challenging and difficult. "Mileage" rides give the rider all kinds of leeway to ride slow or fast, anywhere from four to six hours. Competitive trail rides up the ante somewhat, imposing restrictions and tighter timelines. Finally, endurance rides supremely test your sense of pace and the condition of horse and rider; the leeway for a perfect score may be five minutes at the end of a 50-mile ride.

Stan Alkemade, a laid-back Aussie-born vet with an outback hat, told me that endurance riding is an enormous test of the rider's navigation skills, knowledge of terrain and horsemanship. Sandy ground, like the one at Dufferin Forest, can lead to muscle stiffness. Hard ground is tough on legs. Hills pose their own set of problems. If you fail to train wisely and hard and do not put your horse in peak condition, you pay. If you ride too fast trying to win and overly stress your horse, you pay. Going too slow punishes you the other way. If you fail to provide the right mix of fuel and water and electrolytes, if you fail to cool your horse on hot days, the race is lost. Slow and steady wins the race.

Overly competitive people sometimes lose focus on the horse and pay a price at each of the vet checks—at 12.5, 25, 37.5 and 50 miles.

The ideal horse in such competitions is a sinewy horse, like a long-distance runner. Lean and fast but still with enough fat to act as reserve. Stan Alkemade looks for what he calls "a daisy cutter": a horse with a long slow trot. A horse with a lot of action in his trot means a high-stepper, and all that fancy footwork is uneconomical in the long ride. Paddlers—horses whose feet wing out to the side as they trot—similarly waste precious energy.

You want a horse with naturally low pulse rates, in the 28 to 34 beats per minute range. Forty is what vets like to see at the checks. Any resting pulse in the 20s is a sign that, at least in the cardiovascular sense, you have a special horse. A one-minute trot in a well-conditioned horse should cause no change in the pulse rate.

A bony horse wouldn't do. But the heavier the muscle bulk, the harder it is to cool the horse. Big bone is good, but not a lot of muscle. Neither do you want a leggy horse.

As with cars, water is the best coolant for horses. For years it was thought wise to avoid putting water on the back or rump lest heavy muscles seize up, but much research prior to the 1996 Olympics in hot, humid Atlanta led to some rethinking. Now the wisdom is to put temperate water on these large muscle masses, but then to immediately scrape it off, before repeating the process. A hot horse can heat up a thin layer of water in seconds, thus defeating the purpose.

Smart riders put out pails of water in the sun so that after the race they can bathe their horses in tepid water. Black horses (and this would give pause to owners of traditional, round-barrelled, black Canadians) do not do well in the hot sun. I saw a lot of greys at Dufferin Forest.

I was told that Trakehners are good distance horses as are Morgans and Canadians, but typically they don't recover in the cardiac sense in the way that Arabs do. You want a horse with slow twitch fibre in his muscle, not fast twitch: Thoroughbreds have more of the latter, Standardbreds and Arabs have more of the former.

On the other hand, there are oddballs. Joan Storrey rides a 17-hand, 1,300-pound Arab/Clydesdale called Soaring Eagle who stands out among the sleek Arabs in the way that Big Ben did in show jump-ing arenas. She has to mount him by climbing onto the flatbed of her truck. Conditioning, it seems, matters almost as much as breeding. Soaring Eagle moves with an easy grace, like a huge hydrofoil that skims across the waves.

Some families devote themselves to the sport. Connie Rawski, her husband and three boys, all competed on Sunday. Young Marcus, at seven and in Grade 1, let his mother lead his horse through the vet checks, but he did the riding—all 25 miles—and he has started to make decisions for himself on pace. His brothers, only a few years older than him, have competed in 250-mile events in Michigan stretched over five days. All those miles have accrued, but the Rawskis have a long way to go before equalling the record of one American woman who has ridden some 52,000 miles in competition.

Distance riding is not considered a dangerous sport. The worst combination is an inexperienced rider on an inexperienced and uncontrollable horse. You want one or the other, if not both, to know the ropes. I note that in the OCTRA rulebook a horse known to kick must wear a red ribbon on his tail so that vets doing checks, and even other riders on the trail, are given fair warning. I also learned that a J written in coloured marker on a horse's side signals to all that the rider or horse is a junior-level. N flags that horse or rider as a novice. It tells the judges and vets that the rider may need some extra help, which is always forthcoming.

Dozens of times I looked on as Stan Alkemade, leaned into the horse's side with his stethoscope and pronounced in his broad Australian accent, "Good gut sounds," which the volunteer at his side dutifully noted on her scoring sheet. If it was music to my ears, it was all the more to the rider's. Stan loved to see a horse come in, and after hours of riding, shake himself like a dog. It tells Stan that the horse, despite the rigours of the ride, is still feeling great.

I imagine that doing even a 25-mile competitive trail ride in pouring rain and over boggy ground would be a nightmare.

Sometimes it snows in spring and fall; some riders remember snow falling during an event in June.

The only time tempers flare is when a competitive rider is pulled out of a ride for what he or she considers to be a borderline matter. Otherwise, the mood in these events is relaxed. Riders came in with new Troxel riding helmets, fancy Boz and Orthoflex saddles, or common western ones with a Styrofoam pad taped in place or beat-up English tack.

Nancy Beacon, a sharp-featured woman from Flesherton, Ontario, and a legend among Canada's endurance riders, uses nothing fancier than an English saddle. (In one 100-mile race, someone rode bareback—to make a point, I suppose. Earle Baxter, the doyen of endurance riders in this region with 13,000 miles on his belt, has ridden horses into competition with just a rope as bridle.) Nancy's at the top in her sport, even in her sixties. This is a sport you get into in your late forties, fifties and older.

"It takes two years to know whether you've got a good horse or not," Nancy told me. Her friend, a one-woman pit crew, laughed that Nancy, when considering a horse to buy, hardly looks above the knee. For her, the cannon bone is the critical measurement. If the horse has good bone there, he tends to have it elsewhere. She wants to see eight inches minimum. Long backs tell Nancy Beacon the horse can't do hills. The bigger the feet the better. And attitude: She wants a horse with spirit. Others look for a low standing pulse; the theory being that if it's low to start with, it may stay low even under the stress of running hard and long.

Some riders had sponges inside old nylons attached to the saddle; Earle Baxter had with him a scooper fashioned out of a bleach container. It looked like something you'd find in the bottom of a rowboat, except the bailer in this case was bailing the horse out of overheating and dehydration.

I met a rider named Pat who runs a riding school. She wore red sweatpants (this was at dinner, a $5 beef stew served in disposable bowls) and she said that she liked many aspects of this sport—like the fact that no one cared what you wore. "I noticed," I said.

One young male rider, swarthy and lean, was all in black with a wide light green stripe down the side of his jodphurs. It gave him the look and bearing of a Mountie. Yvette Vinton, a contender for a spot on Canada's Pan American Games endurance team, had fitted her horse with a neon-purple bridle. At the pre-ride talk I noticed one woman's sweatshirt: white with the imprint of a green rocking horse and the name of her farm, Lonesome Acres. One woman wore an Amish-style bonnet, against the sun and in defiance, I would wager, of fashion. Another woman rode in bicycle helmet and pink sweatpants.

A man with an ample middle-aged spread wore his bicycle helmet far back on his head, exposing a vast expanse of forehead. As he held his horse and the vet check ensued, I wondered aloud to the vet if such a helmet would offer any protection at all in a forward fall. In response, she remembered a time riding when a low heavy branch hit her on the front of the head, and the sound it made. Her little story left an impression, I think, on the rider.

"There's no money in long-distance riding," Stan Alkemade observes, "and that keeps it clean. There are lots of $1,000 horses here today, and I'd bet there isn't a single person here who paid more than $5,000 for his or her horse. It's also a sport for older horses and older riders. The real top horses are 9 to 13 years of age, and you don't see many young riders excelling in the sport. It's a true test of horsemanship, and that typically comes with experience." The sport rewards speed all right, but it also rewards those who look after their horses and teach them good manners. Competitors respect, and even help, one another. In a money race last year, said Stan, a lead rider loaned a competitor an Easyboot. "You don't see that in other sports." An Easyboot is a slip-on alternative to nailed-on horseshoes and sometimes serves as a kind of spare tire should a horse throw a shoe in competition.

To prove his point that the endurance sport is seldom a sport for blueblood horses, he tells the tale of American rider Valerie Kanavy who rescued a horse called Cash from a trip to the slaughterhouse and made him into a world champion.

I notice a lot of riders at checkpoints massaging their horse's ears and head, à la Tellington-Jones. Others, says Helen Mason, a writer and a veteran of these competitions today helping at the vet checks, try naturopathy, acupuncture, acupressure, chiropractic, and laser therapy. Some even try reiki, an Oriental therapy that works on energy levels. All those miles can induce soreness in horses, and their riders are open to what works. Helen says that some people can run their hands over a horse's body and, with their eyes closed, see red when they touch on problem areas.

Helen, a tall lean woman in a toque and heavy suede coveralls, was kind and thoughtful, graciously introducing me to vets and judges. She taught me a lot. She took me behind an Arab horse, for example, and pointed out the long, thin muscle structure of his back end.

"Horse people," she explained, "talk about horses as being either steeple-bummed or apple-bummed. Quarter horses tend to the latter shape, and even when they're in terrific condition, the back end retains that round, inverted U-shape. In Thoroughbreds, on the other hand, the bum almost slopes down in a more angular v-shape. Think of people: some are rounded and others, especially marathoners, are long and lean." But a horse's back-end conformation, said Helen, is no guarantee of success in distance riding. "The horse's shape gives the rider a better chance. But lots of horses defy that rule."

An endurance rider is always making decisions. Do I take the saddle off for a vet check, or not? Removing the saddle cools the horse, but may also annoy him if he comes to think his work is over and then you saddle him up again. Some riders use "cloud" stirrups, the Spanish style that offers more support for the rider's feet. A lot of riders had put sheepskin under the saddle, with another sheepskin cover atop the saddle.

Like many horse sports, this is a humbling one. The rider, to do well at all, has to be in decent shape. The rider has to know the idiosyncracies of that horse, the vagaries of terrain and its impact on the horse, which electrolyte drink works, how to ride well and efficiently in cold and rain and summer heat.

I took great pleasure in watching the horses being trotted out to the pink cones and back, trying to see the little hints of lameness or stiffness that vets and judges were spotting. A few horses were pulled out, one wide-eyed Arab shuddering with nervous tension. It was his third competition, but for some reason the horse was completely unnerved and frightened. There was no question or argument; the vet, a petite woman all in blue under a brimmed sun hat, offered advice about calming the horse. The horse was out of the running, but the issue was clearly the horse, not the running.

Sometimes, after a 25- or 50-mile run, the horse is loath to run out to the cones and away from his food and buddies, but he always comes back with alacrity. Horses may form instant bonds with others just met. A tiny older vet with kinky white hair (she had been kicked by a horse earlier in the day and bore her pain with admirable stoicism) told me that horses in competition will sometimes bond with a horse on the trail or with a stranger horse in the trailer coming to the event. The trick then is to pry the lovebirds apart.

I felt I had learned so much in just one day but still only a fraction of what I would need to know to compete. Later, while eating stew with Helen, I was telling her that I had in mind a four- or five-year-old horse to buy. My purchase of Dali was still a few months away. She discreetly suggested rethinking. Competing on a four-year-old, she said, is like asking a 12-year-old boy to run a marathon. "You don't know much," she added, but there was no malice there. The less you know, she as much as said, the more your horse should.

Funny what people said as they ushered their horses through the vet checks. "Good girl," one said approvingly while caressing the horse's ears. "And then there's this little charmer," said one woman, alluding, no doubt, to a day spent arguing about direction and pace with her mount. "Finally," gasped another rider, "we've stopped cantering!" as she explained that her Arab only wanted to go one speed over the 25 miles: flat out.

The farrier was called over to one horse who had picked up a stone in his shoe. The stone was the circumference of a small pancake and twice as thick. When the stone finally came out, the rider slipped it into her jacket pocket, a fat souvenir of a long ride.

Such competitions redefine one's idea of competition and of athlete. The motto of OCTRA is "To finish is to win."

At one point that day at Dufferin Forest I found myself on a lawn chair chatting with veterinarian Art King. He would assist Stan Alkemade, the vet for Canada's endurance team at the Pan Am Games slated later in the summer for Winnipeg and also act as groom for one of the competitors. Looking relaxed and even philosophical in his Labatt's Blue baseball cap, he offered a theory about horse people in general and why they are the way they are. How they sometimes war with each other, especially when they sit in convention halls. I offered the suggestion that perhaps it had to do with the nature of volunteer organizations in which hierarchies form, with those putting in the most time expecting to have the most power.

"Look," he countered, "I've been a member of the Lions Club a long time and nobody fights at our meetings the way horse people do. It has to do with the nature of horsemanship. The rider may weigh 170 pounds, the horse weighs 1,000 pounds or more. So the rider has to control that horse; the whole enterprise makes you conscious of control. So when you put 300 horse people into one room you have 300 controllers."

The more I read about competitive trail riding and distance riding, the more I realized what time it takes to condition a horse, even for a 25-mile ride. And even with the flexible hours I enjoy as a writer, training for competition would essentially double my schooling time on Dali, which already seemed exorbitant. The long rides would have to wait.

Dan Waldman later assured me that training Dali for those long rides would be time well spent. A well-conditioned Canadian horse, he told me, would fare very well, at least on 25- and 30-mile distance rides. "Past that, they're carrying too much weight and they start to lose ground to the Arabs. But I've beaten lots of Arabs on my Canadian."

Waldman, 48, describes himself as "an old stockbroker turned horseman." He and his wife, Christie Riddell, who was shortlisted for the Canadian eventing team at the Montreal Olympics in 1976, own the 40-acre Gahn Ya'ar Farm (Hebrew for Garden Forest), nestled in the Rawdon Hills northwest of Halifax.

"We had been breeding Morgans," he said, "and we happened to run into Ruthanne Hart and her 16.2 Canadian, Charm. The horse is jet-black and as tough as you can ask. We brought her here a few years ago and she did eventing, distance riding, jumping and fox hunting. That's what enamoured us of the Canadians—their versatility."

Waldman and his partner also put special needs students on their horses, and at this the Canadian horse truly excels. Other horses, says Waldman, vary in their sensitivity to these students, and you can rank them on a scale of 1 to 10. The Canadian, he insisted, starts at 5 and goes to 15.

As a distance horse, he said, "they're very easygoing, with tremendous heart. I'm six feet tall and I weigh 255 pounds, so I prefer the heavier lines. When they're well conditioned, their pulse and respiration come back quickly. The only thing is, they have a heavy coat and that can lead to overheating in the spring."

When I told him that my own Canadian, a Fox horse like two of his five horses, is occasionally flighty, he wondered if the horse was simply reflecting the wariness of his rider. "We're Zen horseback people," said Waldman. "Canadians are *so* sensitive. How laid-back are you? If you're at all nervous, he's thinking, 'If my rider is nervous maybe I should be too.'"

Not long after leaving Mount Forest, Helen Mason wrote me the names of some useful books on distance riding, including *Conditioning Sport Horses*, by Canadian vet Hilary M. Clayton. "I heard about this book several years ago when I was riding with some of Australia's top endurance riders," she wrote. "Their son placed eighth at the world championships. They use this book as their bible."

Helen also issued a warning: "These horses get under your skin. It's easy to get addicted."

It's also easy to understand the attraction of distance riding. As my time with Dali steadily mounts, as my horsemanship (or so one hopes) becomes more real and focused, the two of us will grow weary of schooling in rings and even of long hacks. We'll want to test our partnership against that of others in a horse-friendly sport with a motto I admire: To finish is to win.

# DARK FOX DALI IN THE YEAR 2000

LIMESTONE STABLES, JANUARY 31, 2000

*I finally got the scoot I knew would come eventually, the one that would test me
and offer proof of my progress or send me once more tumbling into the dirt.
I was prepared in my way for that hard right turn up the centre, that skittery,
shivery little quick-step dance that took us half the length of the ring
before you could say "Dali!" or "Whoa!"*

OWNING A HORSE, I am discovering, devours time and money. Today, the new year—or the new millennium, as some would have it—only days old, I bought a foam riser pad for the saddle and tendon boots for Dali's hind legs. The tack shop registers my purchase, my face registers disbelief. Ka-ching: $180. Also wrote a cheque for my

Above: Samara Warren with Dali after schooling.

monthly stable fee: $185. Another for use of the arena: $40. Farrier bill of $90 due any day. Ka-ching. Ka-ching. Ka-ching.

Sarah, a friend and a horsewoman, had tried to warn me of what I was getting into when I told her last spring I was buying a horse. "The bleeding is about to start," she said. We both laughed, but it was divided laughter, the sort that occurs when one person understands the joke in a profound way, the other in only a vague way. It seems I am about to join a club and come to understand the phrase "horse-poor."

Sarah talks about having to pay a farrier (admittedly one who once worked for the Canadian equestrian team and likely not known for his cut-rate fees) $195 to have four new shoes put on. In five weeks, the farrier will return and check them, trim the hooves and present her with another bill for $130. Every five weeks, he returns. Every five weeks another bill. "Madame," as Sarah calls her horse Maddy at bill time or after a difficult training session, "gets more shoes than I do."

The boarding fee at Sarah's stable in the rolling horse country north of Toronto, a custom-made saddle, the vet bills: All cut deeply and regularly into a modest salary. She laughed at the absurdity of having to pay the vet $35 to sedate her horse who hates having her teeth "floated" (i.e., rasped)—a $20 procedure. It's like paying $3.50 for Gravol before boarding a $2 ferry.

"You will never spend so much money on a sport as you will once you buy a horse," Sarah cautions me. An "easy keeper" must be like a "maintenance-free house": a sly expression that folds under scrutiny.

I am also angling to spend yet more money on Dali's board, about $2,400 more over the course of the year. My hope is to get in at Limestone Stables down the road, where there is a waiting list, but where the arena is there, on the premises. I need an arena: Too many times in the fall, rain and wind conspired at Lakehead either to cancel the ride or make it an adventure.

And in winter I don't have the time to bundle up my horse and cut paths through snowdrifts to and from the arena. Even at Limestone there is still the grooming, the hot-walking. Riding is becoming a part-time job, but instead of taking in money you lay it out. In great forkfuls.

I think of people like my friend Sarah, who somehow squeeze in horse time evenings and weekends, driving long through city traffic to their barns. And I marvel at their balancing act. The horse seems antithetical to the common pursuits of work and family, and the deeper into the horse world you go, the more these other matters recede.

The horse is innocent of all this. He has no knowledge of such things as, say, stable politics. Riders, I have learned, must contend not just with their horses, but with gossip, with social climbers, with divisions that form all along those stable rows. That stable, someone told me, cuts hay rations. Bring your grain there, said another, and you'll find the tub fast diminishing. So bad are the mice at yet another stable, rumour has it, that coolers left on trunks suffer from rodent chewing and nest-making. Thus are stable reputations trammelled.

I operate on the periphery of all this hot whispering, though not entirely. When I was at Blue Haven, Barb told me one day that several rumours were circulating about me and my horse. One had my horse lame; another had me falling off Dali and breaking my collarbone. There *was* an element of truth in both stories: Dali once had a sore splint and the first-ride buck was fact. But the rumour mill, as usual, was well off the mark. Barb and I laughed.

And it's funny how owning a horse very much gets in the way of *writing* about owning a horse (a Canadian horse, as it happens). I have ambitions in coming months to travel to Quebec and elsewhere as part of my research, but the Dali clock keeps ticking. I worry about losing ground, about keeping him fit and supple, about training for distance rides. I need time to ride, but I need time to write too, and to focus on one is to sacrifice the other.

I think of John Wesley, the 18th century evangelist who rode some 288,000 miles. He always rode on a loose rein, completely absorbed in his Bible as his horse walked on. He can never have had a horse like Dali, or perhaps he did, and went ass over teakettle, saying Praise the Lord as he landed.

January 5, 2000

After a long layoff due to the holidays, a three-week layoff in which Dali got only limited turnout owing to near-incessant rain, I expected a wired horse today. Cousin Kathi and Samara both had the same idea: Let your coach take the reins after such a long layoff. Whatever male pride I possessed in the pre-Dali days has given way to a much stronger instinct for self-preservation. Let the lady ride, let the bald guy ride the pine (jumping poles stacked in one corner of the ring).

In the arena, Dali was fine, even better than fine. He offered a few mini-scoots at noises from inside the stable, and he felt tense, said Samara, in the early going. But he soon relaxed. He sheds conditioning like my dog Dusty sheds fur. The one-hour workout sapped him.

It was the trip over that had him showing the pepper. At one point he just lifted his head, planted his feet and let me know he had no interest in proceeding. I tapped him in the chest to suggest that wasn't on, and even as I did I wondered if he'd simply hightail it back to the barn. He did not. Though he did try the same stuff 10 metres on, before finally acquiescing.

But he was high-headed most of the way, and just before we crossed through the hedgerow—the halfway point in our journey—he heard or saw something in the bush that caused him to rear up a good four feet off the ground. The aggression was not aimed at me, that much I did know. It was a "Put up your dukes" aimed at some unseen terror in the trees. There was, of course, no cougar, no bear, no wolf. The horse-eating monster this day was a chipmunk. I almost—almost, mind you—laughed.

Before these trips, following Samara's advice, I put his bridle on, the halter over that. This sends a signal to Dali that it's work time, and it also gives me a little more purchase and grabbing power should he take a notion to run. For the same reason, I lift the reins forward over his head and tie them up in little knots for fear he would put his foot through the reins if he ever did decide to scoot. I then lead him on, the knotted reins and the shank both in my right hand, held about a foot below his nose, the left hand holding the rest of the lead rope. And though I may later have to swallow these words, I'm becoming more and more confident that while stiff winds and chipmunks and plain high spirit can all make the trip through the fields interesting, I don't think he would bolt. Time will tell.

Samara has suggested I stay away from sweet feed altogether, even the Kentucky Equine Research mix so favoured by Wendy and by our vet, Mark Rutherford. "It's *sweet* feed," Samara argues. "It's sugar, and as I read more and more about what sugar does to the human body, I have to wonder what it does to horses." She's suggesting I try an extruded feed she gives to old Bogi, her nigh-unflappable Arab. I just might give it a try.

The experimentation is a little like pulling up to a gas station and trying various octanes to see which best suits your car. But I now see the car as a less complicated mode of transportation. Choosing the right fuel for my horse is just one of many variables: Too little octane can hurt the engine, too much can hurt the driver. Then again, so can lunar phases, high winds and pilot error, also known as brain deficit.

Next day the wind picked up as the day went on. As a young man I hated wind because it mussed my perfect hair, but eventually I lost my hair and cared less about gusts. Dali has brought me back to my youth, once more cognizant of wind.

The walk to the arena was uneventful, though he did pause and reconnoitre at the spot where that vicious chipmunk resides. The arena creaked and groaned in the wind, and the door at the far end would now and then shudder and flap.

Samara, at my request, rode him again today but felt no need for me to chase him. With the wind howling, I thought she was very brave. Confident is closer to the mark. Dali did make one little feint, a sideways spook when the noises got to him. But he quickly settled and Samara felt he was looser than the day before. She asked him to do little squares, one-quarter pirouettes, something he had never done before. "I like his willingness to try new things," Samara said from the saddle.

But the three weeks off meant that by the end of the hour he was again pooped. Still, Samara managed some canters down the long side. Unlike some trainers, who believe workouts should be compressed, say, four days of riding with three off, she prefers—with young horses—to ride every second day. That pattern lets the horse recover from workouts and may prevent him from souring on work.

"He's a young horse carrying a lot of weight," Samara observed. "I'd be leery of asking him to do too much too soon. When he sets up his canter, his head comes up. He's still working out his balance at that higher speed with a rider on." Her thinking is to build up his conditioning, let the miles accrue.

"He's going to be a sensible horse, and a very good trail horse," she added, and gut instinct told me she was right. By spring, per-haps, there will be no need to chase away those bucks before riding him. The journey continues.

January 10, 2000
Samara trace-clipped Dali today, a move designed to take away some of that great fur coat on his chest, neck and flank, the hot spots that are so difficult to dry once sweat-soaked. It means that hot-walking will be less of a chore, but it also means we'll have to blanket him for turnouts to avoid chills.

I had thought he might act up around the clippers' loud buzz, but he was very brave, very patient. I stood at his head and he would occasionally look back to see what Samara was doing; other times he would bury his head in my chest, content to have his head stroked.

Perhaps his first haircut was more stressful than he let on. The walk to the arena saw Dali pause three or four times for loud whinnies back to his buddies and tiny tantrums that suggested he might just run off. But he wasn't serious about it, and he seemed to sense I knew it. I pretty much ignored him and marched on.

In the ring, with the rain now bucketing down, he was mostly a prince. We tried a thick loose-ring German snaffle bit, a loan from Samara, and he seemed to like it more than the D-ring with the copper rollers I had been using. The latter would end up hanging on a cut-glass doorknob in my home office; I do not miss the mouselike squeaks it made as Dali worried those rollers with his tongue.

He offered one small bout of skittishness, likely occasioned by too much of my heel into his side. "Use your calf and your thigh," Samara advised. "He doesn't like the heel, it gets him worrying. But he respects it too, so save it for when you want him to canter and he ignores you."

I actually *want* him to scoot now. I need to get past one, as a confidence booster. I want assurance that my striving for classic form—straight back, feet under my hips, a straight line from my hands to my elbows to my shoulders and contact with Dali's mouth—will better arm me against these scoots.

"You do look a lot more confident up there," praised Samara.

"When you saw me riding a few weeks back," I replied, "you saw me at my worst." From repeated falls, my body was battered, my psyche at low ebb.

We did serpentines, badly. Mine, ragged and erratically paced, looked nothing like the ones Samara was drawing in the turf a few days ago. Same horse, different rider.

The trip home was through pelting rain, Dali dry enough under a light cotton rug and the heavier one cousin Kathi had bequeathed to me. Still, the water soaked into his neck and mane and dripped through the air holes in my riding helmet, and for some reason, what came to me in that downpour was a small hint of the awful life of the warhorse. How the horses drowned in mud during the First World War, how they were clipped against vermin but shuddered in the snow, how it hurt their handlers to see them suffer so.

I have complained about what I take to be his skittishness, but Dali has much to teach me about patience. It seems to take forever to put on, and take off, his tendon guards, his several blankets, bridle and halter. Today, he tried a little dodge ball in the stable as I doffed his halter and put on the bridle. He was punishing me for being too lazy to leave the reins around his neck. Careless horsemanship invites his games of tag.

But he stands, like a good soldier, in the ring as I blanket him. Samara gave me a useful and important tip today: Always do up blanket straps in a set order, according to whether you're putting the blanket on or taking it off. When I blanket him, say, while he's loose and standing in the arena, I should secure the front buckles first, leg straps last. Were he to bolt as the blanket was being secured, the danger lies in the blanket and straps falling back and entangling his hind legs. You risk a torn blanket, torn muscle, or worse. On the other hand, while removing the blanket, I am to unfasten the leg straps first, then belly straps, front buckles last.

The rule is this: Putting a blanket on, buckle front to back; taking a blanket off, unbuckle back to front.

It's much ado, these blankets. On wind-chill days, I'll secure, with a big bulldog clip bought at an office supply store, a soft quarter-sheet around Dali's neck, followed over the body by the cotton rug and then the big one. He actually likes all this fussing over him. After the ride, and back in the stable, he patiently waits as I make him ready for his stall or for turnout. All this handling, the hours of it, are paying, I am starting to see, a dividend.

January 12, 2000

Another good day in the arena. As my confidence returns and I get looser, so does Dali. We formed squares (badly) and serpentines (well), we trotted over poles, did more transitions and some canter work on the circle. No spooks, only a tiny one that barely measured on the Dali Richter scale.

He likes the loose-ring snaffle, offered a nice forward trot, and even handled himself well in the boogey corner at the far end. In imitation of Samara, and always at that end, I make a low sound produced by vibrating my tongue off the roof of my mouth. The result might be taken for a cat's loud purr or a small fishing motor, but the sound apparently achieves two ends: It forces the rider to take deep breaths in order to make the sound, and the deep breathing calms the horse, for it's a sound that horses themselves make when they attempt to calm each other. Coincidence or not, there were no boogey corner scoots today.

Samara was impressed, and wondered if down the line we'd have any interest in jumping. "Sure," I said, "not because I want to compete in shows, but just because it's fun."

Dali continues to unleash the contents of his bowels the moment I put the saddle pad on him. Is it worry? Is he loosening up in preparation for work? Has he simply settled into a habit? He may step ahead but he otherwise makes no great fuss about saddling, doesn't sidestep or dance, and so I am inclined to ignore his emptying. Were I to adopt a similar habit, *then* it would be cause for concern.

January 13, 2000

Walked Dali through bitter cold to the arena. With wind chill, it felt like −26 Celsius or so. I thought of Dali's ancestors and the winds they would have faced off the St. Lawrence River.

We could have timed the clipping better. His neck and parts of his belly look like a lawn mower was set loose in a hayfield. He went well in the arena, though we kept it light owing to the cold and the fear of pulled muscles.

I stayed at Lakehead all day, kept the car heater on broil and read my newspaper, waiting for the farrier. Terry Osborne is, says Kathi, a blacksmith worth waiting for. He couldn't be specific about when he was coming, and I wanted to be there. And it was good that I was.

Terry had warned me that while Dali was quite good for his first set of shoes and snow pads, he might not be so accommodating for his second. Dali abided the hoof trim, but he objected to the nailing of the shoes. He pushed Terry around, reared a little, snapped one of the cross-ties (which, I should say, was secured by mere binder twine—a safety precaution) and generally issued grief.

"It's not about fear," said Terry, who remained unflappable throughout. "It's more of a temper thing." This was a Thursday, and I had ridden Dali earlier that day. He was to get a long weekend off. When I dropped by the stable Saturday morning, I found him somewhat surly, not keen to let me adjust his turnout blanket, bossing Ras for no apparent reason. He is, as Kathi pointed out when I told her all this, a sensitive horse. "He doesn't let things just slide off his back," she said.

Prediction: He'll be a handful to ride Monday morning.

Wrong again, on several counts. On Monday, a cold blast of air descended on us, so I gave Dali a few more days to the warmth of his barn. The barn radio was reporting that in the Ottawa area the blend of actual temperature and wind chill made it feel like −50 degrees Celsius, besting temperatures then being felt in Antarctica.

Wednesday, the cold diminished somewhat by gentler winds and bright sun, I saddled Dali. He seemed miffed and wary. He even had second thoughts about having his feet cleaned, but I am past being bluffed on that score.

In the indoor ring, he trotted well. Our serpentines get better and better. Samara also had us doing a fancier version of the leg-yield, a precursor to the shoulder-in she calls tail-to-the-wall. You set up your horse in a walk alongside the arena wall, angle his body into the centre of the ring at maybe 30 degrees and keep his hind end adjacent to the wall. Dali did fine going counter-clockwise, but the dreaded going to the right confounded him. The canter work suffered in the same way.

When my repeated attempts failed to achieve the canter transition, Samara hopped on and got it first time. Proof that though Dali was running out of gas and patience, a better guide knew the way.

Echoing others, Samara said that I should expect Dali to continue to be physically awkward under saddle, even flighty, until he's seven. Dog trainers used to tell me that about Dusty: You'll see a big change, they said, when she turns three. She will become less the impish pup who used to flee and tour the village as a lark, more the mature dog who comes when called. They were right. Samara's comment came as I had been berating Dali, suggesting that he's had enough miles that his serpentines *should* be decent by now. Implicit was that I had spent a lot of time and money on this horse and he owed me, at the very least, a serpentine.

But as I rode past her, she in the centre of the ring, Samara defended my horse. There's a Buddha calm about her, and though she's 24 and I'm 50, she is nevertheless the teacher and I am the pupil. And though she is as sweetly disposed a person as I have ever met, I could sense my teacher digging in her heels. Don't even think in those terms, she said. Dali's trot has improved marvellously even in the few weeks she's been watching him. He's been frightened by you coming off him a few times. Don't saddle him with expectations.

Her mantras in the ring are solid ones. Be patient with your horse. Praise him each time he does something right. Support him every way you can: with your quiet hands, by telegraphing your intention, by giving him time to be himself during lessons.

Perhaps I should have left the ring humiliated that she got the canter where I failed. But no, I felt relief. There is no hurry to all this, no deadline to be met, and Dali's seventh birthday is almost a year and a half away. One day he will canter out of a halt. He will be collected and fit and steady, "a made horse" as some trainers say, and his rider might dare to call himself a decent rider with educated hands. All in due time. Dali time.

January 24, 2000

The sweeter side of Dali continues to reveal itself. Last week I rode him only once owing to the cold snap; today marked only the second time I had ridden him in 10 days. Yet I chased him half-heartedly before riding him, somehow knowing he'd be fine.

A few times he whinnied in response to another horse out in the paddock and he felt a little full of himself. He was up, but not overly worried or frantic. The long walk over, through snow-covered fields on a bright day free at last of wind chill, was a joy. I love that slow exhalation he makes, the half sigh that tells me he's relaxed and breathing deeply. And I tell him so. I talk to him always—as I tack him up, as we walk, as I ride.

When the snow is deep, the walk is more like a trek and can take up to half an hour each way. Dali abides my many queries, even turning his head in towards me as if genuinely interested. I ask him about horse time, and how he measures it. Is a day in the paddock longer or shorter than a day in the stall? What does he fear most? The wind? Sounds he cannot fathom? I ask after his pleasures, I pause to wipe some grit near his large brown eyes, I touch him on the nose for no particular reason.

He seems to take comfort in my voice. Sometimes I speak inanely to him, sometimes in French. I tell him that Muhammad Ali used to say, "Ain't I pretty?" and that Dali—if only he could talk—could say the same.

He tries hard to please during schooling. His forward trot is much better, and the canter I couldn't manage last time came today, with a tiny little buck thrown in to let me know the old Dali was still squirreling around in there somewhere.

January 26, 2000

I sent a card to Gilles and Barb, a Krieghoff scene of pastoral 19th century Quebec with the Canadian horse pulling a sleigh. I reported that Dali is well, that he seems to enjoy the routine of walking through the snow-covered fields to the arena and the ride that follows.

He can still go on strike near the end of a lesson, ears pinned, halting at any excuse. But every day he gets a little better at what we ask of him. He even anticipated the canter today. Samara wondered if he surprised himself by getting it, for he held it longer than he has. We also went over a tiny cross-pole jump, Samara taking him over it first, then me.

Later, as I hot-walked him, another boarder at the stable stopped to inquire about him and to admire his "big expressive eyes." It's like I'm falling for him a second time, but on different footing now. I trust him so much more now, and I know the reverse is also true. He lets me into his space longer: Today, after the ride, I saw him scratching the side of his face on a board in his stall and I offered my services. I scratched him for almost a minute, and he luxuriated in that. On other occasions he has allowed such contact, but he'd swing away after a few seconds, then come back. This was different.

Samara has offered to sell me several of her used turnout blankets, too small for her big Nate. And so the one I fancied most is now on Dali and I took home for a wash the old green New Zealand rug Kathi had given me.

I tossed it into the big tub downstairs, filled the tub with soap and water, and thrashed the big thing around in the lather. Up came this brown swill, a fetid foamy brew of mud and manure and who knows what else, the dank and myriad emanations that gather on the woolly undersides of horses and their blankets. The basement, complained Kurt and Ulrike, smells like a barn. Actually, worse than a barn. A horse barn offers hay and the cedar in wood shavings to take the edge off the other smells. What came off Dali's rug had bite. The cellar was days recovering.

Kathi's advice—take a garden hose and strong brush to the rug spread out on the lawn in spring—came too late.

January 31, 2000

I finally got the scoot I knew would come eventually, the one that would test me and offer proof of my progress or send me once more tumbling into the dirt. It came at the boogey end, where a ray of light from an ill-closing door slants across the ring. Dali eyes it every time he passes.

Samara warns me to take care down there, to talk to him. And so I was prepared in my way for that hard right turn up the centre, that skittery, shivery little quick-step dance that took us half the length of the ring before you could say "Dali!" or "Whoa!" I was elated, for it was a serious scoot and I had ridden it. Maybe this is what the first-time surfer feels when he finally catches a big wave and rides it all the way to the beach. Samara paid compliments, to Dali for showing us we should not take him for granted despite his good manners of recent weeks, to me for staying on, and then she sent us right back to the scene of the crime, lest that corner elicit more.

Our lessons have an almost ritualistic shape to them: tentative beginnings, solid middles, miserable ends. Tails to the wall gets better each time out, as do the serpentines. Even the canter shows steady progress and Dali now anticipates it in the corners, and I find myself having to bring him back from unasked-for canters. Call it an embarrassment of riches. For all that, the circle work at the end makes him sour.

The ears go back, he stalls repeatedly like the Fiat I had as a student, and starts up again like that car did in winter, which is to say, reluctantly or not at all. That car invariably needed a push, as Dali does. He cuts into the middle, fusses with his bit, lets the tongue roll out. He operates in a zone one inch removed from a buck. My riding falls apart, I resort to impatient little wishbone kicks and hand pumps and lean like an old cedar.

Samara somehow keeps us focused and calm, finds the little ray of light, not the one that rattles Dali in the boogey end, but the cause for optimism that brings him and me back two days later remembering only the good part of the lesson, those long cheerful trots where we sailed down the long side and looked a very passable horse and rider.

February 6, 2000

Rode him alone, *sans* Samara, for the first time since last November when my horse adventure looked to be coming undone. It was a Sunday afternoon, with Limestone Stables deserted. I had to rouse Dali from a deep slumber in one corner of the paddock. Perhaps, Samara later wondered on the phone, he's too hot under that blanket of his. Maybe he was baking under that sun. He stared somewhat vacantly at me. It was his pal Ras who nickered to me and trotted over, looking for the piece of apple I always save for him.

Only when I got up to Dali and greeted him did I realize I had a lead rope in my hands but no halter. Dali wasn't the only one half-asleep.

As we approached mid-February, the cold of January giving way to milder weather but deeper snow, we fell into a routine, young Dali and I. When I asked him to run a little in the ring the other day, I thought I caught him bowing, a mark of respect that Chris Irwin had talked about. His lazy streak occasionally flashes, but he's going over small X-jumps now and agreeably cantering longer—an entire circle of the arena—when I ask for it. His whole attitude seems more relaxed and confident, perhaps reflecting my own.

Dali seems to be saying, "I see now what my job is, and it's a job I can do." Though I am hard-pressed to tell, Samara insists he's getting leaner. Those long marches through the back fields, the snow a foot or two deep along some stretches, must be muscling us both.

What a pleasure it is to call cousin Kathi and give her such glowing reports.

"Any better and I'd be suspicious," I told her.

"You're cruisin'," she replied.

"For a bruisin'?" I asked.

"Oh yeah," she answered a little mysteriously, and she began to tell me what it's like for her husband, Dick, to hack with their two young and high-spirited eventers at 5 a.m. these winter mornings, after several months of layoff, each horse armed with a pocketful of tricks and spooks and good-fun bucks that only a gifted, long-legged rider like Dick could handle.

"You have no idea," said Kathi, and she was, as usual, right. I have no idea.

February 22, 2000

The other day an old demon looked to have returned. I rode Dali in the ring—after riding, not walking him, over. This was a new development, one that Samara encouraged and the ever deeper snow made almost necessary. After a lesson last week, I decided to ride him home from the arena. I walked him past the barns and outbuildings that make him wary, thinking he'd be calmer in the lane. But he would circle the second I went to put my foot in the stirrup. My heart sank a little, but only a little.

"Dali," I told him, "we're going to get this done." I was in no mood for wading through snowbanks. At first, anger flashed in me, and I snapped his bridle. Then something like the beginnings of horsemanship kicked in, and every time he circled, I put him to work. Made him circle more. Finally, I tossed off his blankets, wondering if they were bothering him. Maybe they were, or maybe I simply outlasted him. He finally let me on, and we had a nice leisurely walk home.

Yesterday, he was first-rate in the ring. His canter, especially, was quick and powerful. He scooted a few times when great sheets of snow peeled off the roof. Kudos for us both. "Two months ago," said Samara, "you wouldn't have sat that scoot. And Dali was actually very brave about the snow coming off the roof. A lot of horses wouldn't have tolerated that."

As for getting back on Dali for the ride through the fields, Samara's advice was to mount him right outside the barn. "Bite the bullet and ride him past those buildings. The problem with the lane is that all he can think about is getting home, and he doesn't want to wait for you." Smart, that Samara.

She also suggested that back at the stable I towel off Dali's head, especially where the bridle touches his skin. The weather had turned exceedingly warm, and she wondered if he might be itchy. Well, I did as she said and Dali practically climbed into my lap. His head got lower and lower, he got all soft. I think I could have rubbed him a long time.

I don't say the mounting demon is gone. Once conjured, demons linger.


I was right about that. Two days later, at that same spot outside the barn, it took me five minutes to get on him. We had done more canter work than normal in the arena and the boy was up. Once again, I waited him out, put him to work when he circled to avoid my foot in the stirrup. Fine, you want to circle, I told him, let's circle.

The blankets may be adding to the problem, for they hide the stirrups, especially the right one. I am reasonably sure he wouldn't run off with me unstirruped, but he does barge. Kathi's suggestion was that the next time he stands agreeably to be mounted, lean down over his neck and offer him a treat. Make him think apple, not barging.

Once mounted, we headed home and for the first time I had a lot of horse under me all the way home. Did the canter excite him? Is he finally getting into shape? Did the ice water we traversed in those back fields act like a bracing cold shower? Hard to say, but at the point in the hedgerow where we once encountered a chipmunk,

Mr. Dali chose to spook. The good news was, I had a powerful sense he would, I anticipated it, and rode it out.

I rode on the trail with Samara and Bogi a few days ago. Dali was tense. "He's got ghosts in his past," was Samara's assessment. Kathi wonders if it's more about spring seemingly in the air—on this warm sunny day the temperature hit 10 degrees Celsius—and being confined to his stall for days at a time.

Late winter/early spring, I am learning, spells hard times for most horses. Just when the sun beckons them out, they're forced to stay in. If the horses were allowed into sodden paddocks, there would be no grass in the spring.

So Dali is stall-bound. On the trail he had a powerful walk. He offered quite a few mini-scoots, and when Bogi crossed a stream right behind him Dali ran on for a bit, as if chased by hounds. Only after about an hour and a half did he relax, but as we got closer to the barn his anxiety resurfaced.

And while I would have wished for more calm, I liked that tremendous sense of power he told me about. I thought of him on the long ride. It seemed to me he could have trotted all day.

March 9, 2000

My nightmare with a young horse such as Dali is essentially the one I conjured that first day I rode him: I am tangled in my stirrups and he is in a full gallop, his terror goaded by that thing in the green helmet banging and dragging at his side. That thing is me. The thought haunts me yet.

More so now.

March 9 is a warm day, with gusting winds. While I was riding Dali through the back fields over to the arena, Samara is outside the arena chatting up my cousin Kathi, who happened to be there on a grain swap, along with Kathie Groenewegen. As I would later learn, Samara was telling the Kaths how well I was doing, how Dali was settling in nicely. But where, she wondered, were they? Larry's never late . . .

At about that moment, perhaps at that very moment, I was hitting the ground hip-first, Dal's saddle was around his belly, and he was tearing off with all the speed he could muster.

Today I got my first taste of what it's like to have a horse bolt, him striking for the barn in a head-down gallop, every fibre twitching. Dali had been cranky as I tacked him up. He's been stall-bound for weeks now, with only 30 minutes a day of turnout. The wind was up, he was up with it, and I was ready, or so I thought, for some antics.

The little scoots and shys and spins I was learning to handle. But this one upped the ante in a heartbeat. To use a military metaphor, Dali had gone from conventional weaponry to the nuclear kind.

And once again, I am afraid, pilot error played a huge role in my hard fall. I'm using an old saddle of Samara's while mine is in for restuffing. The girth seemed tight, but I should have rechecked it up in the saddle. I don't feel safe doing that because Dali sometimes barges on. But we'd better deal with that, because the girth is like a seat belt, and mine wasn't done up properly.

When Dali spooked at something in the bushes on the way to the arena—or claimed he did—he shied hard and quick to the right, causing the saddle to slip hard to the left. This would have compounded exponentially whatever fear had been roused in him. In a nanosecond, Dali spun back in the direction of the barn and there I was in a full hard gallop and listing hard to port. Perhaps I could have fought for position, but it was a losing battle and I bailed out.

My last picture of Dali was him roaring off, the saddle now underneath him, stirrups flailing in the air as the leathers danced, the mud coming up in great black clumps in his wake. Now another nightmare offered itself: Dali hung up in the low branches of a tree, a wide-eyed prisoner of stirrup leather, reins and unforgiving wood.

My left hip screamed, but I ran as best I could down the thin patch of grass, across the field, dreading what I might find up ahead.

But bless him, he was waiting for me just beyond the gate. He was frantic, but he let me slip off the saddle, the buckles at his belly. Pad, saddle, girth were all awash in mud.

Later I would return and retrieve lost items—a stirrup and leather and the quarter sheet—all lying not far from the scene of my hard tumble.

I walked Dali home, saddle hooked over my left arm, covered in mud and shame and misery. And I was left wondering: Did Dali, in fact, spook at something in the bushes? Or had he planned this awful mischief? Was this about ducking work? Does he have that screw loose that some Fox-line horses are said to have? Or was the bolt caused by pure terror, one he feels he must deal with while abandoning all thought of his rider?

"Never underestimate this horse," Barb Wills had said many months ago. I never imagined he would bolt for the barn. Shy and scoot yes, dance a little, sure. But bolt?

I'm calmer now than I have been after previous falls, but I also feel I'm at another one of those crossroads. Cousin Kathi was still at Limestone as I drove in to explain my tardiness to Samara, and we made jokes about where I would place my want ad for the horse I would sell.

Samara was so sweet and understanding, urging me not to beat myself up. But she was frank too, assuring me that there were more falls in the cards. It seems that the lesson of the tight girth has yet to be learned. Even old Bogi, she said, will panic if the saddle starts to slide. Mine was close to 45 degrees. Small wonder Dali lost it.

Sarah, too, offered her shoulder when I called her. And as she did last time, she prescribed arnica gel for the bruising, Vitamin C for the smashed capillaries, and a few tales of her own humiliation to assuage mine.

I wonder how many falls I've got left, how much patience, how much courage.

Cousin Kathi, next day, did her best to put all this in perspective. Look, she said, at where you were four months ago with Dali, and look where you are now. The fact that Dali came back to you, she said, is very unusual and I was to take some consolation in that.

Mary Ann Barrett would later tell me about a friend who failed to check his girth on a hunt, resulting in a similar circumstance—the saddle slipping, the rider falling off and the saddle underneath the horse. But in this case the horse's panic was full-blown. He bolted onto a highway, was hit by a car and had to be put down on the spot. Told of my story, Mary Ann's response was immediate: "You have a very smart horse."

Kathi also pointed out that my list on the pilot-error side was long: sloppy girth, riding him in high wind when I know it rattles him, with a quarter sheet over his hindquarters. Maybe the blanket flared in the wind?

My fall, Kathi told me, caused her to reminisce with Kathie Groenewegen while sitting on the back of her pickup yesterday. They remembered other runaways, Kathi in a body cast for six months. They know all too well what a treacherous mix is spring and the stall-bound horse. But their falls—horse people call them "wrecks"—happened when they were 8 to 15 years old, when horses were all about fun and never about fear, and the notion of mortality was a long way off. I turn 51 on Saturday and I'm wearing a grapefruit on my hip, waiting for the purple bruise to show and thankful I'm not shopping around for a neck brace or a wheelchair.

Each spring, Kathi assured, will be a little less crazy than the one before. In the meantime, she had some advice: "Take baby steps," she said. Maybe that means going back to walking him to the arena, certainly on windy days. Maybe it means hiring Samara to ride him more and tune him up while spring is in the air.

I always feel better after a talk with Kathi. Dali, she says, has no screws loose. But she did wonder if all these falls have jarred a few in my own cranium.

On Friday, the day after my hard fall, the swelling had reached its peak. My left hip looked as though I had applied a wide swath of Mercurachome, that orange-tinted disinfectant my mother, a registered nurse, would use to paint the wounds of my childhood. The one hip had become rounded, almost feminine, and bore no relation to the vertical other. I was not pleased with the effect. Underneath the orange tint, a black-and-purple bruise roiled, like an angry thundercloud, as big as a certain horse's head.

March 23, 2000

For the past two weeks, while my hip slowly healed, Samara has been riding Dali. I get regular reports on how well it's going. The first time she rode him he was "flighty," she said, but he was wonderful after that. Forward in his trot, agreeable, and though wary at that spot where I came off him on the trail, good on the way home. Samara has been riding him to and from the arena, often in stiff winds. I repeat: a rider with confidence.

Yesterday she rode him in the outdoor ring at Lakehead, and had a rocky beginning. Perhaps remembering the last time he and I were out there (another hard fall), he was fearful, and extremely wary of Samara's leg on him. She and I are both beginning to wonder if someone, at some point, has spurred him.

I wanted to know if Samara had worked on adjusting the girth from the saddle, and indeed she had. "Did he walk forward as you did that?" I asked. "Oh, he didn't walk," she said, understated as always. Translation: He ran. But Samara eventually got the job done and he settled well. Even Gerry riding his tractor into the arena didn't faze him.

More troubling, though, was that Dali's right front leg, site of those hairline fractures last summer, is warming again. He may have strained it when he bolted, or while out at play in the paddock, or even getting up after a roll.

I feel a great wash of emotion: worry about the well-being of my clearly smart, sensitive and high-strung horse, worry about my own well-being, and a bitter taste in my mouth that I know is humiliation. Samara spotted the warmth; would I have thought to feel that leg?

She shows great affection for Dali ("He's a good boy," she keeps saying), and has great faith that all will be well. She is certain that ghosts haunt Dali, but equally certain that we can, if not banish them, then park them. You, she told me, have never been rough with him, so it's not like we have to fix both rider and horse. Our task is simpler: Build his confidence.

I hope Samara is right. I hope it's that simple, that Dali learns to trust me, that I have the time, the patience, the skill to pull it off.

March 24, 2000

Like a summer day. Sitting out on the deck talking to the students next door, one of them horsey. She, too, fell off a bolting horse. But her first horse, she recalls, was a 12-year-old, well schooled and calm, the kind of horse they call a "schoolmaster." I nodded.

Got back on Dali for the first time in two weeks. He was good as gold in the arena, but during the walk over—me leading him—he shied at the place where I pulled the saddle off him two weeks previously. It seems that he and Samara encountered a grouse there last week, so now it's a double-boogey spot. He ducked behind me and flew into an enclave of prickly ash, spinning me around and down. I found myself on the ground, looking up into the now-familiar loins of my horse, the small finger on my right hand bloodied, the hand peppered with thorns. Coming home, he did something similar by the sand ring. When will he stop playing the two-year-old?

March 29, 2000

He was so placid as I tacked him up, the rain pelting down outside. But a new caution, a new respect for horsepower, has entered my life with horses, and it will be a while before I ride him to the arena alone.

Yesterday I was driving Margaret Atwood to the train station in Kingston, following a charity fundraiser we were both a part of. We got talking about horses, for she is no stranger to that world. I told her my horse was called Dali and she reacted with a little horror. Salvador Dali the painter, she intimated, was mad. Perhaps, the author suggested, you should call the horse Saroma, after the farm, not Dali, after the surrealist.

The Spanish artist was a tormented man obsessed by decay. He literally tried to paint like a madman, stoking his own paranoia and recording the images that came to mind. Every bit as strange as his art, he annoyed other artists with his bizarre statements and lust for the limelight. H. H. Arnason, in his *History of Modern Art* notes that Dali "made the word surrealism a common noun in all languages, denoting an art that is irrational, erotic, insane—and fashionable."

I wonder if Margaret Atwood has a point. Dali, the horse, I mean, is good in the arena. But he is more than a little animated on the trek between stable and arena. Today he pulled back at some real or imagined threat where the field meets the hedgerow, and when I snapped his lead rope he struck out, more symbolically than anything, with that right front hoof. I cuffed him lightly on the nose and suggested he not do that again.

How cranky he is, I say to myself, wondering if it's all about stall confinement for weeks on end. Or is he just one of those studdy geldings, still full of what Gilles Dupuis would call "attitude"?

In the ring, I let him run, and I chased him a little. He exploded down the long side, occasionally kicking and bucking, the double kick especially full of snap and vigour. Were this a comic strip the words *bam* and *pow* would be encased in a zigzag box. Six months ago I would have been shocked by the outburst; now I take some pleasure in it, and some sense of security too. I'm taking what my vet calls "a little gas out of his tank."

Mark Rutherford, it happened, was there this morning and peeked into the ring. He told me that a saddled horse loose in the ring violated Pony Club rules. "Don't let a kid see you," he said.

"You're afraid he'll roll?" I asked.

He nodded. I assured Mark that I keep the chase on to take away the roll, but I also agreed when he suggested there should be a Pony Club for adults. I'd be in the front row, wide-eyed, taking notes.

As Samara looked over my tack, she noted, but with no hint of reprobation that: 1. The bridle was incorrect, with the noseband on the wrong side of the cheekpiece; 2. I had put the girth on with the elasticized portion on Dali's right side, not on the left where it should be; and 3. The heavy metal snaps, where the stirrup leather attaches to the saddle, were in the vertical position, not horizontal as they should be.

The third item, especially, gave me pause. No one had ever told me, but I should have figured it out. Were I ever to get my foot caught in the stirrup and the horse (we won't name names) is bolting for the barn, you want those stirrups to come away. Otherwise, the rider is dragged, possibly towards a mushy end.

"If you value your life," Samara said brightly, "I'd leave those snaps flat. I noticed you had them vertical. I meant to tell you about that."

I meant to tell you, she was saying, to join the Pony Club. You have a lot to learn.


March 31, 2000

Lunged Dali in the outdoor ring at Lakehead and was reminded of past antics: how right off the bat he moved to canter, shook his head and thought, just thought, about running. I knew to stay calm, kept talking to him, kept my outside hand low and quiet. But I forgot to close the gate and in no time the ring was full of cows and calves, all kicking up their heels. I parked my horse in the barn while Samara played drover.

I rode him, I will admit, with my heart in my mouth. Dali had *scoot* written all over him, but Samara urged me to keep my hands light but in contact, my shoulders back, and the second his eyes or ears wandered to some point outside the ring—a calf playing king of the mountain on the rotten hay pile, some flapping plastic, Gerry's tractor starting up—I was to think about yielding or bending. I felt like a small boy taking his first riding lesson, my brow wrinkled, my head full of questions. Such as, "Samara, how do you stop a runaway horse?" Turns out, she yanks back hard, then releases, to stop the horse from bracing against the bit.

But Dali was wonderful in the ring. No scoots. Well, one. Good canter. I wish I could say he's turned a corner. I know better. With horses, there are no corners, just curves ahead that may lead to pleasant views . . . or precipitous drops.

ICE CUTTING

CHAPTER 17

# THE CANADIAN HORSE HALL OF FAME

---

*"The birthplace of the first Morgan horse was saturated with the blood of the small, blocky,*
*powerful Canadian horse . . . In my opinion, Justin Morgan was a horse of*
*predominant, if not pure, French-Canadian blood."*
—*Bonnie L. Hendricks,* International Encyclopedia of Horse Breeds, *1995*

THERE IS, OF COURSE, NO SUCH THING as the Canadian Horse Hall of
Fame. The sometimes sorry history of the breed suggests that the
horse who did so much for this country—on the farm, on the battlefield, on the track—was often not appreciated on his home turf.
Steadfast, generous and ideally suited to our harsh climate, the
Canadian horse almost slipped into extinction several decades ago, and
only the work of some dedicated individuals brought the breed back.

Above: *Ice Cutting* by Cornelius Krieghoff, circa 1849.

---

Perhaps there should be a place of honour for some of the great Canadian horses of the past 350 years, and their champions. What follows are some horse tales for the selection committee to ponder. I saw no reason to repeat the exploits of some of the great Canadian sport horses described in Chapter 13, but they too merit consideration.

### 1. *On Every Morgan a Maple Leaf*

The little bay stallion called Figure and known to us now as Justin Morgan, sired a magnificent breed called the Morgan, much admired both here and south of the border, where Americans call the Morgan their own.

Justin Morgan, named after his owner, became the pride of Vermont in the early 1800s. In trotting, pacing and pulling he bested every horse in the state who challenged him. He was the little horse that could and he stamped his "get," or offspring, with his own unique quality. The most famous story about him involves a bet.

Then owned by a man named Robert Evans, the horse had done a hard day's work and his owner had stopped in a tavern on his way home. Talk centred on a nearby pine log that other teams of horses had been unable to move to the lumber mill. Evans, cognizant of the incredible pulling strength of his little 14-hand horse, challenged the mill company bosses to bet him a gallon of rum his horse couldn't pull the log onto the landing in three starts. The bet was accepted, and all in the tavern walked outside to see how things would play out.

Perhaps feeling his drink, Evans approached the log but feigned embarrassment at having to hitch his horse to such a meagre load, and he suggested that three of the largest men sit on the log to enliven the wager. In just two pulls, and to the astonishment of everyone, Figure hauled both men and log to the lumber mill. The legend of Justin Morgan was born.

But is the celebrated Morgan breed in fact coursing with Canadian-horse blood? Robert Leslie Jones, a Canadian historian who investigated the matter in the mid-1900s, seemed to think so. The original Justin Morgan, or so it is claimed, was brought from Springfield, Massachussetts, to Randolph, Vermont, in 1795. He was, it was said, the son of a Thoroughbred and a dam of unknown origin. His three most famous sons, Bulrush, Sherman and Woodbury— collectively the alleged sires for all but a few in the Morgan family —were in turn mated with a French-Canadian mare and two dams of unknown origin.

Jones refers to "the puffers of the Morgans in the 1840s" who wanted it known that the Morgan line owed everything to that Thoroughbred. The Morgan, says Jones, likely had some Cleveland Bay in him, plus Suffolk Punch, and certainly "a considerable amount of French-Canadian blood." Thus the excellent legs and feet, and, especially, the heavy, crimpy mane and tail. Champions of the Morgan breed were loath to admit this. But as one Vermonter noted in the *National Live Stock Journal* of 1881, "There was [in the 1840s and 1850s] a terrible fear the Morgan horse would be found to have some French blood in him." The Canadian horse was seen as common, the Thoroughbred as new and desirable.

During the 19th century the Canada/U.S. border at Quebec was very much in dispute and the farm of Justin Morgan, owner of Figure, was actually in Quebec. Similarly, the parents of Justin Morgan (the man) lived in Quebec, then very much the domain of the Canadian horse.

On the other hand, George Barnard, of Sherbrooke, Quebec, that eminent horse authority of the mid-19th century, disputed the Morgan/Canadian connection. He saw differences in the look, the feet, the way of going and the offspring of the two breeds.

At the National Museum of the Morgan Horse in Shelburne, Vermont, the curator, Elizabeth A. Curler, pointed out that between the American Revolution in the 1770s and into the 1820s, Quebec was a major market for nothern Vermonters. Trade, community socializing and family ties all linked Lower Canada's and Vermont's border towns, she wrote in a letter to me. "It was as if there were no boundary line. It is inevitable that there was horse trade. There is evidence of many Morgans going into both Lower and Upper Canada. Most were never heard from again (on this side of the line)."

Joseph Battell, who wrote three volumes on the history of the Morgan in 1905, argues there that some of the finest pacing and trotting horses of the 19th century, such as Pilot and his offspring, were not purebred Canadians as claimed, but suffused with Morgan blood. Battell's books are exhaustively researched but go out of their way to denigrate the Canadian horse while praising the Morgan. Elizabeth Curler dismisses any notion that Justin Morgan, the horse, was a Canadian but does admit the following: "There is evidence of Canadian horses in some Morgan-horse pedigrees."

A modern authority who believes passionately that the Morgan horse owes a lot to the Canadian horse is Bonnie Hendricks, a prominent horse historian and the author of the *International Encyclopedia of Horse Breeds*, published in 1995. In that book, this American author called the Canadian breed "one of the best kept secrets of the twentieth century." Canadian horses, she wrote, "were talented trotters and pacers, and as roads were developed good roadsters were in great demand. Indeed, the New England states were literally saturated with this blood. Yet when writing about the formation of American breeds the Canadian horse has been overlooked by most writers, who refer vaguely to 'horses from Canada that trotted, or paced.'"

She notes that many purebred French-Canadian sires and mares were important as foundation stock for the Morgan, the Standardbred and American Saddlebred. Hendricks is, by her own admission, frank and opinionated in her long entry on the Canadian. Her book tends more to historical fact, but here she weighs in uncharacteristically. Hendricks simply does not buy the argument that Justin Morgan, the horse, was a Thoroughbred/Arab cross as some claim. The horse, she says, looks like neither of those breeds and she wonders if the Thoroughbred connection was invented so that this great horse could claim an august pedigree. On the other hand, she says, the old photos of Canadians and Morgans show a striking similarity. Hendricks writes:

> The birthplace of the first Morgan horse was saturated with the blood of the small, blocky, powerful Canadian horse—an excellent trotter; able to pull far more than its size and weight would indicate; sure of step; curious; bold; given to lively use of eyes and ears; predominantly bay or black; having feet of iron, outstanding strength of legs, and powerful quarters and shoulders; and noted for its crested neck and wavy mane and tail—all qualities possessed by the Morgan horse . . . In my opinion, there is no other possible theory coming close to the obvious, clear ring of truth in regard to his ancestry but that he was a horse of predominant, if not pure, French-Canadian blood.

Justin Morgan sired many fine foals, and the striking thing was how much they resembled him. Some of these offspring went on to found families of their own—the aforementioned Woodburys, Shermans and Bulrushes. But this is where the Canadian connection seems most evident. You can almost sense Hendricks building up a head of steam as she moves down the list:

> Bulrush, one of the most outstanding sons of Justin Morgan, was out of a Canadian mare. Bred to a black Canadian mare, Bulrush got Randolph Morgan. Randolph Morgan, mated to a Canadian mare, produced Jennison Horse (sire of Old Morrill). Woodbury, another famous son of Justin Morgan, was likely from a Canadian mare, and the dam of Black Hawk was a Canadian. Even if Justin Morgan

did not himself carry a preponderance of Canadian blood, it remains that the breed he spawned most certainly did.

Justin Morgan's great-grandson, Black Hawk (out of a Canadian mare), and a great-great-grandson, Ethan Allen, were also celebrated horses in their time. In 1867, Ethan Allen was acknowledged as the fastest trotting stallion in the world when he raced and beat Dexter.

The great bay stallion Justin Morgan died in 1821 at the age of 32 when another horse in his paddock kicked him. The wound was carelessly treated and he died of the ensuing infection. As far as Hendricks is concerned, the Morgan breed's foundation sire is indeed that wonderful bay stallion. But the Morgan line, she insists, was "developed as an American-bred Canadian horse with a bit of mixture to other New England breeds, and with Justin Morgan as the foundation sire."

Hendricks's account of the history of the Canadian horse is both accurate and lavish in its praise. It ends:

> Virtually unknown even in its native country today, the breed is making a strong comeback. A tough working horse, a dependable riding horse, a jumper, and a trotter with fine action, the Canadian is an honest little horse with a big heart and a great deal to offer.

Meanwhile, science is weighing in on the Morgan/Canadian question. The Equine Research Centre at the University of Guelph has conducted several genetic studies, the most recent in 2000. Worried that endangered breeds, such as the Canadian horse, the Newfoundland pony and the Lac LaCroix pony, might one day be vulnerable to inbreeding, researchers wanted to know which other breeds are most closely related. In the event of a "genetic emergency," another breed could serve as a gene pool. The scientists compared the DNA of breeds all over North America and Europe and found that *le cheval canadien*'s closest relative is the trotteur français. One North American breed stood out as the Canadian's close cousin: the Morgan.

Finally, there is this amusing tale from Brigitte Krukowski, of Waterloo, Ontario, and the owner of a Canadian horse called Dexter. "My close friend," she told me, "is a Morgan-horse fanatic and she is continually pestering me to get rid of my Canadian and buy a real horse—she's referring, of course, to a Morgan."

Before Christmas of 1999, the woman sent all her friends a lovely card depicting a 19th century scene of two horses pulling a sleigh through the countryside. She and all her staunch Morgan-owning friends seemed blissfully unaware of two facts: The painter was Cornelius Krieghoff, and the horses on those cards were Canadians.

## 2. The Canadian Horse on Canvas

Even had the Canadian horse disappeared entirely as a breed, its image would have been preserved in grainy old black-and-white photographs, most from the 20th century. But the Canadian is also remembered in 19th century art, art of the most extraordinarily vibrant colour and often depicting hardy little horses pulling sleighs and carrioles.

Cornelius David Krieghoff (1815–1872) painted romantic scenes that capture what seems to us now a simpler time. The winter scenes—Indians hunting, *habitants* enjoying themselves or cutting across the fields in sleds—reveal a very European, and especially German, fascination with certain aspects of 19th century life in North America. Krieghoff was a Dutch-born painter who spent his early life in Germany and only came to North America in 1837 when he was 22 years old. And in many of his paintings, the sturdy little Canadian horse plays a role.

In one, called *Cheating the Toll Man*, young scoundrels in a speeding sleigh thumb their noses at an old tollgate keeper. (This apparently was inspired by Krieghoff's own experience, after a night of drinking, whizzing past the tollgate at Longueuil without paying—much to the chagrin of the one-legged gatekeeper. Krieghoff was much amused by the incident and did 30 versions of the same scene.) The painting may also have powerful political overtones, with the *habitants* literally thumbing their noses at British authority. Farmers would spend a long day peddling vegetables at a market only to see a sizable sum lost to the tolls.

In another painting, called *Merrymaking*, many *habitants* spill out of a country inn after an afternoon of partying while their horses patiently wait outside to take them home in cutters. In *The Habitant Farm*, a bay horse harnessed to a *berline* gets some water and hay prior to work one winter's day.

The value of Krieghoff's 2,000 canvasses has been diluted by appearing on Christmas greeting cards, and his paintings never did earn the high praise of critics, but they are fascinating and detailed records of another time—a time when the Canadian horse was French society's kingpin animal.

Late in 1999, the Art Gallery of Ontario, in Toronto, assembled an imposing collection of 152 Krieghoff paintings, and co-published a handsome, heavy book: *Krieghoff: Images of Canada* by Dennis Reid, the AGO's chief curator. The book and the exhibition lent new dignity to old Krieghoff. Almost one-third of the paintings in the AGO exhibition featured Canadian horses.

Krieghoff's work is a visual reminder of how hard the Canadian horse worked—hauling logs, ice, supplies, people. One painting shows a very wet, very tired Canadian horse after a day of hunting deer in the forest; there's true heaviness in the horse's tread. The patience and steadiness of the breed are apparent: A recurring motif has Canadian horses in harness quietly standing while their drivers converse, or refusing to be alarmed by a yappy dog. Many paintings capture the excitement of racing these *marche donc* (Giddyup) horses across snow- and ice-covered rivers.

But Krieghoff also drew scenes of calamity. In a painting called *Off the Road—The Upset Sleigh*, the horse is down and the contents of the *berline* (four people and a pig) are sent sprawling. *A Winter Incident* has a driver trying to calm his high-headed horse after a firewood-laden sled tips. In *Breaking Up of a Country Ball in Canada, Early Morning*, we see the dangers of blending revelry and horsemanship: another downed horse, another tipped carriole with merrymakers in the snow. And one wonders how long the listing rider shown in the painting will stay in the saddle, and whether his white-eyed horse will kick the violin-wielding man approaching from behind, as he seems set to do.

The Canadian historian Ramsay Cook refers to the painting in an essay in *Krieghoff: Images of Canada*:

> Here is a riot of tipsy action combining in Bruegelesque [sic] fashion many of the familiar elements found in other Krieghoff paintings: colourful dress adorning bourgeois and habitant alike, good *canadien* horses, *berlines* and carioles, snowshoes, barking dogs, escaping pigs, the last few drinks for the road, and hints of hangovers to come.

Krieghoff, who married a Québécoise named Emilie Gauthier, of Boucherville, recognized class differences, and typically painted the British in elegant sleighs being pulled by bigger, more refined trotters with colourful feathered plumes adorning the headpieces of their bridles. The *habitants* used the smaller, more rugged Canadians, often decorating their horses with red or blue ribbon dangling from the bridle near the horses' ears.

In a lecture at the gallery, Cook argued that though Krieghoff's paintings are works of the imagination, they are also documents of that era and reveal much of *habitant* life. The artist was working in a time when 85 per cent of those living in what was then called

Canada East lived in the country. And just as novels such as *Kamouraska*, *Mon Oncle Antoine* and *Maria Chapdelaine* did at the end of the 19th century, Cook said, Krieghoff saw country life in a positive light. And undeniably, the horse—the Canadian horse—figured largely in that life.

An endnote display to the exhibition gathered some of the many products and companies that have featured Krieghoff images: a Carnation hot chocolate container, a CP Air menu, a compact disc, a limited-edition plate, a cookie package, a whiskey container, coasters, a tin of chocolate, greeting cards (of course) and collectible colour postcards that came in packages of Post Bran Flakes in 1954.

As I walked from room to room at the AGO, I was struck by the sense of history that pervades the Canadian horse. Ramsay Cook was right: There is something Breughelesque about Krieghoff's work. The mid-1800s is not so long ago, but the paintings make it seem so. One, called *Ice Cutting*, depicts a horse who looks for all the world like Dali pulling a *berline* laden with six blocks of ice.

A photograph of Cornelius Krieghoff taken circa 1860 shows a mildly befuddled, somewhat fatigued-looking man with thin, worried lips. His mutton chops descend into a Mennonite beard that curls under his chin and must have warred with his starched collar. The painter's greying hair is thick and wild and the round white stains on the slightly blurred albumen print are suggestive of bubbles. Stare at it for a while and you begin to imagine that Krieghoff was slowly descending in a great glass of champagne. The blank stare and turned-down mouth suggest glum resignation.

*Self-Portrait*, painted in 1855, offers a radically different view of a far more elegant man with high forehead, neat black hair and Vandyke beard, arresting brown eyes, an imposing nose and a handsome mouth, all creating a look of intensity.

But he was, apparently, not serious at all. He loved his "whiskey blanc," he was drawn to tavern friendships and taught music. Krieghoff spoke French, English, Dutch and German. All this made him a welcome guest both at the homes of rich clients who bought his work and at country inns where his sense of fun was appreciated.

Krieghoff also befriended the Indians at Sault-St. Louis, now the Kahnawake reserve, and those at the Huron village of Lorette and Montmorency Falls (a favourite subject of his) near Quebec City. At Lorette, the painter got close to Paul Tahourenche, the Huron chief. Another Huron, Gabriel Teoriolen, taught him to prepare vegetable pigments, including a vermilion and a blue that would lend his landscape paintings a distinctive brilliance.

Those of us who admire the Canadian horse but lament his low profile should thank Krieghoff. Most of us have seen the painter's work, and therefore the Canadian horse, without always recognizing either.

## 3. *Albert de Cap Rouge*

When I visited Ross Farm, the Nova Scotia living museum where the Canadian horse is a featured animal, I noticed a black and white photograph of a stallion in one of the tiny offices upstairs. I knew without looking at the fine print who he was. This was Albert de Cap Rouge, an imposing black stud. In her book, *The Canadian Horse: A Pictorial History*, author Gladys Mackey Beattie called him "sire of sires."

Albert de Cap Rouge stood at stud for 19 years and at one time was related to every horse at the Cap Rouge breeding farm, save four. His record at large fairs was astonishing: In 28 exhibition appearances he was first 21 times, and second 4 times. The breeders had no doubt. In terms of conformation, he was the best of the breed.

In one of his reports, Gus Langelier, the former superintendent at Cap Rouge told the story of Albert de Cap Rouge, whose dam, a 1,100-pound mare named Hélène, had "lots of grit, a good gait, and a conformation which gives her more strength than animals two hundred pounds heavier. She is about as tough a piece of horseflesh as ever walked on four legs. Many a time she spent the full ten hours on the corn binder, with a mate weighing nearly fifteen hundred pounds, but never for a moment did her whiffletree get behind the other. Every teamster who worked with her said that she always looked as lively after a hard day as she did in the morning, even when only a couple of weeks before foaling." (A whiffletree was a rounded wooden piece a few inches thick with metal loops hanging on either side of its three-foot length; it lay against the horse's flanks in a team, and a farmer could tell at a glance by its position whether one horse was outpulling the other.)

Langelier reports that Hélène was served by a stallion named Wilfred, a black stud weighing less than 1,200 pounds, "but all horse, to use a common expression." It was thought that the offspring would be small but "brimful of quality, of endurance, of courage."

The colt they produced was Albert de Cap Rouge. He would mature into a horse of 1,300 pounds, a striking specimen noted for his vitality and strength. Many Canadian horses can trace their pedigrees back to him, including Alec Hayward's celebrated stallion, Viger Duc.

4. *The Canadian Horse in the High Arctic*
As a horse breeder, Jérôme Aumond operates on a relatively small scale, but his name keeps recurring in these pages because he has a reputation as a fine and honest horseman.

When three French adventurers arrived in Canada in 1990 with a grand plan—to circumnavigate Cornwallis Island on horse-drawn sleds—they planned to use their own Merens ponies. These compact, sturdy ponies resemble the Canadian and live in the mountains of southern France. But the ponies developed health problems and failed the veterinary screening. It must have been a crushing blow, for the men had spent three years training their horses. Into the breach stepped two Canadian horses.

But not right away. The three men landed at Mirabel Airport in Montreal on March 31, 1990, and set about looking for likely prospects. Horses that sounded promising on the telephone disappointed when actually seen. What they found, too often, were "dozens of horses piled up in sordid box stalls." "*Au Canada*," they later wrote, "*comme ailleurs, un marchand de chevaux est avant tout un marchand.*" (In Canada, as elsewhere, a horse dealer is, above all, a dealer.)

It seems they found a dealer they could trust in one Jérôme Aumond at Ferme Saroma, Dali's birthplace. Pierre and Frédéric Vernay and Jean-Yves Lapaix took two 14-hand Canadian horses, a three-year-old stallion called Valentin and an eight-year-old mare named Prunelle (bought from Jérôme's pal, Michel Joly, also of Messines), on an expedition to Cornwallis Island, Northwest Territories, where temperatures hit –40 degrees Celsius. Their expedition was inspired by the doomed Scott expedition to the South Pole in 1912. On that trek, 17 ponies died in order to keep men and dogs fed.

Pierre Vernay said that after reading Scott's memoirs, he "dreamed of seeing horses, harnessed to a sled, galloping across the ice floes. What a fantastic image!"

The three have embarked on various other Arctic expeditions, including one on skis to Spitzberg, part of the Norwegian archipelago and only 800 kilometres from the North Pole, and a kayak trip around northeast Greenland. They produce films and photographs of their polar adventures, nine to date, to help finance the next one. They always devote at least three months to each journey and insist on complete freedom to go their own way.

Vernay and the two others spent three months trekking around Cornwallis Island's 350-kilometre circumference between April and July. It seems, in retrospect, a dubious enterprise. A similar expedition launched in 1935 towards the South Pole saw all the horses eaten by the starving trekkers.

The Canadian horses clearly suffered in the cold, each pulling a 75-kilogram load, though they did not quit. The mare lost 150 kilograms in the course of the expedition but rebounded afterwards.

They travelled over rock and snow and mud, and faced daylight 24 hours a day.

Getting the horses to Resolute Bay, the departure point, was an adventure in itself. Someone compared seeing horses there to seeing polar bears in Paris. The horses were quarantined in Oka, Quebec, after the trip was successfully completed, but the plan was to take them to France, where, perhaps, the two horses will teach their French cousins something about tenacity.

### 5. *Blackie*

Sir William Francis Butler, an Irish-born military man who served as an intelligence officer with the Red River Expedition that put down the Riel rebellion in 1870, made a 6,000-kilometre trip through the Saskatchewan River country, all described in his book, *The Great Lone Land*, published in 1872.

His horse was a Canadian:

> My horse was a wonderful animal; day by day I feared that his game little limbs were growing weary, and that soon he must give out. But not a bit of it; his black coat roughened, his flanks grew thinner, but still he went gamely on. When I dismounted, to let his companions go on before, he never rested until I mounted again, and then he trotted briskly on until he regained them . . . On the fourth of November we rode over sixty miles, and when we camped in the lee of a little clump of bare willows, Blackie and his comrades went out to shiver through their supper on the cold, snow-covered prairie, the bleakest scene my eyes had ever looked upon.

Blackie's end, after plunging through the ice while crossing the Assiniboine River, makes for grim reading:

The horse kept swimming stoutly round, trying all he could to get upon the ice. All his efforts were useless . . . Never shall I forget how the poor brute looked at me. I rushed back to the camp where my rifle lay and back to the spot where the poor beast struggled with his fate. As I raised the rifle, he looked so imploring that my hand trembled; another moment and the ball crashed through his head. With one look, never to be forgotten, poor Blackie went down under the cold ice. I went back to the camp, sat down in the snow and cried like a child.

6. *The Man Who Championed the Canadian Horse*

Donnie Prosperine, of Maple Lane Farm near Dunrobin, Ontario, had been a horseman all his life, and he was a great admirer of the Hackney. But when he encountered Alec Hayward in 1977 at a meeting of the Eastern Ontario Pleasure Driving Society, Alec told him about Canada's own heritage horse. At that point, he was simply looking for a pair of horses to drive. The breed was little known outside Quebec and the number of purebreds was perilously low.

Prosperine and Hayward had no grand plan, just a notion of raising a few heritage horses on the Ontario side, which then was home to one registered Canadian horse. The two men embarked on a search through Quebec, and it was almost two years before they finally found Windsor Rosine and Windsor Michette. Prosperine bought the mares himself; Hayward bought the stud, Viger Duc, and they purchased two additional mares in partnership.

Clearly, Prosperine loved horses. "He couldn't pass a stall without giving a horse a flake of hay," Alec told me. "And I'd tell him that if he kept doing that I'd supply him with the Vaseline so he could squeeze the horse in past the stall doors."

Donnie Prosperine began showing in 1980 when he took the two Canadian mares to Saratoga Springs, New York. As Hayward remembers, "Donnie got so many compliments about the horses at that show. He got all excited about the breed and fell in love with it fairly rapidly after that point."

He would brook no disparaging words about the breed. One time at the Royal Agricultural Winter Fair, Prosperine got into a heated argument with some Morgan aficionados, who insisted that the Canadian was derived from the Morgan—not the reverse. He called Hayward on the phone and begged him, as an authority on the breed's history, to drive five hours down to Toronto and settle the debate. To which Hayward replied: "Donnie, turn around, face the wall and talk to it. You're going to get as far talking to that wall as you will to those people."

Always promoting the breed, Prosperine helped bring it back to the Royal Agricultural Winter Fair. His own success at shows—he was always in the ribbons—seemed to back his contention that the breed had much to offer. Prosperine helped put together the winning four-in-hand of Nip, Tuck, Black Diamond and Mayflower. Nip and Tuck, two black geldings of fine temperament, would go on to capture the 1987 North American Driving Championship.

For several years, Frank Prosperine, Donnie's son, drove Canadian horses on Parliament Hill, carrying in antique carriages actors in period costume playing the roles of Sir Wilfrid Laurier and Sir John A. Macdonald. Canadian horses participated in parades to open the Ottawa Exhibition and the Ottawa Winter Fair. In one Grey Cup Parade, Canadian horses carried members of the victorious team. Canadian horses and Donnie Prosperine's ever-growing collection of antique carriages were used in movies, television programs, family weddings and all manner of Ottawa functions requiring a touch of history and class.

Meanwhile, the rest of the country was beginning to take notice of the Canadian horse, thanks in no small part to Prosperine's work. He sold horses all over Ontario (where the numbers of Canadians is now several hundred strong), and west to Alberta.

Inevitably, he became involved in the Canadian Horse Breeders' Association, serving as a director for two years, beginning in 1987. That same year he was named "Mr. Canadian Horse," as the man who had contributed most to the breed. The following year the vote to elect him for a second year to the association's board was unanimous.

When he died suddenly in 1989, the breed lost a great friend. But he would, no doubt, be pleased to know that today there are 10 times as many Canadian horses as there were when he and Alec Hayward went looking in backwoods Quebec for a few little horses of iron.

# CHAPTER 18

# THE SWEET SECOND SUMMER

LIMESTONE STABLES, MAY 26, 2000

*I went to Dali's stall window, threw my arms around him, and he settled his great head*
*on my back and left it there while I stroked his neck and shoulder. We stayed that way for*
*a minute or more. This was an unprecedented moment between us. I wondered whether it*
*might count for something some wind-tossed day when old fears begin to grip him.*
*This I do know. I left the stable a happier man than when I arrived.*

DALI HAS A SENSE of humour after all. Today, the day after April Fool's
Day, I sat on my horse in the centre of the ring at Limestone Stables—
Samara looking on—and slowly raised my left leg out of the stirrup and
forward. I was doing what I dread: adjusting the girth from the saddle.

Above: The author and Dali leaping a modest fence at Limestone Stables.

Dali dreads it too. Or was he just playing a little joke? In the blink of a horse's eye, he was in the west end, then the east end, turning hard to the right. All in a quick-step gallop.

I went from one stirrup to no stirrups but I was grimly determined this time to hang on. I pulled back and did not give in, even in that moment on the ring's long side when I felt myself sliding to the left, and I could feel the beginnings of a dump. This time, the saddle held. For a change I didn't utter inane things like *whoa*, just stayed silent and focused on leaning back and applying brakes. I rode out this little storm. We finally came to a halt, Dali wound tight and puffing, me coursing with adrenalin and pride.

It gave me no pleasure to see him scoot. But I was happy not to have kissed the earth for what would have been a sixth time. And when Dali scooted later in the lesson—it was a day of hard rain outside and hard scoots inside—I felt very much in control.

"One day you will laugh at those scoots," Samara predicted.

But my question to her, later, as I hot-walked Dali, was this one: Why do we do this? Why will she in coming weeks don her blue body protector and ride young Nate in the outdoor ring, the same one he bolted from last fall? Is it why others whitewater canoe or scale cliffs? Why do we court danger?

"In the moment," Samara replied, "I have my doubts. But I never question my life with horses."

Frankly, I do. Last night, before Sunday's ride, I had trouble sleeping. While walking Dali over to the arena I sang Ringo Starr's "Act Naturally," not for my benefit, but for his. To mask my worries. To calm him. And it worked.

Only in the ring, the one he knows so well, was he a nut. "Someday," Samara assured, "Dali will be calm." Though she added, "He will always be alert." On his back may I always be the same.

Sometimes life and life with horses converge. Some would call it serendipity, others would dub it fate. But in March 2000, Jane

Smiley entered my world, and hers and mine looked uncannily alike.

I occasionally review books for newspapers and magazines, and so it was that a novel called *Horse Heaven* by the Pulitzer–Prize winning novelist Jane Smiley came my way. It so happened that while I was reading Smiley's book set at the racetrack, *Practical Horseman* ran her article entitled "My Year of Living Dangerously." I had Jane Smiley in stereo.

Smiley, who is my vintage, opened the article on a whimsical note. Everyone I know, she wrote, got a young horse last year—"I'm talking middle-aged women here, buying horses who were still only two. Maybe it was a mass psychosis." Winning the Pulitzer, Smiley once told an interviewer, was nice, but it was having that first baby and buying a horse—when she was, respectively, 42 and 43—that really changed her life. Coming back to horses forced her to ponder "a whole different set of life questions"—about fear, riding, the psychology of the horse. The experience, as wonderful as it was painful, "opened me up. It changed who I am."

Smiley had been obsessed with horses as a child, then lost her interest during the teenage years. But when the passion was rekindled, good sense fled. By age 50, she explained, the old, safe horses owned by her and her friends were either retired or sold, and for reasons not entirely clear were replaced by fiery three-year-olds. There is a pattern here, of people feeling their age but looking to feel younger. I'm coming to understand the needs that come with the middle years: the need to defy time, to get the adrenalin coursing, to feel terribly alive.

I still play hockey, still try to conjure those moments of pure acceleration that, though rare and much diminished from those of my boyhood, take me back to that time. Horses, like hockey, answer my longing for speed and risk.

Smiley had several young horses to contend with. One, a mare named Franny, knocked into her and put her arm through glass, though the cut was "only interesting, not serious." The mare kicked anyone who tried to clean her hooves and later went on strike, refusing to move at all. She reared when ridden on the trail alone and then bit Smiley on the head.

Smiley's other young horse, Persey, reared so much that no trainer would get on her, and she also broke Smiley's finger—"an unimportant ring finger." This was starting to sound vaguely familiar. I had tales that came close to matching hers.

"I got lots of advice," Smiley wrote in the magazine. "Most of it involved intestinal fortitude, force of personality, courage, of course, and danger to my person." The piece ends on an optimistic note, with Smiley riding one or the other horse along with her friends, "amateurs forever, but with a little more force of character than we had a year ago, and not really all that many scars to show for it."

### April 9, 2000

There was Jane Smiley on CBC Radio this morning, telling Michael Enright that a horse's affection is nothing like that of a dog for his owner. The horse is far less attentive than a dog is to his master, but there is something profound and unique, she said, about the feeling that comes from a horse. Smiley has connected with several horses this way. "I felt honoured by it," she said, "and flattered."

In *Horse Heaven*, Smiley shone a bright light into every corner of the horse's mind and I said as much in my review. On the radio, Smiley offered her take on the elusive subject of horse intelligence. She agreed with Enright that the horse has a phenomenal memory, but the smart horse, Smiley argued, is the one able to distinguish between fearful memories and that thing in the moment that triggers those memories. Smiley's ideal horse can park that awful memory in a safe place.

I thought of Dali and how he snorts every time he passes the cow barn at Limestone Stables. He's been passing that same barn for four months now. But I wonder. Is there something in my body language that issues a kind of "barn alert" and sets him off?

Among the characters in *Horse Heaven* was an animal communicator, one supposedly capable of reading the thoughts of horses and putting questions to them. Based on an actual experience with one of these people, Smiley said she has stopped issuing one-word commands to her horses, and now converses with each horse as if the creature were a friendly being quite capable of understanding. She says it works.

I deployed that tactic the next time Dali and I passed the cow barn. I made no effort to calm him, but rather engaged him in a lively discussion of his fear. I told him that he'd been brave and now he could relax. Call it a coincidence, but he was quite matter-of-fact as he walked by that barn.

The inside of my right knee is healing nicely. "You don't give me news of your horse," says my friend David Carpenter. "You give me medical updates." His family and my family own adjacent land in the country southwest of Kingston and it's always been our dream that we will have horses down there after retirement. Two old boys on old plugs—"Not that hellion of yours," he says, for he worries that after one more hard fall my brain will finally turn to mush.

When I rode out Dali's vigorous scoot a week ago, *sans* stirrups, I'm afraid I did it by gripping too much with my knees. By the end of the lesson I had a raw patch inside my right knee the size of a toonie and my green jeans bore a thick red stain about four inches long. Samara rode him a few days later, then he got the weekend off while my knee healed.

Meanwhile, I've bought breeches. Clearly, wearing loose jeans under loose chaps offers scant protection against rubbing and may well encourage it. Perhaps I grip too much with my knees (though why would only one knee get rubbed raw?); perhaps it's the saddle or Dali's conformation. We'll continue working on a deeper seat, me in breeches, no chaps.

I've been reading a wonderful book, one I found in a used bookstore last fall. Called *The Horse*, it's a bibliography of horse books written in Britain after 1851. And I was struck by the listing for a book called *Mount and Man*, written in 1925. The author, someone named McTaggart, has this to say about gripping with the knees: "The rider who looks uncomfortable in the saddle and who is not 'down' in his seat is one whose muscles are not relaxed; one who is anxious and who is, in fact, gripping. Consequently, the way to get a good seat is not to grip, but the very converse: to be free and supple and confident and happy."

Don't worry, be happy. It was my advice to Dali and I should heed it as well.

April 10, 2000

Dali stall-bound is a cranky, wound-up horse. I watched today, amused and delighted, as Samara got him to walk over a single pole on the ground, but only after a five-minute-long discussion. He would dance around the pole, shy, raise his head. But she sat his spooks and spins, and persistently returned to the pole.

"It was good to have that discussion," Samara said later. "The message to him was that we can have these talks, that he wasn't in trouble at the end of it, and we got the job done." As a footnote, she added, "He sure is strong." After their chat, Dali was light and easy in his trot.

I had chased him beforehand and at one point he came off the circle and charged towards me, just for a second, before going back to his circle. A show of force. I chased him with more vigour for that, though he probably deserved a smack on the flank with my dressage whip, a nip to let him know I had noticed and disapproved. It's what a horse above him in the herd hierarchy would have done. What stays my hand is something Chris Irwin once said about "moral authority." I don't think I've earned that yet.

I'm giving myself until fall. When the colours turn, I will have had Dali almost a year and a half. If I am still riding heart in mouth, still lacking moral authority, if he is still too much horse for too little rider, there will be a pause as I strive to become a horseman. Dali will go to someone more skilled than I am. I remember a distance rider telling me it takes two years to know whether you have a good horse or not. Maybe it's as much the horse's decision. Maybe it takes that long for the horse to determine whether he can work with his owner.

At Thanksgiving, then, I will sit amid family at the log cabin and we will either toast my horse, truly my horse now and into the future, or we will say his name and wish him well in his new life.

April 12, 2000

Samara and I are walking wounded, but since she's the younger, far better rider, she's on Dali. My knee is not entirely healed, and it seems a minor groin injury, incurred during the big scoot one week ago, has been exacerbated by a game of hockey. It was fathers versus sons, but the old boys' victory (for me, anyway) was pyrrhic. My entire lower abdomen is home to a dull, wide, hernia-like pain. A single sit-up is beyond me. My doctor says I'll be four to six weeks recovering (in fact, it would be three months before healing was complete).

Samara, meanwhile, has carpal tunnel syndrome after much essay typing and a day in the local rock climbers' gym. I told Dali on the walk to the arena that he had to be gentle with both Samara and me, that since we had shown him only kindness he should show us gratitude. He promptly delivered what Samara declared the best ride he has ever given her. Wonderful squares, elegant serpentines, long canters. At the end, Samara raised her left foot and stirrup towards his head and he was calm about that too. He had truly earned his apple slices.

April 17, 2000

Samara and Dali have fallen into a pattern. The first 10 minutes he totters on the edge of a shy or a spook, then slowly settles in. Today, in the ring, on a cold blustery day that felt like November, he was steady and dutiful.

Lil Grooms said she put Dali out with Bogi and Ras for a longer turnout and she was astonished at Dali's outburst of energy. Leaping high into the air on all fours as if on coiled springs, tearing around like a biker on a Harley. Lil stopped short of saying she was alarmed, but clearly gave that impression. I read into Dali's display pure joy. Dali had felt imprisoned for months, and finally he was free.

May 1, 2000

Dali is now in his new digs at Limestone Stables. For the moment, he's in a stall opposite the tack room and just at the entrance to the arena—in the centre of things. When I dropped him in there a few days ago, he seemed fine with the arrangement. All he could think about on the walk over was the grass, so when he discovered a flake of hay in his stall, courtesy of Shannon Knox, the affable barn manager at Limestone, he looked delighted.

Samara rode him yesterday and thought she would chase him beforehand, since he seemed a little wide-eyed his first time in the Limestone cross-ties. "I've never chased him," she told me on the phone, "so I've never seen him running free in the arena. He can jump! He goes three feet in the air before he bucks. I have never ever seen a horse do that. I could hardly chase him I was laughing so hard. We've got to get him jumping."

He may look like a little pork chop, I replied, but he's a very athletic pork chop. And yes, he can jump all right. Just like his sire.

May 3, 2000

To the sound of two mares squealing at each other in a nearby paddock, Samara schooled Dali in Limestone's outdoor ring. He had, for company, Shannon and her 12-year-old, Frankie, who were taking a few fences.

"He's not as sharp off my leg today as he was on Monday," Samara said as she rode by me, the farm's young chocolate Lab at my ear with a gnarled plastic bone in his mouth. Down the far side they went, and suddenly there was Samara coming off him in slow motion, sliding down his left side and landing in a gentle heap in the sand. Dali seemed in no way alarmed by this. He had stopped, and she was back on him in seconds.

"My fault," Samara explained later. "I had given him a little more leg, he went straight up and forward, I lost a stirrup, and my balance, and down I went."

Dali was turned out yesterday with Shannon's other horse, the 16.2-hand two-year-old, Rocket, who doesn't much like other horses but gets along fine with Dali. I wonder if he is quietly grieving over the loss of his old herd. Early in the lesson today he whinnied mightily in the direction of Lakehead and there was a response, perhaps from Ras.

Samara said she's seen horses reunited after years apart and been amazed by how keenly they renew old acquaintances. I thought I read into Dali's mood today a twinge of sadness. I wish his stall weren't quite so dark, and I wondered if he missed his room with a northern view at the old place.

On the other hand, Samara's steady schooling is paying off. The huge girth I had bought to encircle his bulk is now at its last buckle, a measure of how much belly he has lost. The pork chop is a leaner cut.

May 19, 2000

Today was Saroma Dark Fox Dali's birthday. Six years old he is, and, as far as I can tell, content. Those who deal with him on a daily basis, Kathie and Shannon, both say what a pet he is. I've had him not quite a year, and we have both come a long way.

Dali's in a corner stall now, across from Samara's black Nate, with one east-facing window and another gated window opposite that lets him poke his head into the barn hallway to catch a breeze. Yesterday, after our ride, I spent a few minutes scratching his face and ears and he was happy to have me continue for a minute or more.

Three rides in the arena seem not to have exacerbated my abdominal strain. We've been working, Samara and Dali and I, on getting me into a deeper seat in the canter. Today, moving clockwise, the saddle slipped a little to the left and he scooted. Call it a mid-sized scoot; not one of his wild runs, but no wee dash either. More and more I swallow these darts. I recovered my right stirrup, rebalanced the saddle and went back to the canter. The girth seems tight enough, but it must roll a little when the sweat levels build up on this round horse.

Today there were pigeons in the arena, and when I first chased Dali and he spotted them exploding into flight amid the roof beams, he ran. But then he seemed to factor them in—he is six after all—and settled into a game of chase. The arena, at the moment, houses a huge wagonful of hay—temporary storage while stalls are built for horses Kathie bought after a scouting trip to Holland. I'd be after Dali in the east end and then he'd scoot down to the west end ahead of me, rush to the wagon for a bite of hay, then continue. I swear he was having fun.

Something has changed between us. I find great peace in grooming him, knowing it gives him pleasure. Today I asked him to back up in the cross-ties, using only the French word he knows. *Recule.* I praised him when he did it. His birthday present from me was a little longer hand-grazing outside the ring; by next week, I hope, he'll be out for longer turnout in the paddocks.

The last few times I've ridden Dali in the ring outside, he's scooted, especially in the canter going clockwise. Samara reads into this extreme worry, so perhaps he's remembering times I've come off going that same direction.

Samara's instinct is to de-escalate. Put him back to work when he scoots, but don't heighten his fears. Boost his confidence. Retrace your steps. Even small circles in a clockwise trot bother him now. In tight circles he ignores my inside leg and falls in, making the circle tighter and tighter, and harder for him to accomplish. It's a downward spiral.

I happened to be chatting with Alec Hayward today and he wondered if Dali has yet to learn respect for his rider. Maybe, mused Alec, the horse thinks he can't unseat my instructor but he can dump me all right. I didn't tell him that young Dali has dumped us both.

"The more he has those little scoots and the more they come to nothing," said Samara, "the better he's going to be." Yesterday he gave me two little scoots down the long side of the outdoor ring. I lost both stirrups, but stayed balanced and pulled him up short quite quickly, then talked to him calmly and asked him to hold on while I got back into my stirrups. Samara called me "Velcro-bum," which is, I gather, a high compliment.

We'll see how long I hold that title. Meanwhile, I'm back in a familiar position: actually longing for more scoots so we can get them under our belts. It's not what I imagined longing for when I bought Dali a year ago. But as I tell all who ask: I'm grateful to him. He is indeed teaching me to be a better rider.

May 22, 2000

Dali is still (or once more) a split horse. Smooth and easygoing counter-clockwise; wary, especially in the canter, going the other way. I rode him outside today, the mosquitoes easily penetrating my blue cotton turtleneck. But perhaps we both welcomed the heat, for it has been an unduly cool and grey Victoria Day weekend. I have recently fallen into a small funk, convinced that my flaws as a rider are the prime cause of Dali sometimes coming undone. My intent now is to ride him with more authority. Too much makes him wide-eyed and high-headed; too little and he feels at sea, inclined to second-guess his rider.

"He doesn't let you get away with anything," Samara said today as I voiced my angst over schooling. Here we are, I moaned, a year into schooling and cantering to the right is suddenly a mountain to be climbed. We have gone back to baby steps on that circle to the right: from trot into a few steps of canter and back again. I have discovered—thank you, Samara—how valuable the outside rein is in bringing him back from canter to trot.

But he feels unbalanced going to the right and my aids must be letter perfect or he gets distraught. If my balance suffers and I tilt a little backward, I pull on his mouth. A little forward is not ideal either. An older or less sensitive horse would forgive me my flaws. Not Dali.

"There are riders, many of them," said Samara, in consolation mode, "who simply come out, trot around the perimeter, do a few easy rein changes and call that schooling. I'm asking more—bends, yields, tails to the wall. We want him to be more supple, and some of this stuff he does not find easy."

We want him to respect that inside leg more, so we do lots of 20-metre circles, moving out to 30 metres. It's effortless going to the left; like sculpting granite going right. Still, it's coming.

I remain curious to know how Dali was when they green-broke him at Jérôme's farm in Quebec. Jérôme had sent me a letter on Dali's early days, but it contained more poesy than practical information. No doubt Jérôme gave me what he thought I wanted.

"I would ask Jérôme myself," I told Alec Hayward on the phone yesterday, "but I'm not sure I would understand his reply. Can you ask him?"

"Jérôme's daughters rode him," came the answer a few days later. "They said he was nice, quiet, easy. They're farm girls. They have no fear." And yet they, or someone, must have brooked no nonsense, witness the marks on his mouth when we first brought him to Blue Haven. Someone, somewhere, had been hauling on his mouth.

"And why," I asked Alec, "did you recommend Dali to me? I later heard you didn't much like Fox-line horses."

"That's right," he admitted. "My tendency is to watch the way a horse moves and then ask about his bloodline. I just liked the way your little horse acted. But you're right. There was a time when I wouldn't touch a Fox horse. I have seen very few Fox horses that did not have a vice of some sort. On the other hand, I have had to eat my words," and he proceeded to list three quite wonderful Fox horses he had owned.

The original Fox horse (Alto Fox), said Alec, who knows Canadian horse lines as well as anyone, was "crazy as a bed bug. And he was not a strong horse. He was impotent by the age of 18, which was a good thing. And Fox Larry, the grandsire of your horse, was a real ding-a-ling. And yet I've been told that his son, Dark Fox, the sire of your horse, was a good, athletic horse as long as he was ridden by a strong, experienced rider." Wednesday, the plan is to have Samara videotape one of my rides. I may not like this movie. Will I see a strong, experienced rider? Will Dali be a ding-a-ling like grandpa?

May 24, 2000

Today I lunged him on a much longer line and Dali was nothing short of terrific: responsive, floating over poles on the ground, even granting me the odd bow. I was effusive in my praise.

In the saddle he was mildly skittish, for the paddock next to us had cows and calves kicking up their heels and Dali would take note each time we rounded the far end of the ring. He was strong and forward in the trot, and, at Samara's request, I would give him half-halts as we changed reins and it seemed to work wonders. The alternating tight and wide circles, so worrisome for him a week ago, seemed effortless today. Lastly, we jumped cross-poles and he ducked away from them several times before finally agreeing to the task. You must ride him confidently, while still giving him time to prepare for each little jump. Any hesitation on my part and he takes advantage. If I can remember to talk him through all this, he comes down and relaxes. Time and miles, I tell myself, time and miles.

May 26, 2000

Obsessive by nature, a worrier by inclination, occasionally plagued with doubt, I have climbed inside a little pit where I live with mental images of my horse most hours of the day and not a few of the night. I would welcome a trusted fantasy, maybe a minor ailment to fix on, or a friend seeking advice on some personal woe—anything to offer respite from my blinkered daydreams. Me with my foot inside a stirrup, my body dangling like a noodle.

Me simply riding my horse, doing transitions and striving for perfection as the film rolls on and on.

Me looking down the long driveway at Limestone Stables, feeling a tangle of emotions as a trailer with Dali inside heads for the highway.

I have just over four months to make my decision on Dali, as either the horse of my dreams, or someone else's. We must reach a point where my riding is fine enough that it no longer unsettles him, or he gets so trusting of me that my flaws are of little consequence. Perhaps we can compromise and meet in the middle.

Today I rode him in the indoor ring and tried to keep it simple. I focused on two things only: soft hands and encouraging talk. Perhaps his scoots on the canter were rooted in old fears about me pulling on his mouth in moments of imbalance. And I had seen how useful my voice could be, how it squirted oil on squeaky rein changes. Maybe I am learning how to work him, for he was, this day, a prince.

In the chase beforehand, I had Dali easing up on the short side and lengthening stride on the long side. It was like a piece of music. My lunge whip was the baton and he was the first violin. The chase had a rhythm to it, a flow. I had only to press a little lower to the ground on the long side to urge him on, and he would ease up when I got soft and yielding on the short side. I could stop him, move him forward, with little effort.

Anyone with experience of horses might have looked upon this exercise and the schooling that followed as kindergarten stuff. But in the cross-ties beforehand, Dali had been cranky, curling that foot and sweeping it in little arcs. Were he human I would say he was softly cursing to himself. But I think I responded correctly. I looked at him, told him no and asked that he lift that foot again, and I did so three or four times until he landed it softly and agreeably. If this was a Dali test, it seems to me I passed. I have no fear, none at all, of those feet. Respect, yes. Fear, no.

After the lesson, all the horses in the alleyway got some apple, Dali more than most. I went to his stall window, threw my arms around him, and he settled his great head on my back and left it there while I stroked his neck and shoulder. We stayed that way for a minute or more. This was an unprecedented moment between us. I wondered whether it might count for something some wind-tossed day when his head starts to rise, his eyes grow wide and old fears begin to grip him. Will the trust building between us temper his flight, bring him back a few seconds quicker?

I wonder. This I do know. I left the stable a happier man than when I arrived.

May 29, 2000

Rode outside this brilliant day, again focused on soft hands and a calming voice. Once more he was marvellous.

He gave me a sideways shy early on when he spotted a cow in the adjacent paddock staring at him through the cedars, but I assured him and we moved on.

He impressed by his level-headedness. Shannon and Kathie and Francis leading a great parade of horses to and from turnout—a young grey mare was especially rambunctious once let loose in the next paddock—did not unnerve him. Then a boarder leading a two-year-old was stepped on and yelled loudly for help, which came quickly, but this fuss, too, failed to unravel Dali.

The serpentines, lately troublesome, were easy and fluid. When I thought he had been particularly attentive, I would stop him, ask him to lean around and offer him a piece of apple. Later in the lesson, I stopped him and he eased his head around, inquiring, I suppose, about more apple.

Something Alec Hayward said the other day seems to make sense. He said that while instruction is valuable, it still comes down to you and your horse, and if you had that horse on your property, feeding and seeing him daily, the bonding would have come a lot sooner.

Samara has become a crutch for me, and while her instruction and insight are invaluable, the result in the saddle is a divided focus. I sometimes lose touch with horse or trainer, or both.

May 31, 2000

Samara videotaped today's ride and my sympathy for Dali grew as I watched the video at home. There I was: a skinny guy on a stalwart horse wearing a helmet that made his head look like an oversized button. I appeared relaxed in the walk, occasionally stiff in the trot, often awkward in the canter. Who can blame my horse for being likewise?

You can hear Samara offering encouragement and mild critique. She says I have good hands, and I take the compliment, but the foot is clearly too active and bouncy, the leg too far forward, the forward lean sometimes a problem. My body looks tight when I try putting aids together. The voice of Maria, my old teacher at Wilmarny Farm, comes back to me: "And smile," she would say at the end of some instruction, for that's where the softening begins. From my mouth to the horse's. I had sent a letter to a friend in Vermont, one I still correspond with after a week-long outback ride in Wyoming several years ago. Nancy Okun was responding to a letter of mine in which I described the mixed emotions my first horse was stirring.

She had good advice, and tales to tell. Seven years ago Nancy bought a green Arab gelding named Nicodemus. "I wasn't as experienced," she said, "or I just didn't know how to impart calmness to my horse, so we had great issues. He would be just fine and then for no reason (or at least one I could understand) he would turn, bolt and gallop and buck until I was on the ground. I was hurt very badly a few times. Then the fear set in. I was frightened every time I got on him and he knew it. I sent him for training with the wrong person and things didn't improve. I wound up selling him and feeling defeated. I still see him at competitions and speak to his present owner. She had years of dealing with his bolting, but she had access to a great trainer. He is now terrific, but it's taken seven years. I wasn't the rider to help him over his fears. I would be now, but I wasn't then."

Another horse called Tom Foolery helped Nancy regain her confidence. "Nothing," she wrote, "is going to scare or unseat me if he can't."

Nancy's new horse is another Arab, this one called Rianon, a curious combination of courage and nervousness. On the trail, the horse looks to Nancy for the proper response, and her answer is always "calm and centered." And that was the burden of her advice to me. I had sent her a photo of Dali and she pronouced him "lovely. You two are quite a match! I know it will work out. You have a centered presence around people and horses—and you love him! Don't be afraid to ask for help. Try to be quiet on his back and listen and feel. You will learn to anticipate his moves. Use imagery. Imagine the greatest rider you've ever seen (imagine Skip [the superb wrangler on our Wyoming rides]) and let your body be his. The best advice I can offer is to go lightly on yourself."

I had joked with Samara that the video might offer a before and after. The implication was that perhaps a year from now we can both laugh at me on film in the summer of 2000. "This *is* the after," she countered. The implication was that had we taken the video back in December I might have been truly alarmed at what I saw.

I wonder which way Dali will go—the way of Nicodemus or the way of Tom Foolery. Will I ever gain the knack of calming him? And how important is my affection for Dali in all of this?

I took our dog Dusty to the vet today for routine shots, and a woman in the waiting room pointed out a piece of straw in Dusty's mouth. I smiled, removed it and by way of thanks inquired after her cat, who was meowing in her carrying case. "A tumour," the woman reported, quite suddenly glassy-eyed. "Will they operate?" I asked, instantly regretting this further probe. "Too old," said the woman. Then the tears came and she darted outside.

I wished later I had done this: gone to her and told her how deeply sorry I was. Later in the day I drove to the cabin to cut grass and water a newly planted tree. I love that cabin and plunder any excuse to go there, always with Dusty as company. We go to the point as the sun sets, and though she is not much on swimming she has a comic ritual of dunking her body in the cool waters of Lake Ontario. I will sorrow, truly sorrow, when she goes. But I've had her four years. Will I have four years with Dali?

June 2, 2000

Dali has developed a wariness in one corner of the sand ring. When I lunge him, and he is now consistently fine on the line, his head is nicely dropped for almost the entire circle but rises in that corner.

The good serpentines of a week ago came undone today. Rounding the boogey corner he would curl his head in and drift down the track, refusing to make the bend. My inside rein ends up at my knee; Dali feels trapped, gets high-headed. What a pity that wasn't captured on Samara's camera.

We ended today on some good canter work, but inside the arena where he seems more at ease. We look on the bright side, we hope for better days, we press on.

June 5, 2000

The Canadian horse essentially says, "Ask me right and I'll try it." Those words, once uttered by a driving coach to Will Oddie, a breeder of Canadian horses in Saskatchewan, have come to lodge deeply in my cranium. What willingness Dali, say, possesses, is predicated on the skill of his rider. He is forever saying, in his way, "Ask me right."

Today in the ring, Samara said something that echoed those sentiments. After Dali had balked at something I asked of him, she noted: "He's not doing you any favours." And then there was cousin Kathi's line, how every horse seeks a "worthy leader." All variations on a theme. Ask Dali right, and he's there. Implicit is that asking incorrectly invites trouble.

He is such a sensitive horse that he mirrors my riding. If I unravel a little in a serpentine, he does too. Today I just trotted him up the long side of the ring, forming 20-metre loops to the left as we went. At first he would just duck away to the right. "I'd rather not," he was saying. I'd then do part of the exercise in a walk, half-halt him if he got too strong in the trot, and we worked it through.

When you ask of Dali a difficult task, he needs to be reminded that he can do it, and further, that I will insist—at least to a point. He is a horse who will test the waters. His evasions seem rooted at times in worry or honest confusion, at other times in wilfulness. Dali will second-guess me if he finds me incapable or uncertain. He is generous in his way, but not to a fault. Today was a lovely day to ride. While a strong breeze kept Dali cool and the bugs in the bushes, the sun cast a warm and optimistic light. His winter coat is almost gone; in its stead is a fine sheen. Shannon credits the particular grain mix we both feed our horses.

Samara keeps telling Dark Fox Dali what a handsome guy he is, and I think she means it. Back at his biceps, at the femur, I have noticed a rippled flatness that was not there before, and a certain tucking up, both a measure of the weight he has lost and the fitness he is acquiring from these thrice-weekly rides. He will always retain the blocky build that is his ancestry, but he has a fine, almost delicate head, and soft brown eyes. I put some conditioner in his mane and tail the other day, and now the mane especially seems full and light, rising and falling on either side as we ride, like so many wings. I love this Pegasus touch and the illusions it fosters.

For weeks now I have kept my heavy western chaps in the trunk. Samara wondered if the price of the chaps' grip was a shallow seat and so I ride now in breeches. The closer the contact the deeper the seat. But I have also been wrapping my right knee with about eight feet of gauze as a precaution. The inside of my knee was forever being bloodied, especially after canter work. Lately, I've been forgetting to wrap it, but the rubbing has ceased. Am I now deeper in the saddle? Is Dali's conformation changing? I don't know. I'm just an old guy on a young horse who actually tries to ride by the seat of his pants. "Ride on your pockets," says Samara. "Smile," said Maria. I strive to do both.

Old fears are fading, turning to admiration. I see Dali less and less as a horse with problems to solve, and more like a complex, dignified creature who merits all the understanding I can muster. I sat in my barber's chair a few hours after the ride, closed my eyes as Pat Vecchio, a skilled artisan and a philosopher king to boot, delicately ran his clippers over my beard.

Pat had horses as a boy in Italy and he is always keen to know the latest report on Dali. It was pleasurable to sit in that chair and be, dare I say it, groomed. An image possessed me: that of Dali in the cross-ties, one hind foot tipped in calm repose, his eye gone soft as I run my brush over his body.

June 14, 2000

Dali lame. An odd pairing of words. I have grown accustomed to my own soreness and lameness; the possibility of him lame seemed remote. Even the shin splint never came close.

Last Friday I went to ride him, and cousin Kathi happened to be at the stable, chatting with Shannon. As I wrapped Dali's front legs with black cotton stable bandages over a white cotton wrap, I thought I saw Kathi arch an eyebrow. "Support for that old splint of his," I explained, but I made a mental note to seek her opinion later.

When I lunged Dali in the arena, he hung his head low, held his body tight and shuffled into a stiff trot. He looked to be protecting himself. I was sure he was lame, but I took him out to the ring where Shannon was riding and consulted her, and later, when she arrived, Samara. By now the lameness was pronounced. On the circle Dali would dip his head every time his inner front leg came down. Samara put poultices on both legs to bring down the inflammation; I called the vet.

Next morning Mark Rutherford diagnosed mild tendon strain, both sides. The cause could have been Dali braking hard while playing in the paddock, but Mark, like Kathi, eyed those bandages. No fan of bandages or even of boots, he advised no covering at all unless there is clear evidence of contact between Dali's legs during work. The problem, he said, is getting the tension on those bandages just right: Cotton, unlike polo wraps, has too little give. Even the Woof boots with the Velcro straps, he said, can be put on incorrectly.

But whether his soreness was my doing or his, the fact remains: Dali is lame. Mark prescribed four days of phenyl butasone (equine aspirin, "bute" comes in a pink liquid or powder) to tame the swelling and relieve pain, with stall rest broken by 20 minutes of hand-walking twice a day. My heart sank, and my feeling for Dali rose on these tidings. That I was perhaps the author of his pain caused me not a little anguish.

June 26, 2000

I have passed on to Samara the assignment of working Dali only lightly this week. It seemed a good time to head into Quebec, the heartland of the Canadian horse.

I walked in fields near the village of St-Paulin at the farm of André Auclair with dozens of his soft-eyed mares and their foals, one chestnut mare following me and beseeching that I rub her under the neck just one more time. After a generous lunch, I looked on as André's wide-eyed studs were showcased in the pouring rain and sent bucketing around on lunge lines, each stallion progressively younger and more spirited than the one before.

I sat outside a café at Deschambault, the village just upriver from Quebec City, and got some history lessons from Yves Bernatchez. He took me into an outbuilding behind the café and showed me stone pillars with rings once used to secure Canadian horses in centuries past. In his office above the café we pored over his old books on the history of *le cheval canadien*.

Southeast of Trois-Rivières at Trottier Mills, where the Appalachians begin their rise, I was offered lodging at the farm of Gilles Racette and his wife, Anne Bélanger. I leaned on a fence and looked into a sand ring as two young riders jumped little Canadians under Anne's guidance. All week long I eyed Canadian horses in fields and barns, huddled with breeders, and talked of little else but the horse of iron. It was like a massive infusion.

Gilles Racette has been defending and promoting the Canadian horse for decades. He sat on a rocking chair in his reading room, a patchwork quilt as cushion, and told me that people call him often looking for a suitable Canadian horse.

"Black, no Fox," they say, meaning they want a black horse but not one from the Fox line. Dali's line.

Distance always gives me perspective, and during a week in which I put 1,500 kilometres on the car I had ample time to ponder my horse from afar. On the meditative grounds of *le vieux presbytère* overlooking the St. Lawrence River from the heights at Deschambault, I smoked my pipe and thought of him. North of Trois-Rivières I pulled onto a dirt road under crackling hydro lines to relieve myself and again pondered him. Sitting in Montreal traffic, snarled after an overpass had collapsed with deadly results, my thoughts went to Dali.

Is he the right horse for me? Why, after a year of schooling, of getting professional help and trying to work his worries through, has our progress been so slow? Why can I not, as a friend once phrased it, "impart calmness to him?" Is he, as Gilles Dupuis once bade me consider, too much horse for someone with weekend-rider skills?

I had thought that by now we'd be jumping, riding the trails, competing in distance events. This morning on the telephone I voiced some of these frustrations to cousin Kathi and Samara, two of the most sympathetic horse people I know. Both said much the same thing: Dali has taught you much, and you are a far better rider now than you were a year ago. But it should be fun, and clearly it's not.

"You could do it," said Samara. "Invest another year in him, and he would become more calm, more willing to work. But he will always have that edge." Kathi said an old horseman once told her that the horse you see in the first minutes of your first encounter is essentially the horse he will be for the rest of his life.

The Dali I saw at Ferme Saroma was a wide-eyed horse who looked suspiciously at the western saddle Jérôme put on him. Jérôme rode him with a strong hand only briefly before handing him over to me, and in minutes I was airborn. And when Dali was finally brought back to me he was white with lather and tight with dread. I got on him, felt relief when I didn't get bucked a second time, and perhaps recklessly concluded at home a day later, "That's the horse for me."

Was it optimism or idiocy that informed my decision? These days I ride defensively, and a good day is one without scoots or falls. I wish we could focus on accomplishments, such as dressage figures or vaulting modest fences or long conditioning treks on trails; instead, I am grateful after a ride that things *didn't* happen. This was not my vision when I embarked on this journey.

Samara concedes that Dali makes even her a little nervous, and she is happy to know that I have, for the moment, parked plans to train for distance events. I still feel I need Samara, but I resent that fact and am determined to limit her help to once weekly. As for the back fields, where I rode Dali with Wendy 10 months ago, they seem, for the moment, beyond us. You should feel no shame, both

Kathi and Samara say, in admitting that perhaps he was not the best choice. And Kathi well remembers trying to dissuade me from buying a young green horse.

Dali is like a sharp knife I have too often mishandled, and the memory is fresh of my cuts. I am forever "taking the edge off him," knowing that time off renders him bored and energized. Cousin Kathi does not dispute my assessment—she calls the match of Dali and Larry a mismatch, "like some marriages I know"—but she also wonders if a free lease might be the ticket. Share the responsibility of riding Dali with a kind-hearted but experienced rider who will help me put the miles on him. Kathie G., told of all this, says she has someone in mind.

But for all the distress he has caused me, the thought of selling Dali induces in me a heavy, palpable dread. If keeping him is the wrong thing, so is not keeping him. This must be, I tell myself, male menopause.

My friend Sarah is facing a similar test of her passion for horses. "The honeymoon," she tells me, "is over. Stone-cold reality has set in." Sarah has endured a somewhat stormy three-year relationship with her 11-year-old Thoroughbred mare, Maddy, but they enjoyed great success in eventing competitions last summer. Spring hormones have always posed a challenge, and in the early summer of 2000, during some hill work, the mare bucked Sarah off and high-tailed it to the stable. Bruised and shaken, Sarah finds herself engaged in mustering more self-discipline and determination than she ever thought herself capable. "You have to ride with confidence," her coach tells her, and not just hide your fears, but lose them.

Like me, Sarah is an amateur rider who can devote perhaps three rides a week to her horse. And like me, she wonders if that's too little for so much horse. Owning any horse, I now know, exacts an emotional, physical and financial toll, but a certain kind of horse can amplify the burden, make it seem overwhelming. "Riding," a young but sage equestrian recently wrote in *Practical Horseman*, after watching friends embrace and then abandon riding, "is all about time."

Horse ownership has caused me to ponder the exclusivity of the horse-rider relationship, and how time spent with my horse takes me away from family and other things I love—travel, cabin, writing and reading. Dali occupies a great and weighty space in my life and at times I wish that were not so.

Still, says Sarah, selling her horse, or swapping for another (more Ford than Ferrari) feels too much like giving up. *No mas*, the Spanish say—No more. *J'en ai marre*, say the French—I've had enough. The English say, *I quit*. She's stubborn is Sarah, and I admire that in her. The Canadian horse has stubbornness in spades and I will concede to owning some myself. And yet another voice is urging us caution, warning of danger.

Sarah and I possess knowledge we did not possess before. It's knowledge born, in part, of bruises and adrenalin and fear. Years ago when I rode, at times with gleeful abandon, in the mountains and plains of Wyoming, it never occurred to me that my rental quarter horse would buck or bolt. I knew nothing of his demons and so rode with utter confidence. Now, like Sarah, I know my horse almost too well and find myself having to reconstitute my boldness.

I long for the kind of riding I did in the Alberta foothills and with friends on trails in southeastern Ontario, enjoying the sun on my face, watching hawks and admiring the land beyond and below, finding sustenance in the gentle blowing of the horse I was on. The simple joy of riding.

It had all seemed so uncomplicated a year ago when this odyssey began. When my then 13-year-old son, Kurt, made a foot-high rocking horse in his woodworking class and painted it in Dali's colours— the one white sock on the right hind foot pleased me no end—I placed it in a high location where I could see it out of the corner of my eye as I wrote this book. The red heart painted midway on the rockers augured for the kind of partnership I dreamed of.

But dreams get as tangled as lunge lines. I am not giving up on Dark Fox Dali. I am not even giving up on me as rider. It is only this: His spirit requires more time than I have to give.

And so as I write this, I am at one of those crossroads that all horses and riders arrive at sooner or later, and the way seems unclear. And I wonder. If I sell Dali or swap him for an older, calmer horse, which will I feel more strongly? Sadness, or relief?

July 29, 2000

A month later and much has changed. Dali has been wonderful all month, as if he had somehow intuited my thoughts of selling him. More likely, it is the summer doldrums and the fact that after three months he's settling in at Limestone. Frankie, big laid-back Frankie, is clearly Dali's paddock boss, but Dali gets on well with Rocket and Nate too. The tall boys. This morning as we, I on Dali, Samara on Bogi, rounded the barn after a buggy trail ride, Frankie called out a hearty greeting to him. Even Shannon's to-ing and fro-ing in the barn on the John Deere manure-mobile, which used to unsettle him, does no longer.

Dali has been brave and steady on the trail, generous in the ring. Still, he needs miles and I have neither the time to log them myself nor the money to pay a trainer to help amass them, though were I deeper of pocket I would give the job to Samara in a heartbeat. Instead, I have a loose arrangement with a rider named Shannon Offord to ride Dali when I'm away and otherwise share him. Ideally, he'll get ridden six times a week.

Shannon is 24 and simply cannot afford a horse at the moment. Kathie has recommended her, lets her ride her mares, and that's a blessing I put confidence in. In August, while my family and I were away on holidays, Shannon often rode Dali four times a week. She would supple him and turn him using only cues from her leg. She even had him backing up nicely, something he loathes, until some stubbornness kicked in. But when I came back late in August and rode him, he was as happy and willing as I had ever seen him.

The new, agreeable Dali continued to show himself all through September. One day I asked him to back up, using only the French word and keeping the reins almost slack. This discussion took about two minutes, and I kept repeating his name, asking him softly to do as I asked. He finally turned around to look at me, offered a little sigh and backed up half a step. No nose in the air, no balking, no ears back. Just a sign that said, "You're my buddy, and I'll give it a shot. Just this once, mind." I could have kissed him.

By mid-October, he was backing up nicely and consistently, and we were, with Samara's guidance, jumping two-foot fences and cross-poles in sets of three. Happy horse, happy rider. I'm not sure what lies ahead for the two of us, but right now I see him, and he sees me, as a pal.

Few at the stable call him Dali anymore, perhaps because Dali was too close to Dolly, and there's nothing girlish about him. Shannon, the ever even barn manager, calls him Dallers but to most of us he's Dal now, one of the boys in the gelding paddock. "Hey Dal," I always say to him by way of greeting out there, and his response is just as ritual-istic: He closes his eyes for a second or two and drops his head gently into my outstretched halter. I scratch him under his neck, I chat him up and ask after his health, and we walk up the lane. The mares we pass like him and call out a greeting. Trudeau, the cocky little chestnut foal—I call him the WalMart greeter with attitude—nickers to him, too. Dal is a lucky horse to call this home, and I think he knows it.

Out of curiosity and using a stick at Limestone, I measured Dal in mid-October. He was 15.1 hands. He was a little taller now, and though it was all in my head, I walked a little taller myself.

Saroma Dark Fox Dali, six-and-a-half years old as I pen these words, has had 18 months to get to know me. It would be a stretch to call him mellow or laid-back, as many of his kin truly are. But neither is he delinquent, as I once feared him to be. Dali is more relaxed now than I have ever seen him.

As I write this, the leaves turned and falling and the air cool and crisp in the last days of autumn in the year 2000, our partnership feels solid. Kathi watched me ride him and remarked on how soft his eye was, how he had lost that worried look. I, too, have lost that worried look and I ride Dali more happily and more securely than ever.

At one point in our adventures, I lamented that I had picked a too spirited, too nervous horse, and not at all a fair choice to focus on as representative of the breed. In truth, no one horse can be said to carry the colours of an entire breed. Dali is Dali, and his character owes something to his bloodline, to my own strengths and weaknesses as rider and trainer, and even to circumstance. It likely worked against him that he was schooled late, not early, in his youth.

And yet there are many aspects to him that speak of his heritage. The high cheekbones, the sturdy build, the generous mane and tail, those magnificent feet, the great shaggy coat he sports all winter. People new to the barn will stop and take a second look when they're told he's a Canadian.

Some things about Dali will never change. He will always be smart and sensitive, alert and careful, inclined to worry about some things. I still would not put my 14-year-old son, who has had minimal riding instruction, on Dali. This horse still asks too much of his rider. But his early haughtiness and almost studdy disposition have given way to trust. He is a favourite at his stable because he's kind and mannered and gets on well with his paddock mates. And as he matures and I put more miles on him, his natural athleticism will serve us both well on the long rides that I hope lay ahead.

In the final days of writing *Little Horse of Iron*, I learned some important details of Dali's family history. All that hot Fox blood he is supposed to possess has, it appears, a gentle counter on his dam's side. René Bélanger of St-Antonin, Quebec, owns Ranch-L Nicot Ukraine, Dali's dam, who is now 13. "A wonderful horse, very gentle," he told Patricia Cooper. "My son was seven when we bought her and he could do anything with her. You can ride her, drive her.

She has good conformation and temperament and she's had three foals, all good."

And this mare's bloodlines, it seems, are also quiet. At the farm of John Litjens in St-Armand Ouest, Madame Litjens well remembers both La Gorgendière Barreau Nicot and Ranch-L Kaiser Nadia, the sire and dam of Ranch-L Nicot Ukraine. The stud, she told Patricia Cooper, was bought at the Deschambault sale in 1981 and proved to be a good and gentle stallion who finally died in 1999 after siring 40 foals. As for Ranch-L Kaiser Nadia, "She was very very gentle and her foals were all quiet." She was descended from the Henryville line, one noted for its docility.

I look back and I wonder how much of Dali's antics were rooted in something as simple as unsettling change. Dali moved from Ferme Saroma to Blue Haven to Lakehead Stables to Limestone Stables—all in the space of a year. A hard year, as it happened.

All the books I had read on horsemanship, all the riding masters at whose feet I have sat, the several instructors who sought to teach me to ride better—all pale beside what I learned in a year and a half with this young horse.

I may yet call myself a horseman, and when I do, I will have Dali to thank for it.

So, we have come to a sweet turn in the road, Dal and I. In the fall of 2000 I still lunged him before riding him, but for only a minute, and more as a matter of routine than to take the measure of him. By December of that year, I stopped the lunging, for there was no need. The work to supple Dali, my blocky horse, is never-ending but the partnership between us feels more solid than it's ever been. I ride him four times a week, he's fitter now, and once a week Samara coaches us over small jumps. We have come far, he and I, and there's a long road ahead.

I have a history now, of both the Canadian horse as a breed and of this one horse, to call upon. The other day I saw Kathi and Dick at a lakeside family reunion and when I told her how swell things were with Dal, she smiled and made a roller-coaster motion with her hands. Dick assured me that those hills and valleys will become over time less pronounced, roll more gently. He looked out over the water as he spoke, trying to find the words to describe moments of exhilaration and delight, when a tiny adjustment in balance, say, achieves a wondrous and unforeseen result in the saddle. He and Kathi are eyeing two colts, which would bring their herd to seven and extend their connection with horses into retirement and beyond.

"Every ride," says Dick, "has something to offer." When I shared that insight with Patricia Cooper, she heartily agreed and suggested that even, or maybe especially, disastrous rides and drives have something to offer. "I'm learning," she told me, "every time I go out to drive Tom or China—learning about driving and my horses. Maybe that's why we love our horses and our equestrian sports. There is always another challenge." I understand what Dick and Patricia are saying in a way I would not have in the pre-Dal days. My little horse of iron, he of the round frame and muscled neck and expressive brown eyes, merits that degree of scrutiny. Perhaps this is a better form of accounting, one that measures the horse-human equation in shades of wonder and gratitude, one ride at a time.

# EPILOGUE

SPRING 2001

*The Canadian horse has survived and endured, mostly on its own merits. Various govern-ments and the breeders' association have all played a role in keeping the breed going, but in recent decades it's come down to a few believers singing the praises of a virtuous horse and hoping that some of us would listen. A modest plan, but it seems to have worked.*

THE MAY 6, 1999 EDITION OF THE *OTTAWA CITIZEN* contained yet anoth-er story about a separatist/federalist squabble. The government of Canada and the government of Quebec were both claiming an element of history as their own. What they were fighting over was a horse—the Canadian horse.

The photo accompanying the story features a striking black stal-lion, Beckett's Creek Calypso Ferari galloping across a paddock. He's

Above: Front page of *The Ottawa Citizen*, May 6, 1999.

sleek and muscled and that distinctively long mane and tail are whipping in the wind. "Politics in the Paddock," one headline reads. "A Truly Canadian Horse Race," reads another.

For a breed of horse that almost disappeared off the face of the earth a few decades ago it may speak of a brighter future that two governments now raced to adopt him as their own.

In 1999, an Ontario Liberal MP named Murray Calder introduced a private member's bill calling for the House of Commons to recognize officially the oldest breed in Canada as the national horse. But Calder needed unanimous consent among political parties in the House of Commons before the bill could be considered. Only the Bloc Québécois voted against it.

It should have come as no surprise that the Bloc blocked. The Parti Québécois, just a week previously, had voted at a convention to designate the Canadian horse as Quebec's own horse. There's a certain irony in a separatist government lusting after a Canadian horse. But one can understand their claim: The cradle of the Canadian horse is the province of Quebec. For close to 350 years, the horse was bred there almost exclusively. On the other hand, the horse is called the Canadian, and were it not for the efforts of certain breeders outside Quebec two decades ago, the breed may well have vanished.

The PQ—the same government that cut funding and thereby ended the last sponsored breeding program of Canadian horses at Deschambault in 1981—were quite serious about getting to the Canadian first. The PQ's Proposition 16 looked to have a better chance of getting to the finish line than Calder's Bill C-454. And so it did. On December 15, 1999, the government of Quebec declared the Canadian horse, the Canadian cow and the Chantecler chicken as their own.

"It did bug the Péquistes that the horse is called the Canadian horse," Yves Bernatchez told me. "Politicians like simple concepts and this made it hard to explain to constituents." Bernatchez is the one to whom Radio Canada goes as the authority on the Canadian horse, and small wonder. Decades ago he moved his family and law practice to Deschambault to be closer to the experimental farm there, then central to the future of the Canadian horse.

Murray Calder, meanwhile, continued to press his private member's bill as the year 2000 wound down. It is, he admits, a Sisyphean task. Private member's bills almost always fail. But in his revamped bill, the horse would be called the *Canadien* horse, out of respect for its roots in old Quebec. Breeders, even those in Quebec, he told me, believe that the Canadian horse would be more valuable if promoted as a national, not a provincial, breed. Québécois breeders, then, regardless of their political stripe, might lobby the Bloc to support the bill. Capitalism might prevail over patriotism.

The question, Who owns the Canadian horse?, has been a source of controversy for a long time. As early as 1900, the federal government moved to take control of the Canadian horse, apparently seeking to secure a steady supply of warhorses. But Dr. Joseph-Alphonse Couture, that champion of the breed then working as a vet for the federal government, resisted it. He eventually saw some financial advantages in allowing federal involvement. And so, by 1906, the Canadian horse was in Canadian, not Quebec, hands. In 1935, the Canadian Horse Breeders' Association (CHBA), as recorded in its own documents, "agreed to designate the breed as 'Canadian' instead of 'French-Canadian' as formerly, and all offical records have since been printed accordingly." (Murray Calder would no doubt emphasize this detail as he lobbies fellow MPs.)

Still, responsibility for the Canadian horse was shared in those days. At the breeding farm near St. Joachim, Quebec, in the 1920s and 1930s, for example, the federal government paid the costs of running the operation, the provincial government paid the rent, and the Canadian Horse Breeders' Association had organizational duties.

The association, unfortunately, is given to squabbling. Reading old newsletters of the CHBA, and of its Ontario wing, the Upper Canada District, or UCD, I have to wince at all the infighting. In a very Canadian way, it is language that often sets tempers aboiling.

November 10, 1996. At issue was whether the UCD should launch its own newsletter, and whether it should appear in both French and English. "Newsletter with both languages so we don't fall apart," the minutes record one francophone member as saying. "Bickering has to stop."

Another UCD member in 1996 introduced a plea from another member not present: "He would like to see the member and stallion bashing stop. He says there are members running down other members' horses, blood lines etc. and he says it's getting out of hand. If you don't have anything good to say about another member and their horses to a prospective client then you should not say anything." Seems to me a rabbit in the Walt Disney film, *Bambi*, uttered something similar: "If you don't have somethin' good to say," he says his mother told him, "don't say nuthin' at all."

The December 1997 issue of *Le cheval canadien* carried a headline suggesting that the CHBA was at a turning point, and referred vaguely to the previous years' internecine struggles. The association, curiously, had never had so many members (639) and the horse's fortunes looked good. In 1970, only 49 Canadian foals were registered; in 1995, the figure was 300, rising to 476 in the year 2000. Such numbers did nothing to douse the flames.

The UCD traditionally holds its annual general meeting in the basement of a Belleville motel, where the black-and-white-checkerboard motif on the ceiling is sometimes more interesting than proceedings themselves. But in the way that a sleepy horse in a paddock can explode into a canter when a groundhog darts from his hole, the dull readings of minutes and seconding of motions at UCD AGMs can take a lively turn, as I saw firsthand in April 1999 when I sat in.

Some years beforehand, a UCD member, fed up with the politics that often mar small organizations like this one, ran a large ad in her local newspaper offering the services of her stallion. In tiny print at the bottom, it read: "Not affiliated with the Upper Canada District Canadian Horse Breeders' Association."

Letters were sent, apologies demanded. The board of directors, convinced that the "professionalism" of their organization had been maligned, unilaterally revoked her membership. Years later, the incident still has life, the way the ground below a barn fire stays dangerously hot long after the charred cinders have gone cold. The rank and file, at least those in attendance, fire verbal darts at the head table. One member even asks that the board apologize to the aggrieved member, who sits in the audience. The last time I squirmed in my seat this much was at a wedding where the best man's speech—a blue and tasteless locker-room roast—left us all shaking our heads.

But this pot never really gets to boiling. The horsewoman is not only welcomed back into the fold, but voted in as vice-president to sit on the very board that chastised her. With the marking of this curiously tidy circle, the matter seemed closed. But in a comic postmortem, the UCD newsletter later reported that the appointment had fallen through: The vice-president's membership dues were not in order.

Early in the year 2000, an Ontario group of Canadian horse owners sought to form a new association. Another splinter from a tiny piece of wood. "This association," read its letter of introduction, "is for breeders and admirers of 'the little iron horse' who are dedicated to the preservation of the breed and to ensure the Canadian Horse remains pure to its heritage."

Alec Hayward told me that he and other owners had grown increasingly alarmed at the horses being accepted into the stud book. Numbers are up, he said, but the quality is down. The old government standard, said Hayward, calls for male horses no taller than 15.3 hands, and for females 15.2 or smaller; yet horses of 16 and 17 hands are now being registered as Canadians. Ever since the late 1980s, he contends, when it became clear that there was money to be made from selling Canadian horses, the breed standard has dipped. Hayward has no interest in becoming active in the new organization, only in helping to launch it. But in a related matter, he's very much in the thick of things. Since the mid-1990s Alec has been involved in a bitter dispute with the CHBA after it dropped his horses from the registry. He sued for damages, and both sides have been racking up enormous legal bills ever since.

As Alec puts it, "When they threw a rock at me, I was standing in front of their window. The proper standard for the Canadian horse was set by the Canadian government, and the government never got out of the business. The Morgan association, the Arab association, they can change their breed standard any way they want. But the Canadian is the only breed in North America where the standard was set by the government, and that's still the case."

Gilles Racette, who presided over the national association when the standard was adjusted by general council in 1991, now wonders if Alec's position has some merit. He would not be averse to seeing the standard changed back. And Gilles finds it darkly ironic that Alec Hayward, one of the great defenders of the breed, had to battle the very association formed 100 years ago to preserve the breed.

(In 2000, round one of Hayward versus the CHBA was settled, with a judge awarding Alec $15,000 in damages. Meanwhile, more trouble was brewing. The national association was reporting in its fall 2000 newsletter that it would no longer recognize its Quebec wing, whose president is Gilles Racette. The reasons are tangled and beyond the scope of this book, but my own sense is that old grudges and power struggles are stoking the fire, with both sides convinced they have the best interests of the breed at heart. I was given to ponder anew the veterinarian Art King's insight that horsemanship is about control, and that a room full of horse people is a room full of controllers.)

Racette has seen meetings of the CHBA become so acrimonious that fist fights seemed likely. "I've had more arguments on the board than 30 years on the police force," he told me. Lately the most bitter fights have pitted those who prefer the blocky Canadian against those who want taller, finer horses. "A good horse is a good horse," André Auclair likes to say, "but a good horse is not necessarily a Canadian." Gilles Racette offers this analogy: "If you like antiques but you also like chrome, you're not an antique lover. The Canadian horse is a legacy from our ancestors."

Jean-Paul Paré, now a trainer in Toronto, agrees that a 17-hand Canadian is excessive, but he argues that there is a middle ground. With the right breeding, the Canadian could become a world-class sport horse.

And so, some 350 years later, it's still a burning question: What does a Canadian horse look like?

Meanwhile, it's clear that the profile of Canadian horses has been rescued from obscurity, and demand for them is much up from what it was. I talked to those who know the breed, seeking to know why. Some say the quality of the horse finally asserted itself after years in the dark. A flurry of magazine and newspaper articles about the Canadian horse no doubt stirred interest just when many members of the boom generation—nearing retirement and with time and money on their hands—either discovered or rediscovered horses. The Canadian horse seemed a natural choice.

Intense American interest in the Canadian horse has also stirred the pot. It is an old (and, to some, an aggravating) truth that we on this side of the border only value something when those below the border do. The lesson of history is that Americans have been valuing the Canadian horse for almost two centuries.

Nationalist feeling, in both Quebec and Canada, has also fuelled the market. And as demand increased, prices rose. Some show people, unable to afford a $10,000 or $20,000 sport horse and seeking modestly priced eventers, jumpers and distance horses, have shown increasing interest in the rugged all-purpose Canadian. But English riders want taller, finer horses, and thus the pressure on breeders to produce them and the internecine struggles that plague an association already given to squabbling.

And though the numbers of Canadians left remains low, the gene pool, at least for now, is adequate. In their study, presented at the Sixth World Congress on Genetics Applied to Livestock Production, in January 1998 (pity I missed it), three Canadian researchers wanted an answer to this question: At what point is the gene pool of an endangered species simply too small to ensure preservation? Is the Canadian horse, for example, rare enough that the breed risks genetic diseases, inbreeding and decreased productivity?

It appears not. The study compared the levels of inbreeding and genetic variability in 11 breeds: the Appaloosa, Arabian, American Saddlebred, Belgian, Canadian, Miniature Horse, Morgan, Quarter Horse, Standardbred, Thoroughbred and Tennessee Walking Horse.

The study found that the Canadian has not suffered a loss in genetic variation due to its small population size, nor is it more inbred than more popular breeds. "The Canadian," says a precis of the study, "does appear to be more genetically distinct from popular race and riding horse breeds, reinforcing the need to consider making the conservation of this breed a high priority."

I spoke to Ruthanne Hart of Margaree Centre, Nova Scotia, who had some interesting thoughts on the breed at this critical juncture in its history. Hart may be to Nova Scotia what Alec Hayward is to Ontario: a goodwill broker who connects interested parties to Canadian horses in her region. But she strikes me as a clear-eyed woman, not one to extol the breed's merits beyond what is real and true.

"I like the Canadian," she told me, "not because they're the best horse in the world but because they're Canadian. I would go to horse shows and hear horses being introduced. This one was from Oklahoma, this one was from Germany. You had the sense that the import was always seen as better, and that the homegrown was a kind of leftover. Why not look at our own breed?

"The Canadian is a great all-round horse. There are quieter horses, and faster horses—though I doubt there are smarter horses—than the Canadian. You can trail-ride them, jump with them, drive them, use them on the farm. And you can compete at a very high level with them."

But in the excitement of past decades, some breeders have come to celebrate the Canadian in a way that distorts. Hart worries that some owners could be headed for a fall if they believe all the hype.

Hart is in a position to weigh into this matter. She has owned Canadians for 10 years and currently owns four, and has been active for a decade in the Maritime wing of the CHBA, first as president and now as secretary-treasurer.

"The Canadian should not be advertised as the quietest horse you can get," she says. "Some are, some are not. You shouldn't think of the Canadian horse as a teddy bear. I've been around other breeds, Thoroughbreds, warmbloods, and I would say that the Canadian is smart, has a sense of humour, and is honest. They like to learn and they're easily bored."

Hart has a friend who rode on the German equestrian team several decades ago. This woman helped train Hart's filly while coincidentally training her own Thoroughbred. "She loved my filly," said Hart. "She said my horse lacked the gaits of the Thoroughbreds and Trakheners she had worked with, but she said my filly was one of the smartest horses she ever worked with."

The downside, warned Hart, is that such a horse learns the right thing and the wrong thing at the same speed. Thus Hart would never sell certain Canadians to a novice or someone not equipped to handle a spirited one.

Hart's four Canadians are all quite different in character. One, were you simply to speak harshly to her, would pout in the corner of her stall for days. Another, incapable of holding a grudge, would accept either a firm hand or the sternest voice commands.

Ten years ago Hart was seeking a companion horse for the one at the inn where Hart worked as a cook. She knew of a bunch somewhere and selected one called Colonel, a 14-year-old half-Canadian. "He's kinda strange," said his owner in a thick Scottish brogue, "and it's been quite a while since he was ridden." That was an understatement: It had been 12 years, and though Colonel at first backed away when Hart went to mount him, he was otherwise good under saddle.

Since then it's been all Canadians for Hart. Gilles Racette in Quebec got her started, and every three years now at her farm on the west coast of Cape Breton Island she raises a foal.

The Canadian horse has survived and endured, mostly on its own merits. Various governments and the breeders' association have all played a role in keeping the breed going, but in recent decades it's come down to a few believers singing the praises of a virtuous horse and hoping that some of us would listen. A modest plan, but it seems to have worked.

The Canadian horse deserves to be preserved, just as heritage architecture and heritage seeds warrant special protection. The merits of the little horse of iron, I hope, should be clear by now and this book was written in praise of him. These sturdy horses, on whose powerful bodies the history of the nation has been etched, are *our* horses. For that reason alone, they deserve a future and not just a glorious past.

# BIBLIOGRAPHY

CHAPTER 1

Beattie, Gladys Mackey. *The Canadian Horse: A Pictorial History.* Lennoxville, Quebec: Sun Books, 1980.

Bernier, Paul. *Le cheval canadian.* Sillery, Quebec: Les éditions du Septentrion, 1992.

Bluche, Francois. *Louis XIV,* Oxford: Basil Blackwell, 1990.

Burke, Peter. *The Fabrication of Louis XIV.* New Haven and London: Yale University Press, 1992.

Cross, Michael S. and Kealey, Gregory S. *Economy and Society During the French Regime to 1759: Readings in Canadian Social History, Vol. 1.* Toronto: McClelland & Stewart, 1983.

Dicks, Stewart K. *Les Canadiens: The French in Canada 1600–1867.* Scarborough, Ont.: Prentice-Hall, 1980.

Douville, Raymond and Casanova, Jacques-Donat. *Daily Life in Early Canada from Champlain to Montcalm.* New York: Macmillan, 1967.

Gendron, H. Mario. "Quelques Notes Historiques Sur Les Chevaux Canadiens." St-Alban, Quebec: Société des éleveurs de chevaux canadiens, 1994.

Gillmor, Don and Turgeon, Pierre, *Canada: A People's History.* Toronto: McClelland & Stewart, 2000.

Hendricks, Bonnie L. *International Encyclopedia of Horse Breeds.* Norman: University of Oklahoma Press, 1995.

Jones, Robert Leslie. *History of Agriculture in Ontario, 1613–1880.* Toronto: University of Toronto Press, 1946.

Jones, Robert Leslie. "The Old French-Canadian Horse: Its History in Canada and the U.S.," *Canadian Historical Review,* Volume XXVIII, No. 2, 1947, 125–155.

MacDonald, Robert R. *The Sun King: Louis XIV and the New World.* New Orleans: The Louisiana Museum Foundation, 1984.

Parkman, Francis. *Pioneers of France in the New World: France and England in North America, Part First.* Williamstown, Mass., Corner House Publishers, 1970.

Ross, Cecily. "The Little Horse That Could." *Harrowsmith Country Life* Vol. XIX, No. 119, December 1994, 40–46.

Skeoch, Eric. *Life in New France.* Toronto: Grolier, 1980.

Thorne, J.O. and Collocott, T.C., ed. *Chambers Biographical Dictionary.* Edinburgh: Hazell, Watson and Viney Ltd., 1974.

Williams, R.S. "The Angel Without Wings." *Canadian Living* Vol. 22, No. 11, November 1997, 52–56.


CHAPTER 2

*The Economist.* "The Lawn-Ornament Trade: Horses in the West." May 23, 1998, Vol. 347, No. 8069, 27–28.

Groleau, Leon. "Screenplay: The Conformation of Horses: An Essential Tool for Selection." Ministère de l'Agriculture, des Pêcheries et de l'Alimentation du Québec, Fifth version, September 1, 1992.


CHAPTER 3

Atwood, Margaret. *Days of the Rebels 1815–1840.* Toronto: Natural Science of Canada Ltd., 1977.

Herbert, Henry William. *Hints to Horse-keepers: A Complete Manual for Horsemen.* New York, A.O. Moore & Company, 1859.


CHAPTER 5

Brereton, J.M. *The Horse in War.* London: David & Charles, 1976.

Catton, Bruce. *Stillness at Appomattox. (The Army of the Potomac Trilogy).* New York: Doubleday, 1953.

Crowninshield, Benjamin W. *A History of the First Regiment of Massachusetts Cavalry Volunteers.* (Reprinted as the tenth volume of the *Army of the Potomac Series*). Baltimore, Maryland: Butternut and Blue, 1995.

Dwyer, Christopher S. "Raiding Strategy: As Applied by the Western Confederate Cavalry in the American Civil War." *The Journal of Military History,* 63 (April 1999), 263–281.

Ellis, John. *Cavalry: The History of Mounted Warfare.* New York: G.P. Putnam's Sons, 1978.

French, Cecil. *A History of the Canadian Army Veterinary Corps in the Great World War 1914–1919.* Guelph, Ontario: The CAV Barker Museum of Canadian Veterinary History and Crest Books, 1999.

Jamieson, Perry D. *Crossing the Deadly Ground: U.S. Army Tactics 1865–1890.* Tuscaloosa: University of Alabama Press, 1994.

Katcher, Philip. *Civil War Source Book.* New York: Facts on File, 1992.

Merritt, William Hamilton. *The Canadian Rangers: Canada in the South African War, 1901–2.* Toronto Public Library, Special Collections (C.S.L.: S.N., 1900–1905).


CHAPTER 6

Irwin, Chris. *Horses Don't Lie: The Magic of Horse Whispering.* Winnipeg, Man.: Great Plains Publications, 1998.


CHAPTER 7

Langlier, G.A., "The French-Canadian Horse: Bulletin No. 95." Dominion of Canada, Department of Agriculture, Ottawa, 1920.

Langlier, G.A., "The French-Canadian Horse: Bulletin No. 27-New Series." Dominion of Canada, Department of Agriculture, Ottawa, 1927.

MacEwan, J.W.G. *The Breeds of Farm Live-Stock in Canada.* Toronto: Thomas Nelson & Sons, 1941.

Pelletier, J.R. "Twenty-One Years' Work (1919–1940) for the Improvement of the Canadian Horse Breed as carried on at the St. Joachim Horse Farm, Quebec." Department of Agriculture, Ottawa, 1943.

Rutherford, Dr. J.G. "Cheval Canadian: Report of the Select Standing Committee on Agriculture and Colonization, First Session, Eleventh Parliament." House of Commons, Ottawa, 1909.

Rutherford, Dr. J.G. "The French Canadian Horse: Evidence of Dr. J.G. Rutherford Before the Select Standing Committee on Agriculture and Colonization, 1909." Printed by Order of Parliament, Ottawa, 1909, 61–73.

Street, David. *Horses: A Working Tradition*, Toronto: McGraw-Hill Ryerson, 1976.


CHAPTER 9

O'Brien, Laird. "A Horse Uniquely Ours from the King of France." *Canadian Geographic,* Vol. 111, No. 1, February/March 1991, 76–81.

CHAPTER 10

Self, Margaret Cabell. *Horsemastership: Methods of Training the Horse and the Rider*. New York: A. S. Barnes and Company, 1952.

CHAPTER 11

Christie, Barbara J. *The Horses of Sable Island*. Lawrencetown Beach, Nova Scotia: Pottersfield Press, 1995.

CHAPTER 13

Bienvenu, Paul and Sylvie. "The Origins of Horse and Carriage in Quebec." *The Carriage Journal*, Vol. 20, No. 2, 57–75.

Cauz, Louis E. *The Plate: A Royal Tradition*. Toronto: Deneau, 1984.

Chartrand, René. "Following the Horses" in Horizon Canada, Vol. 8. Laval University, Quebec: Centre for the Study of Teaching Canada, 1987.

Kumin, Maxine. *Inside the Halo and Beyond: The Anatomy of a Recovery*. New York: W.W. Norton & Co., 2000.

Plumb, Charles S. *Types and Breeds of Farm Animals*. Boston: Ginn and Company, 1906.

Veevers, Terry. "From the Box Seat: A Look at Competitive Driving." Equine Video Productions, Milgrove, Ont., 1990.

CHAPTER 16

Arnason, H.H. *History of Modern Art*. Englewood Cliffs, N.J.: Prentice Hall, 1978.

CHAPTER 17

Acker, Alison. "A Noble Canadian." *The Beaver*, February/March 1997, Vol. 77:1, 4-6.

Barnard, George. *The Cultivator*, Vol. 9, 1842, p. 33.

Battell, Joseph. *Morgan Horse and Registry, Volumes I and II*. Middlebury. Vermont: American Publishing Co., 1905.

Braider, Donald. *The Life, History and Magic of the Horse*. New York: Grosset & Dunlap, 1973.

MacEwan, Grant. *Heavy Horses: Highlights of their History* (Chapter 7, "The Canadien: Little Horse of Iron"). Saskatoon, Sask.: Western Producer Prairie Books, 1986.

Mongibeaux, Jean-François. "Prunelle: Cheval d'Orgueil." *Le Figaro.* Le 8 septembre, 1990.

Reid, Dennis. *Krieghoff: Images of Canada.* Toronto: Douglas & McIntyre and the Art Gallery of Ontario, 1999.

de Roussan, Jacques. "A Muse Among the Habitants" in Horizon Canada, Vol. 2. Laval University, Quebec: Centre for the Study of Teaching Canada, 1987.


CHAPTER 18

Grimshaw, Anne. *The Horse: A Bibliography of British Books 1851–1976.* London: The Library Association, 1982.

Smiley, Jane. *Horse Heaven.* New York: Alfred A. Knopf, 2000.

Smiley, Jane. "My Year of Living Dangerously." *Practical Horseman*, Vol. XXVIII, No. 4, April 2000, 65–73.


EPILOGUE

Pritchett, Jennifer. "Politics in the Paddock: A Truly Canadian Horse Race." *Ottawa Citizen,* May 6, 1999, p. 1.

# IMAGE CREDITS

Frontispiece: Photograph of Dali © Patti Gower, *The Globe and Mail*.

Chapter 1: Reprinted by permission of the Pinacoteca, Turin, Italy.

Chapter 2: © Shawn Hamilton.

Chapter 3. Artist unknown, 19th century. From *The Horse in the Stable and the Field: His Management in Health and Disease* by J.H. Walsh, circa 1871.

Chapter 5. Algernon M. Talmage. Oil on canvas. Reprinted by permission of Canadian War Museum (Ottawa), catalogue number 8735.

Chapter 7. © Yves Bernatchez.

Chapter 8. © Paul Orenstein.

Chapter 14. © Patti Gower, *The Globe and Mail*.

Chapter 17. From the private collection of Peter Winkworth and reprinted with his permission.

Chapter 18. © Patti Gower, *The Globe and Mail*.

*All other chapter images © Lawrence Scanlan.*

# ACKNOWLEDGEMENTS

THE ONE PERSON WHO HELPED ME most through the roller-coaster ride that was my first year of owning a horse was Kathi Bayly, an accomplished horsewoman who, mercifully, lives nearby and who happens to be my cousin. She would laugh, not unkindly, at my more egregious errors, encourage me when I was down, warn me when I grew cocky. I called her almost every week with some query and she invariably had answers and advice—about tack and schooling and the horse's mind, my horse's mind in particular. Kathi was my Pony Club.

*Little Horse of Iron* is equal parts history and personal quest. If Patricia Cooper in Palgrave, Ontario, offered the initial idea and the lion's share of research for the history, Kathi Bayly offered invaluable help and hands-on guidance for the quest. This book is dedicated to both Patricia and Kathi, and, of course, to my horse Dali, who insisted early on that I ride with a deep seat, soft hands and a steady heart, or face certain consequences.

Many people read the manuscript closely and I am grateful for their insightful commentary: Kathi Bayly, David Carpenter, Patricia Cooper, Carol Risbridger and Samara Warren. Gilles Dupuis, Samara Warren and Barb Wills played important roles in the education of both Dali and his rider and I remain in their debt.

Many people helped along the way and my naming them here pays small homage to their various kindnesses—from answering with patience my endless questions, to offering a fine home-cooked meal and sometimes even lodging to a virtual stranger. Thanks to: Jérôme and Sara Aumond, André Auclair, Mary Ann Barrett, Yves Bernatchez, Claudine Carpenter, Elizabeth Curler, Sandra Gulland, Alec Hayward, Alan and Bernice Hiltz, Helen Mason, Gail Mosher, Sue Mott, Deb Ottier, June Pelot, Gilles Racette and Anne Bélanger, Ginny Sealy, Terry Veevers and Barry Ward.

Donna Hoffman in Ontario and Noël Vinet in Quebec both spent years diligently gathering historical documents on the Canadian horse and merit special thanks. The various publications of La société des éleveurs de chevaux canadiens (the Canadian Horse Breeders' Association) as well as the newsletters of the association's various chapters in Ontario, the Maritimes and the West were all useful sources of information.

My literary agents Jan Whitford and her successor, Jackie Kaiser, are friends and mentors both, and I take my riding hat off to each.

I owe heartfelt thanks to my son, Kurt, and my partner, Ulrike Bender, who have tolerated and even quietly encouraged my passion for horses, trusting that my basic instincts as an athlete (well, former athlete) would safely see me through the rougher parts of my journey. Ulrike, as always, read the manuscript and nudged it towards greater clarity.

Finally, I am grateful to Sarah Davies and all her colleagues at Random House Canada, for believing in the book and guiding it with such care from beginning to end. Sarah is not just a fine editor, but a fine rider, too, and she lent a sympathetic ear and wise counsel on both counts. Book designer Scott Richardson lent his usual grace to the look of *Little Horse of Iron*; copy editors Liba Berry and Mary Patton did wonders to purge the manuscript of its infelicities.

If I neglected to thank my horse overly much in the book's diary entries, let the record show that I thank Dali now, and every little horse of iron who came before him.

# INDEX

Adams, Charles Francis Jr., 60-61

Africa (horse), 219

African Lion Safari, 135, 161, 166-167

Albert (horse), 228

Albert de Cap Rouge (horse), 102, 299-300

Alkemade, Dr. Stan, 253-254, 255, 257-258, 260

Allen, Janet, 24

American Saddlebred horse, 97, 292

Andalusian horse, 9

April (horse), 172, 177-178

Arab horse, 9

in distance riding, 250, 253, 254

Arctic expedition, Canadian horses in, 300-302

Argall, Samuel, 8, 170

Ariss (horse), 162, 167, 169

Arnason, H. H., *History of Modern Art*, 286

Arnold, Benedict, 38

Art Gallery of Ontario, Cornelius Krieghoff exhibition, 296, 298

Asmon (horse), 220

Atkins, George, 102, 130

Atwood, Margaret, 286

*Days of the Rebels 1815-1840*, 44-45

Auclair, André, 127, 326, 342

Aumond, Jérôme, 48, 49, 50, 51, 74, 78, 134, 136, 137, 142, 167, 246, 300, 301, 317, 328

Aumond, Sara, 142

Ayre, Elaine, 235-236

Barnard, Edouard-André, 98-99

Barnard, George, 39, 41, 291

Barney (horse), 130

Barrett, Mary Ann, 74-76, 283

Battell, Joseph, 292

Battle of the Breeds, Calgary, 54, 55

Baxter, Earle, 256

Bayly, Dick, 52, 90, 93, 157, 232-233, 235, 278, 334-335

Bayly, Kathi, 22, 26, 52, 73, 92-93, 116, 122, 144, 146, 157, 201-202, 205, 233, 235, 240-241, 278, 283, 334-335

Beacon, Nancy, 256

Beattie, Gladys Mackey, *The Canadian Horse: A Pictorial History*, 54, 299

Beautel (horse), 162, 167, 169

Beckett's Creek Calypso Ferari (horse), 336-337; photo, 336

Bélanger, Anne, 126, 327

Bélanger, René, 333-334

Benoit, Alain, 223

Bernatchez, Yves, 99, 127, 128-129, 327, 337-338

Bianca (horse), 136

Big Ben (horse), 77, 161

Billings, John D., 61

Black Creek Pioneer Village, 182

Black Diamond (horse), 304

Black Hawk (horse), 63, 293, 294

Black Horse Ale Percherons, 102

Blackie (horse), 302-303

Blue Bull (horse), 214

Blue Haven, 72, 82-83

Boer War

and Canadian horse, 66-69

number of horses killed in, 66

Bogi (horse), 206, 235, 267, 282, 331

Bougainville, Louis-Antoine de, 14

*Box Seat, The* (video), by Terry Veevers, 218

Braithwaite, Jack, 224

Brannaman, Buck, 154

*Breaking Up of a Country Ball in Canada, Early Morning*, painting by Cornelius Krieghoff, 297

Breeding programs to restore Canadian horse, 101-103

Brereton, J. M., *The Horse in War*, 62

Brio de la Victoire (horse), 127

Brother of Bruno (horse), 214

Brown Hal (horse), 215

Brunette (horse), 214

Brunner, Erica, 219

Brunner, Kirsten, 219

Bruno (horse), 214

Bulrush (horse), 291, 293

Butler, Dr. Larry, 77, 79, 80-81, 115-116

Butler, Sir William Francis, *The Great Lone Land*, 302-303

Buying a Canadian horse
author's experiences, 17-35, 47-57
looking at horses, 23-25, 31-34, 53
what to look for, 26-29

Calder, Murray, 337, 338

Canadian Driving Society, 217

Canadian horse, illustration, 36
ancestors' characteristics, 9

ancestors' passage across Atlantic, 7-9
at exhibitions, 100-101, 168, 304
breeding in New France, importance of, 13
Canadian or Québécois, politics of, 336-338
characteristics, 4, 12, 15, 19-20, 34-35, 55-56, 87, 134, 136, 166, 170, 171, 176, 181, 182, 224-225, 344-345
conformation and stud-book standards, 27, 30, 100, 340-342
contribution to breeding of racehorses, 213-215
crossbreeding and dilution of breed in 19th century, 37, 39, 40-41, 99
decline in late 19th century, 97-98
decline in mid-20th century, 103-104
dispersal with Francophones in 19th century, 45-46
drain to U.S. in 19th century, 36-37, 38, 44, 59-60, 61
earliest uses in Canada, 11-15
early development and proliferation in Canada, 11, 13
feet, 15, 42-43
gene pool, adequacy of, 343
"Hall of Fame," 289-305
history, 17th century, 5-11
history, 18th century, 11-15

history, 19th century, 36-46, 59-66
history, 20th century, 66-70, 96-104, 130-138, 159-182, 336-345
in Arctic expedition, 300-302
in Battle of Plains of Abraham, 14-15
in Boer War, 66-69
in Civil War, 59-61
in combined driving, 217, 219, 220
in distance riding, 249-250, 254, 261
in First World War, 69-70
in liberty performance, 161-162
in paintings of Cornelius Krieghoff, 295-299
in wars, 14-15, 58-70
Louis XIV and, 6, 8, 10
praise for in 19th century, 41-43
prepotency of, 41
racing of, 5, 12, 38-39, 212-213
relationship to Morgan horse, 290-295
relationship to Thoroughbred, 40, 291, 292-293
revival in early 20th century, 98-103
revival in present times, 20-21, 130-138, 159-182, 336-345
versatility, 11-15, 211

*Canadian Horse, The: A Pictorial History*, by Gladys Mackey Beattie, 54, 299

Canadian Horse Breeders' Association (CHBA), 20, 98, 129, 131, 305, 133-134, 138
internal difficulties, 338-342

Canadian Horse Breeding Syndicates, 101

Canadian Pacer, 39

*Canadian Rangers, The: Canada in the South African War, 1901-1902*, by John Innes, 67-69

Cap Rouge experimental station, 101

Carpenter, Claudine, 114

Carpenter, David, 114, 310

*Carrousels* of Louis XIV, 6-7

Cash (horse), 258

Catton, Bruce, *A Stillness at Appomattox*, 63

Cavalry tactics
in Boer War, 67
in Civil War, 63-64

Charm (horse), 261

CHBA (Canadian Horse Breeders' Association), 20, 98, 129, 131, 305, 133-134, 138, 338-342

*Cheating the Toll Man*, painting by Cornelius Krieghoff, 295-296

Chew's Pilot (horse), 215

China (horse), 335

Chipperfield, Jimmy, 167

Chivas (horse), 219

Chocolate (horse), 2

Christie, Barbara, *The Horses of Sable Island*, 170

Civil War, horses in, 59-66

  shortage, 61-62

  number killed, 65

Classic (horse), 31-32, 33

Clayton, Hilary M., *Conditioning Sport Horses*, 262

Clearbit (horse), 214

Cleveland Bay, 291

Clydesdale horse, 12, 171

Colbert, Jean Baptiste, 9, 10

Collection in horses, 155

Colonel (horse), 345

Combined driving, 208-209, 215-225

*Conditioning Sport Horses*, by Hilary M. Clayton, 262

Conformation of Canadian horse and stud-book standards, 27, 30, 100, 340-342

*Conformation of Horses* (film), 27-28

Conqueror (horse), 40

Cook, Ramsay, 45, 297-298

Cooper, Patricia, 3-4, 222-223, 333, 334, 335

Copperbottom (horse), 214

Corbeau (horse), 214

Cormack, Dr. Ray, 223-224

Cornwallis Island, Canadian horses in expedition to, 300-302

Costs of owning and training a horse, 263-264

Couture, Dr. Joseph-Alphonse, 98, 338

Crossbreeding of Canadian horse and dilution of breed in 19th century, 37, 39, 40-41, 99

Curler, Elizabeth A., 291-292

Dahms, Trish, 55

Dailley, Carole, 219

Dailley, Ginny, 133, 135

  role in revival of Canadian horse, 160-170

  training methods, 163-166

Dailley, Gordon, 166-167

Dali, 16; photos, 47, 71, 105, 139, 183, 263, 306

  and traffic, 202-205, 206

  attitude, 108, 120-121

  author's decision to buy, 113

  author's decision to take on trial, 56-57

  author's falls, 193, 203-204, 226-227, 230, 231-235, 280-282, 285

  author's first meeting with, 50-52

  author's thoughts of selling, 311-312, 319, 327-331

  bloodline, 49, 54-56, 88-89, 104, 126-127, 129, 235-236, 318, 333-334

  dental work, 112-113, 150

  first trail ride, 199-200

  foot sensitivity, 86, 89, 91, 92-93, 106, 107-108, 109-110, 111, 155

  going left, 142, 149-151

  mounting problem, 151, 157-158, 184, 186, 278, 279

  mouth sensitivity, 81-82, 90, 94, 106, 107, 110, 142

  splint bone fracture, 80-81, 110, 112, 113, 115-116, 121, 284-285

  trailering, 74, 78-79, 187

  training, 84-95, 105-124, 139-158, 183-207, 226-248, 263-288, 306-307, 311-325

  veterinary check, 79-81

  weight, 116-117

Dali, Salvador, 286

Daniel Boone (horse), 214

*Days of the Rebels 1815-1840*, by Margaret Atwood, 44-45

Dealers

  American, in 19th century, 38, 44

  Québécois, modern, 133

Dehydration in horses, 250, 252

Depreciation in value of horses, 29-30

Deschambault, 14, 49, 127-128, 327
  horse show, photo, 96
  experimental station, 101, 103-104

Desrochers, Dr. Jean, 27

Deuter (horse), 216

Diamond (horse), 137

Dick Turpin (horse), 65-66

Disorders of horses, 26-27

Distance riding, 249-262
  competitive trail rides, 253
  endurance rides, 253
  ideal horses for, 253-254, 256
  mileage rides, 253

Dobbie, Dave, 182

Dolly (horse), 172, 173, 177; photo, 159

Doris (horse), 219

Dorrance, Tom, 52, 72

Douglas, Henry Kyd, 65-66

Doyle, Sir Arthur Conan, *The War in South
  Africa*, 67

Drennon (horse), 214

Driving. See Combined driving

Du Coteau Lalou Caesar (horse), 209-211,
  219, 225; photo, 208

Ducat Major Nancy (horse), 56

Dupuis, Gilles, 72, 81-94, 106-123, 151-
  152, 154, 155, 157-158, 184, 186, 190,
  191, 234, 328; photo, 71

Ecker, Gayle, 252

Ed (horse), 23-24

Endurance rides, 253

Enright, Michael, 309

Equine Research Centre, University of
  Guelph, 294-295

Ethan Allen (horse), 294

Evans, Robert, 290

Evans, William, 43

Evergreen Farm, 118

Faillon, Etienne Michel, 42

Farro (horse), 162, 164-165, 169

Fédération Equestre Internationale (FEI), 216

Feet
  Dali's sensitivity, 86, 89, 91, 92-93,
    106, 107-108, 109-110, 111, 155

of Canadian horse, 15, 42-43

Figure (horse), 290-295

Filon (horse), 23-24

First Regiment of Massachusetts Volunteer
  Cavalry, 59-60

First World War and Canadian horse, 69-70

Flynn, Leonard, 240

Forester, Frank, *Horse and Horsemanship of
  the United States and British Provinces of
  North America*, 41-42

Forrest, General Nathan Bedford, 64

Fox line, 56, 126, 127, 165, 179, 180, 318

Frankie (horse), 313, 331

Frannie (horse), 172, 173, 177, 181;
  photo, 159

Franny (horse), 308-309

French, Captain Cecil, 69-70

Frenchers, 40

Friesian horse, 9

Gail (horse), 182

Garland, Pat, 20

Gauthier, Emilie, 297

Gauthier, Jean-Paul, 210, 220

Genetic studies
  gene pool of Canadian horse, 343
  of endangered horse breeds, 294-295

Gift (horse), 214

Ginger (horse), 179-180

Girling, Captain T. A., 69

Gourde, Léo, 131

Graham, Bill, 209, 216, 217, 223-225

*Great Lone Land, The*, by Sir William
  Francis Butler, 302-303

Grierson, General Benjamin, 64

Groenewegen, Francis, 189

Groenewegen, Kathie, 189, 200, 201, 280,
  283, 329, 331

Grooms, Chris, 189, 229

Grooms, Gerry, 188-189, 196

Grooms, Kellie, 189

Grooms, Lil, 187, 188-189, 313

Guillaume (horse), 181

*Habitant Farm, The*, painting by Cornelius
  Krieghoff, 296

Harrison, Tom, 71

Hart, Lyn, 87

Hart, Ruthanne, 261, 343-345

Hayward, Alec, 32, 34, 48-49, 52, 53, 54, 102, 129-134, 136, 167, 182, 220, 221, 300, 303-304, 316, 317-318, 321, 340-341

    role in revival of Canadian horse, 130-133, 160

Hélène (horse), 299-300

Hellyer, Terry and Walter, 219

Hendricks, Bonnie, 5

    *International Encyclopedia of Horse Breeds*, 292-294

Henryville line, 56, 181, 334

Herbert, Henry William, *Hints to Horse-Keepers*, 42-43

Heritage Park Historical Village, 182

Hilltop Stables, 2

Hiltz, Allan, 173, 175-176, 178-179

Hiltz, Barry, 176

Hinrich, Anne, 167

*Hints to Horse-Keepers*, by Henry William Herbert, 42-43

*History of Modern Art*, by H. H. Arnason, 286

Hobbyhorse Larry's Dark Fox, 49, 54-55, 56, 104, 235-236, 318

Hochgeschurz, Udo, 210

Hoffman, Donna, 133

*Home, Farm and Business Cyclopedia, The*, 42

*Horse and Horsemanship of the United States and British Provinces of North America*, by Frank Forester, 41-42

*Horse Heaven*, by Jane Smiley, 308, 309-310

*Horse in War, The*, by J. M. Brereton, 62

*Horse, The*, 310

*Horsemastership*, by Margaret Cabell Self, 155, 185

*Horses Don't Lie*, by Chris Irwin, 92, 117

*Horses of Sable Island, The*, by Barbara Christie, 170

Hunt, Ray, 72, 114

*Ice Cutting*, painting by Cornelius Krieghoff, 298; image, 289

Ice-racing of Canadian horse, 38-39, 212. See also Racing of Canadian horse

Innes, John, *The Canadian Rangers: Canada in the South African War, 1901-1902*, 67-69

*Inside the Halo and Beyond*, by Maxine Kumin, 216

*Instruction du Roi, L'*, by Antoine de Pluvinel, 10

Insurance, liability, 227

*International Encyclopedia of Horse Breeds*, by Bonnie Hendricks, 292-294

Irwin, Chris, 121-124, 147, 151, 190-191, 218, 277, 311

    *Horses Don't Lie*, 92, 117

Jennison Horse (horse), 293

Jenyns, Colonel Soame, 66

Jerry (horse), 67-68

Jimmy Peach (horse), 219

Johnson, Dr. Richard, 137-138

Joly, Michel, 301

Jones, Robert Leslie, 9, 38, 40-41, 43, 97, 290-291

Joyce, Greg, 181-182

Justin Morgan (horse), 290-295

Kalm, Pehr, 11, 15

Kanavy, Valerie, 258

Kerr, Morris, 217, 219

Kilpatrick, General Judson, 65

King, Dr. Art, 260, 341

King's Landing Historic Settlement, 182

Kitchener, Lord, 67

Kittrel's Tom Hal (horse), 215

Knox, Shannon, 313

Krieghoff, Cornelius David, 5, 45, 295-299

    *Breaking Up of a Country Ball in Canada, Early Morning*, 297

    *Cheating the Toll Man*, 295-296

    *Habitant Farm, The*, 296

    *Ice Cutting*, 298; image, 289

    *Merrymaking*, 296

    *Off the Road—The Upset Sleigh*, 297

    *Self-Portrait*, 298

    *Winter Incident, A*, 297

*Krieghoff: Images of Canada*, by Dennis Reid, 296, 297

Krukowski, Brigitte, 295
Kumin, Maxine, 93, 228
    *Inside the Halo and Beyond*, 216
La Gorgendière Alto Fox (horse), 129,
    318
La Gorgendière Barreau Nicot (horse), 334
La Gorgendière Fox Kosmos (horse), 180
La Gorgendière Fox Larry (horse), 49, 88-
    89, 126-127, 129, 180, 318
La Gorgendière Fox Miria (horse), 179
La Vallière, Louise de, 7
Laberge, Germain, 210
Lac LaCroix pony, 294
Lady Moscow (horse), 39
Lakehead Stables, 73, 188-189
    Dali's move to, 186-187
Lalonde, Ray, 33, 228
Lalou line (Lou line), 56, 126, 127
Lambert, Gérard, 136, 219
Lambert, John, 44
Lambert Rex Apollo (horse), 137
Langelier, Dr. Gustave, 102, 299-300
Lapaix, Jean-Yves, 301-302
Lee, General Robert E., 63
Lemieux, Gérard, 131-132
Liberty performance with Canadian horses,
    161-162
Limestone Stables, 235, 264
    Dali's move to, 313
Lindblad, Di, 251
Lion du Canada (horse), 98
Litjens, Madame John, 334
Little Brown Jug (horse), 215
Loiselle, Camille, 136
Longleat, 167
Lou line (Lalou line), 56, 126, 127
*Louis at Maastricht*, portrait by Pierre
    Mignard, 7; image, 1
Louis XIV, 5-10
    role in bringing Canadian horse to
        Canada, 6, 8, 10
    role in developing ancestors of Canadian
        horse, 10
Louisbourg, Fortress of, 181-182
Lyndon, Jane, 220

Mackenzie, Greg, 219
Maddy (horse), 153, 221, 329
Mambrino Pilot (horse), 214
Maple Lane Rebel Tom (horse), 222, 223
*Marche donc*, 15
Mason, Helen, 258, 259, 262
Mayflower (horse), 304
McBurney, Margo, 118
McCallum, Gerald, 220
McCullough, Wendy, 191-192, 199, 200,
    201, 202, 206, 232, 233
McNeil, Elaine, 135
Merens pony, 300
*Merrymaking*, painting by Cornelius
    Krieghoff, 296
Midnight (horse), 33-34
Mileage rides, 253
Millar, Ian, 3, 90
*Mobile Veterinary Unit in France, A* (1919),
    image, 58
Montcalm, Marquis Louis-Joseph de, 14-15
Montmagny, Sieur de, 8
Morgan horse, 4, 63, 97, 254
    relationship to Canadian horse, 290-295
Morgan, Justin, 291
Morgan, Paul, 90-91
Mosby, Colonel John S., 64
Mosher, Gail, 31-33, 76, 94-95, 133, 195
Mott, Ken, photo, 208
Mott, Sue, 209-211, 219, 225; photo, 208
*Mount and Man*, by McTaggart, 311
Mounting problem with Dali, 151, 157-
    158, 184, 186, 278, 279
Mouth, Dali's sensitivity, 81-82, 90, 94,
    106, 107, 110, 142
Mr. Canadian Horse (Donnie Prosperine),
    305
"My Year of Living Dangerously," by Jane
    Smiley, 308
Narragansett Pacer, 39, 213
Nate (horse), 237, 314, 331
National Museum of the Morgan Horse,
    291
Native (horse), 215
Newfoundland pony, 294

Nicodemus (horse), 321-322
Nigger Baby (horse), 215
Nip (horse), 220, 304
Northern Dancer (horse), 161
OCTRA (Ontario Competitive Trail Riding Association), 30, 250, 251
Oddie, Will, 135-137, 323
*Off the Road—The Upset Sleigh*, painting by Cornelius Krieghoff, 297
Offord, Shannon, 331
Okun, Nancy, 321-322
Old Tecumseh (horse), 215
Ole Bull (horse), 215
Ontario Competitive Trail Riding Association (OCTRA), 30, 250, 251
Osborne, Terry, 272
Ottawa Valley Large Animal Clinic, 77
Ottier, Deb, 250
Pacers and Canadian horse, 39
Packers, 47-48, 92
Papineau, Louis-Joseph, 45
Paré, Jean-Paul, 127, 342
Payback from a horse, 205
Pelletier, J. R., 101-102
Pelot, June, 34-35, 133, 135
Pelot, Lloyd, 34
Percheron horse, 9, 12, 102, 171
Persey (horse), 309
Peterson, Carol, 188, 190
Philip, Prince, 219
Pilot (horse), 214-215, 292
Pilot Jr. (horse), 215
Plains of Abraham, Battle of, Canadian horse in, 14-15
Plumb, Charles, 214, 215
Pluvinel, Antoine de, *L'Instruction du Roi*, 10
Politics and Canadian horse, 336-338
Postage stamp, attempt to get image of Canadian horse on, 160-161
Poutrincourt, Sieur de, 8
Prime Time (horse), 147, 186, 229
Prosperine, Donnie, 32, 88, 220, 221
named Mr. Canadian Horse, 305
role in revival of Canadian horse, 130-133, 303-305

Prosperine, Frank, 88-89, 136, 221, 304
Prosperine, Judy, 222
Prunelle (horse), 301-302
Quarter horse, 258
Queen's Plate, 5
Racehorses, contribution of Canadian horse to breeding, 213-215
Racette, Gilles, 126, 127, 134, 136, 175-176, 182, 327, 341-342, 345; photo, 125
Racette, Louis Philippe, 126
Racing of Canadian horse, history, 5, 12, 38-39, 212-213
Rainey (horse), 130
Ranch-L Kaiser Nadia (horse), 334
Ranch-L Nicot Ukraine (horse), 49, 56, 333-334
Randolph Morgan (horse), 293
Ras (horse), 191-192, 199, 201, 206, 230, 277
Rawski, Connie, 255
Rawski, Marcus, 255
"Reading" horses, 117, 123-124
Reid, Dennis, *Krieghoff: Images of Canada*, 296, 297
Revival of Canadian horse
in early 20th century, 98-103
in present times, 20-21, 130-138, 159-182, 336-345
Rianon (horse), 322
Riddell, Christie, 261
Roanaki (horse), 215
Roberts, Monty, 72
Rocket (horse), 314, 331
Rocky (Peterson horse), 188
Rocky (Wills horse), 113, 185, 186
Ross, Cecily, 4-5, 86, 89
Ross Farm Museum, 171, 175, 176-177, 178-179, 299
Royal Agricultural Winter Fair, 304
Rumours and gossip in horse world, 265
Russell, Gordon, 180-181
Rutherford, Dr. J. G., 99-100
Rutherford, Dr. Mark, 111-113, 115, 150, 287, 326

Rysdyk's Hambletonian (horse), 214
Saddles, 87, 90-91, 118-120, 143, 144,
146
St. Clair (horse), 214
St. Joachim Farm, 101, 103, 338
St. Lawrence (horse), 39, 214
St. Lawrences, 40
Ste-Anne de la Pocatière experimental station, 101, 103
Ste-Justine de Newton, combined driving
competition at, 216-219
Sale of Canadian horses to U.S. in 19th
century, 36-37, 38, 44, 59-60, 61
Saroma Dark Fox Dali (horse). See Dali
Saroma Surprise Etoile (horse), 137
Scanlan, Kurt, 330
Scanlan Lawrence, photos, 105, 226, 306
decision to buy Dali, 113
decision to take Dali on trial, 56-57
experiences buying a Canadian horse,
17-35, 47-57
falls, 193, 203-204, 226-227, 230, 231-
235, 280-282, 285
first meeting with Dali, 50-52
thoughts of selling Dali, 311-312, 319,
327-331
training, 84-95, 105-124, 139-158, 183-
207, 226-248, 263-288, 306-307,
311-325
*Wild About Horses*, 74
Schleese, Jochen, 118-120, 143
School horses, 47-48, 92
Sealy, Joe, 164
Sealy, Kevin, 164-165
Self, Margaret Cabell, *Horsemastership*, 155,
185
*Self-Portrait*, painting by Cornelius
Krieghoff, 298
Sherman, General William Tecumseh, 62,
64
Sherman (horse), 291
Skate (horse), 68-69
Smiley, Jane, 307-310
*Horse Heaven*, 308, 309-310
"My Year of Living Dangerously," 308

Smith, Titus, 43
Smuggler (horse), 214
Soaring Eagle (horse), 254-255
Spierenburg, Suzanne, 54-56
Splint bone fracture (Dali's), 80-81, 110,
112, 113, 115-116, 121, 284-285
Sport, Canadian horse in. See Combined
driving; Distance riding; Racing of
Canadian horse
Stamina of Canadian horse, 12
Standardbred horse, 4, 97, 254, 292
Star Pointer (horse), 215, 213
*Stillness at Appomattox, A*, by Bruce Catton,
63
Stoneman, General George, 65
Storrey, Joan, 254-255
Street, David, 212-213
Stud book for Canadian horse, 98-100
present-day controversy over standards,
340-342
revision of standards in (1907), 99-100
Suffolk Punch, 291
Tahourenche, Paul, 299
Talon, Jean, 9
Tarka (horse), 34
Tecumseh (horse), 215
Tennessee Walking Horse, 97
Teoriolen, Gabriel, 299
Thoroughbred horse, 97, 166, 254, 258
relationship to Canadian horse, 40, 291,
292-293
Time involved in owning and training a
horse, 265
Tom (horse), 335
Tom Crowder (horse), 215
Tom Foolery (horse), 322
Tonnerre (horse), 126
Trail riding, competitive, 249-262. See also
Distance riding
Trailering Dali, 74, 76-79, 187
Trakehner horse, 254
Tralee, 223
Traveler (horse), 63, 65
Tremain, Bob, 74, 77, 78
Trudeau (horse), 332

Tuck (horse), 220, 304

Upper Canada Village, 182

Valentin (horse), 301-302

Vecchio, Pat, 325

Veevers, Terry, 19-20, 167
   *The Box Seat* (video), 218

Vélo (horse), 220

Vernay, Pierre and Frédéric, 301-302

Versatility of Canadian horse, 11-15, 211

Veterinary check of Dali, 79-81

Veterinary checks in distance riding, 252

Vézina, Jean-Yves, 127, 129

Viger Duc (horse), 131-132, 167, 300, 303

Vinton, Yvette, 257

Waldman, Dan, 261

*War in South Africa, The*, by Arthur Conan Doyle, 67

Ward, Barry, 171-175, 176, 177; photo, 159

Warren, Samara, 235, 236-239, 241-247, 266-273, 275-280, 282, 284-285, 287-288, 307, 311, 313, 315, 317, 321, 322, 324, 328, 329, 331; photo, 263

Wars, Canadian horse in, 14-15, 58-70

Wesley, John, 266

*Wild About Horses*, by Lawrence Scanlan, 74

Wilfred (horse), 300

Wills, Barb, 72, 73, 81-94, 106-123, 139-151, 154-157, 185, 186, 188, 190, 196-197, 198, 200, 201, 228, 231, 234, 265, 282; photos, 71, 139

Wilmarny Farm, 48, 115

Wilson, Dan, 138

Windsor Michette (horse), 132, 303

Windsor Rosine (horse), 132, 303

*Winter Incident, A*, painting by Cornelius Krieghoff, 297

Withybrooke buggy, 222

Witteveen, Harry, 218

Wolfe, General James, 15

Woodbury Morgan (horse), 291, 293

World Singles Driving Championships, 208-209

Xector (horse), 53

Young's Pilot (horse), 215

Zenith (horse), 209, 216, 217

Zephyr (horse), 162, 164, 165-166, 169

Zeta (horse), 182

Zircon (horse), 137